CRIMINOLOGICAL THEORY

SECOND EDITION

For our children and grandchildren

Catherine
Jordan
Charlie and Mike
Stephen and Christopher

SECOND EDITION

CRIMINOLOGICAL THEORY

CONTEXT AND CONSEQUENCES

J. Robert Lilly
Francis T. Cullen
Richard A. Ball

Under the editorship of
James A. Inciardi

SAGE Publications
International Educational and Professional Publisher
Thousand Oaks   London   New Delhi

For information address:

SAGE Publications, Inc.
2455 Teller Road
Thousand Oaks, California 91320
E-mail: order@sagepub.com

SAGE Publications Ltd.
6 Bonhill Street
London EC2A 4PU
United Kingdom

SAGE Publications India Pvt. Ltd.
M-32 Market
Greater Kailash I
New Delhi 110048 India

Printed in the United States of America

Library of Congress Cataloging-in-Publication Data

Lilly, J. Robert.
    Criminological theory: context and consequences /authors, J.
Robert Lilly, Francis T. Cullen, Richard A. Ball.—2nd ed.
        p. cm.
    Includes bibliographical references and indexes.
    ISBN 0-8039-5900-1.—ISBN 0-8039-5901-X (pbk.)
    1. Criminology. 2. Crime—United States. 3. Criminal behavior—
United States. I. Cullen, Francis T. II. Ball, Richard A., 1936-
        III. Title.
HV6018.L55 1995
364.973—dc20   94-22985
                                                                       CIP

98 99 00 01 10 9 8 7 6

Sage Production Editor: Yvonne Könneker

CONTENTS

1

THE CONTEXT AND CONSEQUENCES OF THEORY

Crime is a complex phenomenon, and it is a demanding, if intriguing, challenge to explain its many sides. Often commentators (some, but not all, public officials come to mind) suggest that using good common sense is enough to explain why citizens shoot or rob one another and, in turn, to inform us as to what to do about such lawlessness. Our experience—and we trust this book, too—teaches that the search for answers to the crime problem is not so easy. It requires that we reconsider our biases, learn from the insights and mistakes of our predecessors who have risked theorizing about the causes of crime, and consider clearly the implications of what we propose.

But the task—or, as we see it, the adventure—of explaining crime is an important undertaking. To be sure, crime commentary frequently succumbs to the temptation to exaggerate and sensationalize, to suggest that crimes that are exceptionally lurid and injurious compose the bulk of America's lawlessness, or perhaps to suggest that most citizens spend their lives huddled behind barricaded doors and paralyzed by the fear that local thugs will victimize them. There is, of course, an element of truth in these observations, which is why they have an intuitive appeal. Yet most Americans—particularly those living in more affluent communities—do not have their lives ripped apart by a brutal assault or tragic murder, and although many citizens lock their doors at night, install burglar alarms, and perhaps buy weapons for protection, they typically say they feel safe in and close to their homes (Cullen, Clark, & Wozniak, 1985; Scheingold, 1984).

These cautionary remarks, however, do not detract from the reality that crime is a serious matter that deserves, we believe, study and understanding. If most Americans escape the type of victimization that takes their lives or destroys their peace of mind, too many others do not share this good fortune. Thus media reports of Americans killing Americans are sufficiently ubiquitous that many of us have become so desensitized to the violence in our communities that we give these accounts scarcely more attention than the scores from the day's sporting events. And it is likely that most of us have friends, or friends of friends, whom we know have been seriously assaulted or perhaps even murdered.

Statistical data paint an equally bleak picture. Each year the FBI publishes the *Uniform Crime Reports* in which it lists the number of crimes that have become known (mostly through reports by citizens) to the nation's police departments. For 1992 alone, over 20,000 U.S. citizens were murdered and nearly 1.9 million others were either robbed, raped, or seriously assaulted; an additional 12.5 million citizens, the FBI's figures revealed, had their houses burglarized or their property damaged or stolen (Federal Bureau of Investigation, 1993, p. 58).

It is disturbing that these statistics capture only part of the nation's crime problem. Many citizens, perhaps one in two, do not report crimes against them to the police, and thus these acts do not appear in the *Uniform Crime Reports*. For instance, the National Crime Victimization Survey, a study in which citizens are asked if they have been victimized, "estimated that there were 33.6 million crimes committed against individuals or households in the United States in 1992" (Bureau of Justice Statistics, 1994, p. 15).

Further, the FBI's statistics include data only on serious street crimes. Yet we know that minor crimes—petty thefts, simple assaults—are even more widespread. "Self-report" surveys in which respondents (typically juveniles) are asked how many offenses they have committed consistently indicate that the vast majority of people have engaged in some degree of illegality. More important, however, there are other realms of criminality—not only quite prevalent but also quite serious—that traditionally have not come to the attention of police because they are not committed on the streets. Domestic violence—child abuse, spousal assault; that is, the violence that occurs "behind closed doors"—is one of these areas (Straus, Gelles, & Steinmetz, 1980). Another such area is white-collar crime, the crimes committed by affluent people in the course of their occupations (Sutherland, 1949). As recent revelations suggest, corruption in the business and political communities takes place regularly and has disquieting consequences (Cullen, Maakestad, & Cavender, 1987; Simon & Eitzen, 1986).

More statistics and observations could be added here, but this only would belabor the point: Crime is a prominent feature in our society. Indeed, as Elliott Currie noted, lawlessness—particularly violence—is higher in the United States than in any other industrialized Western nation. Making cross-cultural comparisons is difficult; for example, nations differ in what they consider to be illegal and in their methods of collecting crime data. Even so, Currie's (1985) review of available statistical information revealed that as of the late 1970s "about ten American men died by criminal violence for every Japanese, Austrian, West German, or Swedish man; about fifteen American men died for every Swiss or Englishman; and over twenty for every Dane" (p. 25).

But why is crime so prevalent in the United States? Why in some of our communities but not others? Why do some types of people break the law, although others are law-abiding? Why do the affluent, not just the disadvantaged, commit illegal acts? How can these varied phenomena be explained?

Over the years theorists have endeavored to address one or more of these questions. In this book, we attempt to give an account of their thinking about crime—to examine its context, its content, and its consequences. Before embarking on this story of criminological theorizing, however, it is necessary to discuss the framework that will inform our analysis.

Theory in Social Context

Most Americans have little difficulty in identifying the circumstances that they believe cause people to engage in wayward conduct. When surveyors ask citizens about the causes of crime, only a small percentage of the respondents say they "have no opinion." The remainder of those polled usually remark that crime is caused by factors such as unemployment, bad family life, or lenient courts (Flanagan, 1987).

Most people, then, have developed views on why crime occurs, that is, they have a "theory" of criminal behavior. But where do such views, such theories, come from? One possibility is that citizens have taken the time to read extensively on crime, have sifted through existing research studies, and have arrived at an informed assessment of why laws are disregarded. But only the exceptional citizen develops his or her views on crime—or on any other social issue—this way. Apart from those who study crime for a living—criminologists—the rest of the people do not have the time, nor some the inclination, to investigate carefully the crime problem.

This observation may not seem particularly insightful, but it is important in illuminating that most people's opinions about crime are drawn less from rational thought and more from the implicit understandings they have come to embrace during their lives. Attitudes about crime, as well as about other social issues, can come from a variety of sources: parents, church sermons, how crime is depicted on television, whether one has had family or friends who have turned to crime, and whether one has experimented with criminal activity oneself or perhaps been victimized. In short, social experiences shape the way in which people come to think about crime.

This conclusion allows us to offer three additional points. First, members of the general public are not the only ones whose crime theories are influenced by their life experiences. Academic criminologists and government officials who formulate crime policy have a professional obligation to set aside their personal biases, read the existing research, and endorse the theory that the evidence most supports. To an extent, criminologists and policy makers let the data direct their thinking, but it is equally clear that they do not do so fully. Like the general public, they too live in society and are shaped by it. Before ever entering academia or public service, their personal experiences have provided them with certain assumptions about human nature and about the way the world operates (thus some will see themselves as liberals; others as conservatives). After studying crime, they often will revise some of their views. Nonetheless, few ever convert to a totally different way of thinking about crime; how they explain crime remains, if only in part, conditioned by the experiences they have had.

Second, if social experiences influence attitudes about criminality, then as society changes—as people come to have different experiences—views about crime will change also. We illustrate this point throughout this book, but a few brief examples might help to clarify matters for immediate purposes.

It will not surprise many readers to learn that Americans' views on crime have changed markedly since the settlers first landed on the nation's shores. Indeed, at different times in our history, Americans have attributed the origins of crime to spiritual demons and the inherent sinfulness of humans, to the defective biological constitution of inferior people in our midst, to the denial of equal opportunity, and to the ability of the coldly rational to calculate that crime pays. As we will see, each of these theories of crime (and others as well) became popular only when a particular set of circumstances coalesced to provide people with the experiences that made such reasoning seem logical or believable.

Thus for colonists living in a confined, highly religious society, it "made sense" for them to attribute crime to the power of demons to control the will of those who fell prey to the temptations of sin. For those in the late 1800s who witnessed the influx of foreigners of all sorts and learned from the social Darwinists that natural selection determined where each individual fell in the social hierarchy, it made sense that people became poor *and* criminal because they were of inferior stock. For those of the 1960s, however, who were informed that systematic barriers had prevented minorities from sharing in the American dream, it made sense that people became criminal *because* they were poor—because they were denied equal opportunity. In more recent times, as society has taken a turn in a conservative direction and it has become fashionable to blame social ills on a permissive society, it has made sense to more and more Americans that people commit crimes because they know they risk, if ever caught, only a slap on the wrist.

In short, social context plays a critical role in nourishing certain ways of theorizing about crime. If the prevailing social context changes and people begin to experience life differently, there will be a corresponding shift in the way they see their world and the people in it. Previous theories of crime will lose their appeal, and other perspectives will increasingly make sense to larger numbers of people. Note that all this can take place—indeed, usually does take place—without systematic analysis of whether the old theory was, in fact, wrong or if the new theory represents an improvement!

But does any of this relate to you, the reader? Our third point in this section is that your (and our) thinking about crime undoubtedly has been conditioned by your social experiences. When most of us look to the past, we wonder with a certain smugness how our predecessors could have held such strange and silly views about crime or other things. In making this type of remark, however, we not only fail to appreciate how their thoughts and actions were constrained by the world in which they lived but also implicitly assume that our thoughts and actions are unconstrained by our world. Our arrogance causes us to accept our interpretations, our theories, as "obviously" correct; we forget that future generations will have the luxury of looking at us and assessing where we have been strange and silly.

This discussion suggests the wisdom of pausing to contemplate the basis of your beliefs. How have your social experiences shaped the way you explain crime? Asking and seeking answers to this question, we believe, opens the possibility of lifting the blinders that past experiences often strap firmly around one's eyes. It creates, in short, the exciting opportunity to think differently about crime.

Theory and Policy:
Ideas Have Consequences

Theory is dismissed frequently as mere empty ruminations—fun, perhaps, but not something for which practical men and women have time. But this is a short-sighted view, for as Thomas Szasz (1987) has cautioned, "ideas have consequences" (Weaver, 1948). Theory matters.

When it comes to making criminal justice policy, there is ample evidence of this maxim (Sherman & Hawkins, 1981). Lawlessness is a costly problem; people lose their property and sometimes their lives. The search for the sources of crime, then, is not done within a vacuum. Even if a theorist wishes only to ruminate about the causes of theft or violence, others will be ready to use these insights to direct efforts to do something about the crime problem. Understanding why crime occurs, then, is a prelude to developing strategies to control the behavior. Stephen Pfohl (1985) has captured nicely the inherent relationship between theory and policy:

> Theoretical perspectives provide us with an image of what something is and how we might best act toward it. They name something this type of thing and not that. They provide us with the sense of being in a world of relatively fixed forms and content. Theoretical perspectives transform a mass of raw sensory data into understanding, explanations, and recipes for appropriate action. (pp. 9-10)

This discussion also leads to the realization that different theories suggest different ways to reduce crime. Depending on what is proposed as the cause of illegal behavior, certain criminal justice policies and practices will seem reasonable; others will seem irrational and perhaps dangerously irresponsible. Thus if offenders are viewed as genetically deranged and untrainable—much like wild animals—then caging them would seem to be the only option available. But if offenders are thought to be mentally ill, the solution to the problem would be to give them psychotherapy. Or if one believes that people are moved to crime by the strains of economic deprivation, providing job training and access to employment opportunities would seem to hold the promise of diminishing their waywardness.

This is not to assert that the relationship between theory and policy is uncomplicated. Sometimes theories emerge and then the demand to change policy occurs; sometimes policies are implemented and then attempts are made to justify the policies by popularizing theories supportive of these reforms; often the process is interactive with the theory and policy legitimating one another. In any case, the important point is that support for criminal justice policies will collapse eventually if the theory on which they are based no longer makes sense.

An important observation follows from this discussion: As theories of crime change, so do criminal justice policies. At the turn of the century, many Americans felt that criminals were "atavistic reversions" to less civilized evolutionary forms or, at the least, feebleminded. The call to sterilize offenders so that they could not pass criminogenic genes to their offspring was accepted widely as prudent social action. Within two decades, however, citizens were more convinced that the causes of crime lay not within offenders themselves but in the pathology of their environments. The time was ripe to hear suggestions that efforts be made to "save" slum youths by setting up neighborhood delinquency prevention programs or, when necessary, by removing juveniles to reformatories, where they could obtain the supervision and treatment they desperately needed. More recently, numerous politicians have climbed on the bandwagon that claims that crime is caused by the permissiveness that has crept into the nation's families, schools, and correctional system. Not surprisingly, they have urged that efforts be made to "get tough" with offenders, to teach them that crime does not pay by sending them to prison for lengthier stays and in record numbers.

We must remember, however, not to decontextualize criminological theory: The very changes in theory that undergird changes in policy are themselves a product of transformations in society. As noted above, explanations of crime are linked intimately to social context—to the experiences people have that make a given theory seem silly or sensible. Thus it is only when shifts in society occur that theoretical models gain or lose credence and, in turn, gain or lose the ability to justify a range of criminal justice policies.

We hope as well that the reader will find the discussion of some personal relevance. We have suggested that thought be given to how your own

context may have shaped your thinking; now we suggest that similar thought
be given to how your thinking may have shaped what you have thought
should be done about crime. The challenge we are offering is for you to
reconsider the basis and consistency of your views on crime and its control—to reconsider which theory you should embrace and the consequences this idea should have. We hope that our book will aid you as you
embark on this adventure.

Context, Theory, Policy:
Plan of the Book

"Perhaps the clearest lesson to be learned from historical research on
crime and deviance," Timothy Flanagan (1987) reminds us, "is that the
approach to crime control that characterizes any given era in history is
inexorably linked to contemporaneous notions about crime causation"
(p. 232). These remarks are instructive because they capture the central
theme of our book: the interconnection among social context, criminological
theory, and criminal justice policy making. As we progress through
the subsequent chapters, this theme will form the framework for our
analysis. We will discuss not only the content of a theoretical perspective,
but also its context and consequences.

The scope of the enterprise, however, should be clarified. Our purpose
here is to provide a primer in criminological theory—a basic introduction
to the social history of attempts, largely by academic scholars, to explain
crime. In endeavoring to furnish an accessible and relatively brief guide
to such theorizing, we have been forced to leave out historical detail and
omit discussions of the many theoretical variations each perspective on
crime typically has fostered. As a result, this book should be viewed as a
first step to understanding the long search for the answer to the riddle of
crime. We hope that our account encourages you to take further steps in
the time ahead.

Our excursion into the story of criminological theory commences, as
most stories do, at the beginning. Chapter 2 discusses early efforts, to use
Ysabel Rennie's (1978) words, "to search for the criminal man." Most of
these attempts, as we shall see, argued that the causes of crime lay within
men and women: in their soul, their will, or their bodily constitution.
Chapter 3, by contrast, focuses on scholars who argued that the answers
to crime were to be found not within people, but in the social circum-

stances in which people must live. Some of these scholars asserted that the seeds of crime were rooted in the fabric of slum life; others felt that the very nature of American society was criminogenic.

Chapters 4, 5, and 6 examine theoretical models that largely (though not exclusively) emerged and then gained force in the 1960s and 1970s. To some degree, each model was an attempt to move beyond previous sociological theories of crime. Thus in Chapter 4 we learn about "control" theorists, who suggested that the question was not so much why people's social environments motivated them to commit criminal acts—the traditional question criminologists asked—but why such circumstances *stopped* them from breaking the law. In Chapter 5 we discuss "labeling" theory. Scholars in this perspective offered the bold argument that the main cause of committed involvement in crime is not society per se, but rather the very attempts that are made to reduce crime by stigmatizing offenders and processing them through the criminal justice system. And in Chapter 6 we review theorists—often called "conflict" or "radical" scholars—who have gone so far as to suggest that the embrace of capitalism is what induces high rates of lawlessness among both rich and poor.

Chapter 7, a new chapter for this edition, explores the development of feminist criminology in North America and Britain. It also examines the early development and extension of Britain's "new criminology" into what is known now as "left realism." We present these theoretical orientations as new directions in "critical" theory.

The eighth chapter brings our story up to date and to a close. Here we explore the theoretical trends that have gained in popularity during the last decade and which are having an increasing sway on the nature of criminal justice policy. We discover that many of these theoretical explanations are attempts to revitalize—dressed in new language and with more sophisticated evidence—the models of crime that were popular closer to the turn of the century. Thus we see that claims are being made once again that the sources of crime lie deeply within the individual and not within the social fabric. The ramifications of this theoretical shift are immense, and, we argue, merit our close assessment.

2

THE SEARCH FOR
THE "CRIMINAL MAN"

Before we examine the content of this chapter, it is important to remember a few of the cautionary comments offered in Chapter 1. By keeping these ideas in mind we more than likely will be successful in accomplishing the goal of introducing you to the context and consequences of criminological theory.

We want to remember that the search for explanations of criminal behavior is not easy because we must guard constantly against our biases, mistaken perceptions, and prejudices. Unless we maintain our intellectual guard against these problems, our learning will be severely limited, and that is unwanted. This will become obvious as we study the following chapters and learn that many theories of crime that have experienced popularity with the public and professional criminologists also have been criticized for having serious blind spots. Unfortunately, the blind spots often have contributed to the creation and implementation of official policies that have produced results as undesirable as crime itself. Although it is impossible to develop perfect policies, we must keep in mind the fact that theories do influence the policies and practices found in criminal justice systems.

It is important to remember that the explanations of crime, whether they are created by the public or professional criminologists, are influenced by the social context from which they come. This means that the social context will consist of perceptions and interpretations of the past as well as the present. It may mean also that the explanations of crime include some thoughts about what crime and society will look like in the not-too-distant future. This is exactly what Bennett (1987) offered in *Crimewarps,* a study of what crime will look like in the next 20 to 50 years. A brief examination of the social context that influenced her writing of *Crimewarps* will help illustrate what we mean by the importance of social context. As you will see, the context includes general sociological factors such as time and place. It also includes the author's career experiences and opportunities.

By the time Bennett began to work on *Crimewarps,* she had completed a doctorate in sociology (1972) and was an accomplished scholar, researcher, teacher, and journalist with more than 20 years of work on the topic of crime. In addition, she was an associate of the Center for Policy Research and the Center for Investigative Reporting. She also had worked as a network correspondent for NBC News, and she had been a talk show host for PBS television. In other words, we can say that Bennett was experienced and therefore prepared to study major trends. In fact, her book was an outgrowth of having been asked by the Insurance Information Institute to be a consultant and media spokesperson on the topic of "the state of crime in the future" (Bennett, 1987, p. vii). Bennett's experiences and the consulting work for the Insurance Information Institute occurred within a shifting social context that she connected to crime by using the term *crimewarps.* She used this term to refer to "the bends in today's trends that will affect the way we live tomorrow" (p. xiii). Essentially her thesis is that much of what we have come to regard as basic demographic features of our society's population and crime trends are changing dramatically. She referred to these crimewarps as representing a "set of major social transformations" (p. viii). Altogether she identified six "warps." For example, she labeled one warp "the new criminal." This refers to the fact that today's "traditional" criminal is a poor, undereducated, young male. By relying on demographic information and dramatic news accounts of current crimes, Bennett argued that the traditional criminal will be displaced by "older, more upscale offenders." These will include, among other trends, more women involved in white-collar crime and domestic violence. In addition, she argued that teenagers will commit fewer crimes although senior citizens "will enter the crime scene as geriatric delinquents" (p. xiv).

The importance of this example lies not in the accuracy of Bennett's claims, her career experiences, or the fact that she was invited by the Insurance Information Institute to work on the future of crime at a time when our society is experiencing dramatic demographic transformations. Rather, the lesson to keep in mind is that all of these factors coalesced in such a manner to allow Bennett to write a book on crime that makes sense because it is timely in view of what we know about society today and what we think it may look like in the future. Remember, writers—like ideas—are captives of the time and place in which they live. For this reason alone, it is impossible to understand criminological theory outside its social context (Rennie, 1978). It remains to be seen how Bennett's book will be evaluated in 20 to 50 years, and it remains to be seen if the "criminal man" of the future fits Bennett's predictions.

One more cautionary comment needs to be made. Just as today's social context has made a book like Bennett's possible, the context of previous historical eras made different kinds of theories about crime possible. Early theories of crime tended to locate the cause of crime not in demographic shifts as has Bennett, but within the individual: in their soul (spiritualism/demonology), their will (classical school), or their bodily constitutions (positive school). We will examine each of these theories in this chapter. We are now ready to begin our search for the criminal man. We start with the earliest explanation, spiritualism.

Spiritualism

As an explanation of criminal behavior, spiritualism provides a sharp contrast to the scholarly explanations used today. Unlike today's theories, spiritualism stressed the conflict between absolute good and absolute evil (Tannenbaum, 1938). People who committed crimes were thought to be possessed by evil spirits, often referred to as demons.

Although the genesis of this perspective is lost to antiquity, there is ample archaeological, anthropological, and historical evidence that this explanation has been around for many centuries. We know, for example, that primitive people explained natural disasters such as floods and famines as punishments by spirits for wrongdoings. This type of view was used also by the ancient Egyptians, Greeks, and Romans. Much later, during the Middle Ages in Europe, spiritualistic explanations had become well organized and connected to the political and social structure of feudalism. One important reason for this particular development is that, originally, crime was a private matter between the victim or the family of the victim and the offender(s). Unfortunately, this means of responding to offenses had a tendency to create long blood feuds that could destroy entire families. There was also the problem of justice: A guilty offender with a strong family might never be punished.

To avoid some of these problems, other methods were constructed for dealing with those accused of committing a crime. Trial by battle, for example, permitted the victim or some member of his or her family to fight the offender or some member of the offender's family (Vold & Bernard, 1986). It was believed that victory would go to the innocent if he or she believed and trusted God. Unfortunately, this arrangement permitted great warriors to continue engaging in criminal behavior, buttressed by the belief they would be found always "innocent." Trial by ordeal determined guilt or innocence by subjecting the accused to life-threatening and painful situations. People, for instance, might have huge stones piled on them. If they were innocent, it was believed that God would keep them from being crushed to death. If they were guilty, a painful death would occur. People also were tied up and thrown into a river or pond. If they were innocent, God would allow them to float; drowning meant they were guilty (Vold & Bernard, 1986).

Compurgation represented another means of determining innocence or guilt based on spiritualism. Unlike trial by battle or ordeal that involved physical pain and the threat of death, compurgation allowed the accused to have reputable people swear an oath that he or she was innocent. The logic was based on the belief that no one would lie under oath for fear of God's punishment (Vold & Bernard, 1986).

The same fear of God's punishment formed the explanation of crime and deviance for what Erikson (1966) has called the "wayward Puritans," citizens in the early American Massachusetts Bay Colony. And later when our penitentiaries were constructed they were thought of as places for "penitents who were sorry for their sins" (Vold & Bernard, 1986, p. 8). Today we have many groups and individuals who believe crimes and other wrongs can be explained by the devil. In early 1987, for example, when "prime time preacher" Jim Bakker of the famed PTL Club (Praise the Lord and People That Love) confessed to an adulterous one-night stand with a former church secretary, some of his followers said it was the result of the devil's work (*Newsweek*, 1987a). And on one occasion when Internal Revenue Service auditors revealed that several millions of dollars were unaccounted for by the PTL organization, Bakker's then wife Tammy Faye said the devil must have gotten into the computer (*New York Times*, 1987a). Others who have been caught for criminal acts have turned to God for a cure for their behavior. Charles Colson of Watergate fame, for instance, has taken the Christian message to prisoners as a solution to their problems.

It is important to remember that even though people may criticize "the devil made me do it" argument as quaint or odd, it nevertheless makes sense for some people who try to understand and explain crime. In fact, it even may be argued that the public's interest in this type of explanation grows at the same rate as our population growth. According to the National Council of Churches, church membership grows gradually at approximately the same rate as the nation's population. Altogether nearly 70% of the population say they are involved with a church, a figure that has remained steady in recent years (*New York Times*, 1987b, p. 13).

The major problem with spiritualistic explanations, nonetheless, is that they cannot be tested scientifically. Because the cause of crime according to this theory is otherworldly, it cannot be verified empirically. It is primarily for this reason that modern theories of crime and social order rely on explanations that are based on this world. These theories are called natural explanations.

Naturalistic theories and spiritualistic explanations have in common their origin in the ancient world. Despite this common origin, the two perspectives are very different. Thus, by focusing on the physical world of facts, naturalistic theories seek explanations that are more specific and detailed than are spiritualistic theories. This approach to thinking and explanation was very much part of the Greeks, for instance, who early on in their search for knowledge philosophically divided the world into a dualistic reality of mind and matter. This form of thinking is still prevalent in the Western world as evidenced by reasoning that restricts explanations of human behavior to either passion or reason.

An early example of a naturalistic explanation is found in "Hippocrates' (460 B.C.) dictum that the brain is the organ of the mind" (Vold, 1958, p. 7). Additional evidence of efforts to explain phenomena by naturalistic reasoning was present approximately 350 years later in the first century B.C. in Roman thought, which attempted to explain the idea of "progress" with little reliance on demons or spirits (Vold, 1958, p. 7). The existence of this reasoning, however, does not mean that demonic and spiritualistic explanations had begun to wane by the time of the Roman Empire. In fact, these explanations reigned high well into the Middle Ages.

On the other hand, naturalistic explanations persisted in spite of the spiritualistic perspective's dominance, and by the 16th and 17th centuries several scholars were studying and explaining humans in terms known to them (Vold, 1958). Their efforts are identified collectively as the classical school of criminology. Later in this chapter, we will consider a second influential naturalistic theory, the positivist school of criminology.

The Classical School: Criminal as Calculator

The most important feature of this school of thought is its emphasis on the individual criminal as a person who is capable of calculating what he or she wants to do. This idea was supported by a philosophy that held that human beings had free will and that behavior was guided by hedonism. Individuals, in other words, were guided by a pain and pleasure principle by which they calculated the risks and rewards they would receive for their actions. Accordingly, punishment should be suited to the offense, not to the social or physical characteristics of the criminal.

If this sounds familiar, you should not be surprised; one of the basic tenets of our legal heritage is that people should be given equal treatment before the law. People should not be punished or rewarded just because they happen to have the right name or be from a powerful family. Equality is one of the powerful ideas that was endorsed widely by the 18th- and 19th-century Enlightenment writers who influenced our founding fathers. Of particular interest here is the scholar most often identified as the leader of the classical school of criminology: Cesare Bonesana Marchese de Beccaria (1738-1794), an Italian mathematician and economist. It is Beccaria who pulled together many of the most powerful 18th-century ideas of democratic liberalism and connected them to issues of criminal justice.

Although it is true that Beccaria was born into an aristocratic family and had the benefit of a solid education in the liberal arts, there is little if any evidence in his background that would have predicted that his one small book on penal reform, *On Crimes and Punishments,* would be acknowledged eventually to have had "more practical effect than any other treatise ever written in the long campaign against barbarism in criminal law and procedure" (Beccaria, 1764/1963, p. ix). Indeed, one biographical overview of Beccaria indicates that his education failed to produce a modicum of enthusiasm for scholarship except for some attraction to mathematics (Monachesi, 1973). But this interest soon passed and what seems to have emerged is a discontented young man with strong arguments against much of the status quo, including his father's objections to his marriage in 1761 (Beccaria, 1764/1963, p. xii). To understand Beccaria's great contribution we must examine the social context of his life.

Unlike the United States' concern for protecting its citizens through equal protection, due process, and trial by one's peers, the criminal justice system of Beccaria's Europe, especially the ancient regime in France, was "planned to ruin citizens" (Radzinowicz, 1966, p. 1), a characterization that applied to the police, criminal procedures, and punishment. The police of Paris, for example, were "the most ruthless and efficient police marching in the world" (p. 2). They were allowed by the French monarchy to deal not only with criminal matters, but also with the morals and political opinions of French citizens. They relied heavily on spies, extensive covert letter opening, and the state-approved capacity not only to arrest people without warrants but also to pass judgment and to hold people in custody indefinitely on unknown charges.

Once arrested the accused had few legal protections. He or she was cut off from legal assistance, subjected to torture, and kept in secret from family and friends. Witnesses against the accused testified in secret. Once guilt was determined, punishments were severe, "ranging from burning alive or breaking on the wheel to the galleys and many forms of mutilation, whipping, branding and the pillory" (Radzinowicz, 1966, p. 3). Death by execution in early 18th-century London took place every 6 weeks, with 5 to 15 condemned hanged on each occasion (Lofland, 1973, p. 35).

Beccaria became familiar with these conditions through the association and friendship of Alessandro Verri, who held the office of Protector of Prisoners in Milan, Italy, where Beccaria lived. Outraged by these conditions and recently having become familiar with the writings of such scholars as Montesquieu, Helvetius, Voltaire, Bacon, Rousseau, Diderot, and Hume, Beccaria was encouraged by a small group of intellectuals to take up his pen in behalf of humanity. He was not eager to write, however, because he did not enjoy writing and because he worried about political reprisals for expressing his views. He so feared persecution from the monarchy for his views that he chose to publish the book anonymously (Monachesi, 1973). It took 11 months to write, but once published, the volume excited all of Europe as if a nerve had been exposed. By 1767, when the book was first translated into English, it already had been through several French and Italian editions. But what did it say? What caused all of the excitement?

Beccaria's tightly reasoned argument can be summarized in relatively simple terms (Radzinowicz, 1966; Vold, 1958). First, in order to escape war and chaos, individuals gave up some of their liberty and established a contractual society. This established the sovereignty of a nation and the ability of the nation to create criminal law and to punish offenders. Second, because criminal laws placed restrictions on individual freedoms, they should be restricted in scope. They should not be employed to enforce moral virtue. To prohibit human behavior unnecessarily was to increase rather than decrease crime. Third, the presumption of innocence should be the guiding principle in the administration of justice, and at all stages of the justice process the rights of all parties involved should be protected. Fourth, the complete criminal law code should be written and should define all offenses and punishments in advance. This would allow the public to judge how and if their liberties were being preserved.

Fifth, punishment should be based on retributive reasoning because the guilty had attacked another individual's rights. Sixth, the severity of the punishment should be limited, and it should not go beyond what is necessary for crime prevention and deterrence. Seventh, criminal punishment should correspond with the seriousness of the crime; the punishment should fit the crime, not the criminal. Fines, for example, would be appropriate for simple thefts, although the harsher sanctions of corporal punishment and labor would be acceptable for violent crimes. Eighth, punishment must be a certainty and should be inflicted quickly. Ninth, punishment should not be administered to set an example; neither should it be concerned with reforming the offender. Tenth, the offender should be viewed as an independent and reasonable person who weighed the consequences of the crime. Offenders should be assumed to have the same power of resistance as nonoffenders. Eleventh, for Beccaria, the aim of every good system of legislation was the prevention of crime. He reasoned it was better to prevent crimes than to punish them.

Beccaria was not, however, the only scholar in his time to consider these issues. Jeremy Bentham (1748-1832), an English jurist and philosopher, also argued that punishment should be a deterrent, and he too explained behavior as a result of free will and "hedonistic calculus" (Bentham, 1948). John Howard (1726-1790), also English and a contemporary of Beccaria and Bentham, studied prisons and advocated prison reform (Howard, 1792/1973). His work is credited often with having influenced the passage of England's Penitentiary Act of 1779, which addressed prison reform.

The influence of these writers, however, went far beyond the passage of specific laws. Their ideas inspired revolutions and the creation of entirely new legal codes. The French Revolution of 1789 and its famous Code of 1791 and the United States Constitution each were influenced by the classical school. However, by the 1820s crime still was flourishing, and the argument that bad laws made bad people was being questioned seriously (Rothman, 1971). Also, the argument that all criminal behavior could be explained by hedonism was weakening as the importance of aggravating and mitigating circumstances increased. Nor did the new laws provide for the separate treatment of children. Nevertheless, the classical school did make significant and lasting contributions. The call for laws to be impartial and specific and for punishment to be for crimes instead of criminals, as well as the belief that all citizens should be treated fairly and equally, now have become accepted ideas. But what caused crime remained a troubling question unanswered by the Enlightenment's "rather uncomplicated view of Rational Man" (Sykes, 1978, p. 11), a view based primarily on armchair thinking. The result was a new search for the "criminal man," with emphasis given to action being determined instead of being the result of free will. The advocates of this new way of thinking created what came to be known as the positivist school of criminology.

The Positivist School:
Criminal as Determined

The most significant difference between the classical school and the positivist school is the latter's search for empirical facts to confirm the idea that crime was determined by multiple factors. This is a clear shift away from the reasoning of Beccaria and Bentham, who thought crime resulted from the free will and hedonism of the individual criminal. As will become apparent, the 19th century's first positivists wanted scientific proof that crime was caused by features within the individual. They primarily emphasized the mind and the body of the criminal, thus to some extent neglecting social factors external to the individual. (Later these factors became the focus of sociological explanations of crime; more about this type of explanation later.)

However, the search for causes of crime in fact did not begin with the 19th-century positivists. Early examples in literature, for instance, connect the body through the ideas of beauty and ugliness to good and evil behavior. Shakespeare's *Tempest* portrays a deformed servant's morality as offensive as his appearance, and Homer's *Iliad* depicts a despised defamer as one of the ugliest of the Greeks. This form of thinking is present still, as evidenced by contemporary female beauty contests in which contestants vie with one another not only by publicly displaying their scantily clothed bodies but also through rendering an artistic performance of some sort. A beautiful woman is expected to do good things. Although an example of sexist thinking, the connection between physical features and behavior is less than scientific.

The Birth of the Positivist School:
Lombroso's Theory of the Criminal Man

The modern search for multifactor explanations of crime is usually attributed to Cesare Lombroso (1835-1909), an Italian often called "the father of modern criminology" (Wolfgang, 1973, p. 232). A clue to his work and the social context of his life is gleaned from his self-description as "a slave to facts," a comment that could not have been made by writers of the classical school. In the century that separated Beccaria's graduation from the University of Pavia (1758) and Lombroso's graduation from the same institution (1858) with a degree in medicine, secular, rational-scientific thinking and experimentation had become increasingly more acceptable ways to analyze reality.

An essential clue to understanding Lombroso's work is to recognize that in the last half of the 19th century the answer to the age-old question, "What sort of creatures are human beings?" had begun to depart from theological answers to answers provided by the objective sciences, particularly biology. It was here that humans' origins as creatures were connected to the rest of the animal world through evolution (Vold, 1958). No other 19th-century name is associated more often with this connection than Charles Darwin (1809-1882), the English naturalist who argued that humans evolved from animals. His major works, *Origins of the Species* (1859/1981), *The Descent of Man* (1871), and *Expression of Emotion in Man and Animals* (1872), each predate Lombroso's. For Lombroso the objective search for explaining human behavior meant disagreement with free will philosophy. He became interested in psychiatry "sustained by close study of the anatomy and physiology of the brain" (Wolfgang, 1973, p. 234).

Lombroso's interest in biological explanations of criminal behavior developed between 1859 and 1863 when he was serving as an army physician on various military posts. During this time he developed the idea that diseases, especially cretinism and pellagra, contributed to mental and physical deficiencies "which may result in violence and homicide" (Wolfgang, 1973, p. 236). He also used his position as a military physician to measure systematically approximately 3,000 soldiers in order to document the physical differences among inhabitants from various regions of Italy. From this study, Wolfgang tells us, Lombroso made "observations on tattooing, particularly the more obscene designs which he felt distinguished infractious soldiers" (p. 235). Later Lombroso used the practice of tattooing as a distinguishing characteristic of criminals. He started to publish his research on the idea that biology could explain criminal behavior in a series of papers that first started to appear in 1861. By 1876 he published his findings in *On Criminal Man* (1876), a book that went through several Italian editions and foreign language translations.

The central tenet of Lombroso's early explanations of crime is that criminals represent a peculiar physical type, distinctively different from noncriminals. In general terms, he claimed that criminals represent a form of degeneracy that was manifested in physical characteristics reflective of earlier forms of evolution. He described criminals as atavistic, a throwback to an earlier form of evolutionary life. For instance, he thought ears of unusual size, sloping foreheads, excessively long arms, receding chins, and twisted noses were indicative of physical characteristics found among criminals.

Lombroso classified criminals into four major categories: (a) born criminals, people with atavistic characteristics; (b) insane criminals, who included idiots, imbeciles, and paranoiacs, as well as epileptics and alcoholics; (c) occasional criminals or criminaloids, whose crimes are explained primarily by opportunity, although they too have innate traits that predispose them to criminality; and (d) criminals of passion who commit crimes because of anger, love, or honor. They are characterized by being propelled to crime by an "irresistible force" (Wolfgang, 1973, pp. 252-253).

To Lombroso's credit, he modified his theory throughout five editions of *On Criminal Man,* with each one giving attention to more and more environmental explanations, including climate, rainfall, sex, marriage customs, laws, the structure of government, church organization, and the effects of other factors. However, he never completely gave up the idea of the existence of a born criminal type, and although he is most often thought of as the person who connected biological explanations to criminal behavior, he in fact was not the first person to do so.

This idea, for instance, was developed in the 1760s by the Swiss scholar Johann Kaspar Lavater (1741-1801), who claimed there was a relationship between facial features and behavior. Later, Franz Joseph Gall (1758-1828), an eminent European anatomist, expanded the idea and argued that the shape of one's head could explain an individual's personal characteristics. This explanation was called *phrenology,* and by the 1820s it was stimulating much interest in the United States. One book on the subject, for instance, went through nine editions between 1837-1840 (Vold, 1958). It is instructive to note that as phrenology increased in popularity, its explanatory powers were expanded; more and more different forms of human conduct, it was claimed, could be explained by the shape of the head. The importance of phrenology for us is that it indicates the popularity of biological explanations of behavior nearly 50 years before Lombroso received his degree in medicine in 1858 and long before he ever was called the father of modern criminology. In fact, Ellis (1913) identified almost two dozen European scholars who had pointed to the relationship between criminals' physical and mental characteristics and their behavior before Lombroso. So why should Lombroso be studied and remembered?

Although his biological explanation of crime is considered simple and naive today, Lombroso nevertheless made significant contributions that continue to have an impact on criminology. Most noteworthy here is the attention he gave to a multifactor explanation of crime that included not only heredity but social, cultural, and economic variables. The multiple factor explanation is common in today's study of crime. Lombroso is credited also with pushing the study of crime away from abstract metaphysical, legal, and juristic explanations as the basis of penology "to a scientific study of the criminal and the conditions under which he commits crime" (Wolfgang, 1973, p. 286). We are indebted to Lombroso also for the lessons he taught regarding methods of research. He demonstrated the importance of examining clinical and historical records, and he emphasized that no detail should be overlooked when searching for explanations of criminal behavior.

Lombroso's Legacy:
The Italian Criminological Tradition

Enrico Ferri. Lombroso's legacy of positivism was continued and expanded by the brilliant career and life of a fellow Italian, Enrico Ferri (1856-1929). Born into the family of a poor salt-and-tobacco shopkeeper, Ferri came to be one of the most influential figures in the history of criminology (Sellin, 1973). In the words of Thorsten Sellin, one of the world's most eminent criminologists, who as a young man in November 1925 heard Ferri lecture at the age of 70, "Ferri the man is as fascinating as Ferri the scholar" (Sellin,

1973, p. 362). He was a scholar with brilliant ideas and strong passions who believed that life without an ideal, whatever it may be, was not worth living. By the age of 16, Ferri was developing his lifelong commitment to the "scientific orientation," having come under the influence of a great teacher who himself was of strong convictions. Ferri gave up the clerical robe for the study of philosophy.

Ferri was just 21 when he published his first major work, *The Theory of Imputability and the Denial of Free Will.* It was an attack on free will arguments, and it contained a theoretical perspective that was to characterize much of Ferri's later work on criminality, as well as his political activism. Unlike Lombroso who gave more attention to biological than to social factors, Ferri gave more emphasis to the interrelatedness of social, economic, and political factors that contribute to crime (Vold, 1958). He argued, for example, that criminality could be explained by studying the interactive effects among physical factors (such as race, geography, and temperature), individual factors (such as age, sex, and psychological variables), and social factors (e.g., population, religion, and culture). He also argued that crime could be controlled by social changes, many of which were directed toward the benefit of the working classes. He advocated subsidized housing, birth control, freedom of marriage, divorce, and public recreation facilities, each reflective of his socialistic belief that the state is responsible for creating better living and working conditions. It is not surprising that Ferri was also a political activist.

He was elected to public office after a much publicized lawsuit in which he successfully defended a group of peasants accused of "incitement to civil war" after a dispute with wealthy landowners (Sellin, 1973, p. 377). He was reelected 11 times by the Socialist Party and stayed in office until 1924. Throughout his career Ferri attempted to integrate his positivistic approach to crime with political changes. For example, he tried unsuccessfully to have the new Italian Penal Code of 1889 reflect a positivistic philosophy instead of classical reasoning. And after Mussolini came to power in the early 1920s, Ferri was invited to write a new penal code for Italy (Vold, 1958). It reflected his positivistic and socialistic orientation, but it too was rejected for being too much of a departure from classical legal reasoning. After nearly 50 years as a socialist-liberal, Ferri changed his philosophy and endorsed fascism as a practical approach to reform. According to Sellin (1973), fascism appealed to Ferri because it offered a reaffirmation of the state's authority over excessive individualism, which he had criticized often.

Although it is puzzling to try to understand Ferri's shift from socialism to fascism, some insight is provided by considering that he was living at a time of great social change, and as a person with humble origins, he wanted the changes to produce a better society. To accomplish this reform he felt that individuals must be legally responsible for their actions, instead of being only morally responsible to God. This approach to responsibility represented a radical departure from tradition because it was offered within a theoretical framework that called for "scientific experts" not only to explain crime but also to write laws and administer punishment. In essence, it was a call for the state to act "scientifically" in matters of social policy.

Ferri's call for legal responsibility was offered when Italy was experiencing much unrest caused mostly by industrialization in the late 1800s and later by the social disorder stemming from World War I. Evidence of Ferri's response to the changing conditions in Italy is found in the fact that in the first four editions of *Sociologia Criminale,* he had only five classes of criminals: (a) the born or instinctive criminal whom Lombroso had identified as the atavist; (b) the insane criminals who was clinically identified as mentally ill; (c) the passion criminal who committed crime as a result of either prolonged and chronic mental problems or an emotional state; (d) the occasional criminal who was the product of family and social conditions more than abnormal personal physical or mental problems; and (e) the habitual criminal who acquired the habit from the social environment. For the fifth edition of *Sociologia Criminale* (1929-1930) he added a new explanation of crime, the involuntary criminal. Ferri explained this phenomenon as "becoming more and more numerous in our mechanical age in the vertiginous speed of modern life" (Sellin, 1973, p. 370).

We must understand also that Ferri's interest in fascism did not occur in a social void absent of public support. It took only 5 years from the time Benito Mussolini formed the Fasci del Combattimento in 1919 until the first elections in Italy under the fascists in 1924, when he received 65% of the vote. When Mussolini asked Ferri to rewrite the Italian code, Ferri's response was consistent with the mood of the times.

Raffaele Garofalo. After Lombroso and Ferri, Raffaele Garofalo (1852-1934) was the last major contributor to the positivist or the Italian school of criminology. Unlike Lombroso's emphasis on criminals as abnormal types with distinguishable anatomic, psychological, and social features, or Ferri's emphasis on socialistic reforms and social defenses against crime,

Garofalo is remembered for his pursuit of practical solutions to concrete problems located in the legal institutions of his day and for his doctrine of "natural crimes."

In many ways his work represents more clearly than either Lombroso or Ferri the currents of interests in late-19th-century Europe. This is the result of three different phenomena, each interconnected. First, Garofalo was born only 6 years before Lombroso received his degree in medicine. Thus, by the time he was an adult, enough time had passed since the publication of Lombroso's and Ferri's major works to permit some degree of reactive evaluation. Second, Garofalo was both an academician and a practicing lawyer, prosecutor, and magistrate who faced daily the practical problems of the criminal justice system. Accordingly, he was in an excellent position to be familiar with the great attention Lombroso's and Ferri's works had received in both academic and penal circles and with the practical policy implications of their writings. Third, at the time Garofalo published the first edition of *Criminology* (1885) at age 33, the social Darwinian era was at the peak of its existence, with numerous suggestions from biology, psychology, and the social sciences on how society could guarantee the survival of the fittest through criminal law and penal practice (Hawkins, 1931).

Garofalo's theoretical arguments on the nature of crime and on the nature of criminals were consistent with social Darwinism. He argued, for example, that because society is a "natural body," crimes are offenses "against the law of nature." Criminal action was therefore crime against nature. Accordingly, the "rules of nature" were the rules of right conduct revealed to humans through their reasoning. It is obvious here that Garofalo's thinking also included some influence from the classical school and its emphasis on reasoning. For Garofalo the proper rules of conduct came from thinking about what such rules should allow or prohibit. He nevertheless identified acts that no society could refuse to recognize as criminal and repress by punishment: natural crimes. These offenses, according to Garofalo, violated two basic human sentiments found among people of all ages, namely the sentiments of probity and pity (Allen, 1973, p. 321; Vold, 1958, p. 37). *Pity* is the sentiment of revulsion against the voluntary infliction of suffering on others; *probity* refers to the respect for the property rights of others.

The social Darwinian influence on Garofalo's thinking is apparent also in his explanation of where the sentiments of probity and pity could be found. They were basic moral sensibilities that appear more or less in "*advanced form in all civilized societies*" (Allen, 1973, p. 321; emphasis added), meaning that some societies had not evolved to the point of advanced moral reasoning. Similarly, the Darwinian influence is present in Garofalo's argument that some members of society may have a higher than average sense of morality because they are "superior members of the group" (p. 321).

Garofalo's notion of the characteristics of the criminal also revealed a Darwinian influence, but less so than when he addressed the issue of punishment and penal policies. In developing this portion of his theoretical arguments, he first reconsidered the Lombrosian idea of crime being associated with certain anatomical and physical characteristics and concluded that although the idea had merit, it had not been proved. Sometimes physical abnormalities were present; sometimes not. He argued instead for the idea that true criminals lacked properly developed altruistic sentiments (Allen, 1973). True criminals, in other words, had psychic or moral anomalies that could be transmitted through heredity. However, the transmission of moral deficiencies through heredity was a matter of degree. This conclusion led Garofalo to identify four criminal classes, each one distinct from the other because of deficiencies in the basic sentiments of pity and probity.

Murderers were totally lacking in both pity and probity and would kill or steal when given the opportunity. Lesser criminals, Garofalo acknowledged, were more difficult to identify. He divided this category based on whether criminals lacked sentiments of either pity or probity. Violent criminals lacked pity, which could be influenced very much by environmental factors such as alcohol or the fact that criminality was endemic to the population. Thieves, on the other hand, suffered from a lack of probity, a condition that "may be more the product of social factors than the criminals in other classes" (Allen, 1973, p. 323). His last category contained cynics or sexual criminals, some of whom would be classified among the violent criminals because they lacked pity. Other lascivious criminals required a separate category because their actions stemmed from a "low level of moral energy" rather than from a lack of pity (p. 329).

Garofalo's reliance on Darwinian reasoning is obvious nowhere more than when he considers appropriate measures for the social defense against crime. Here he again uses the analogy of society as a natural body that must either adapt to the environment or be eliminated. He reasoned that because true criminals' actions revealed an inability to live by the basic human sentiments necessary for society to survive, they should be eliminated. Their death would contribute to the survival of society (Barnes, 1930). For lesser criminals, he proposed that elimination take the form of life imprisonment or overseas transportation (Allen, 1973).

It is clear that deterrence and rehabilitation were secondary considerations for Garofalo. However, he favored "enforced reparation" and indeterminate sentences, which indicates that Garofalo's social defenses against crime were modeled to some extent on the psychic characteristics of the offender. In this regard his position of punishment is more in line with the free will reasoning of the classical scholars than Garofalo might admit. One conclusion about Garofalo is clear, however, and that is his position on the importance of society over the individual. To him the individual represented but a cell of the social body that could be exterminated without much, if any, great loss to society (Allen, 1973). By giving society or the group supremacy over the individual, Garofalo and Ferri were willing to sacrifice individual rights to the opinion of "scientific experts," whose decisions might not include the opinions of those they were evaluating and judging, nor the opinion of the public. Not surprisingly, their work was accepted by Mussolini's regime in Italy because it lent the mantle of scientific credence to the ideas of racial purity, national strength, and authoritarian leadership (Vold, 1958).

The work of the Italian positivists also suffered from serious methodological research problems. Their work, for instance, was not very statistically sophisticated. As a result, their conclusions about real or significant differences between criminals and noncriminals were in fact highly speculative.

This problem was addressed by Charles Goring's (1913) study on 3,000 English convicts and a control group of normal males. Unlike Lombroso, Ferri, and Garofalo, Goring employed an expert statistician to make computations about the physical differences between criminals and noncriminals. After 8 years of research on 96 different physical features, Goring concluded that there were no significant differences between criminals and noncriminals except for stature and body weight. Criminals were found to be slightly smaller. Goring interpreted this finding as confirmation of his hypothesis that criminals were biologically inferior, but he did not find a physical criminal type.

The Continuing Search for the Individual Roots of Crime

Body types and crime. The search for a constitutionally determined "criminal man" did not stop with Goring's 1913 conclusions. Kretschmer (1925) took up the theme as the result of his study of 260 insane people in Swabia, a southwestern German town. He was impressed with the fact that his subjects had definite types of body builds that were associated, he thought, with certain types of psychic dispositions. First published in German in 1922 and translated into English in 1925, Kretschmer identified four body types: asthenic, athletic, pyknic, and some mixed, unclassifiable types. He found asthenics to be lean and narrowly built, with a deficiency of thickness in the overall body. These men were so flat-chested and skinny that their ribs could be counted easily. The athletic build had broad shoulders, excellent musculature, deep chests, flat stomachs, and powerful legs. They were the 1920s counterpart of the modern "hunks" of media fame. The pyknics were of medium build with a propensity to be rotund, sort of soft-appearing with rounded shoulders, broad faces, and short, stubby hands. The asthenic and athletic builds, Kretschmer argued, were associated with schizophrenic personalities and the pyknics were manic-depressives.

Four years after the English translation appeared in the United States, Mohr and Gundlach (1929-1930) published a report based on 254 native-born, White male inmates in the state penitentiary at Joliet, Illinois. They found that pyknics were more likely than asthenics or athletics to have been convicted of fraud, violence, and sex offenses. Asthenics and athletics, on the other hand, were more likely to have been convicted of burglary, robbery, and larceny. However, Mohr and Gundlach were unable to demonstrate any connection between body build, crime, and psychic disposition.

Ten years later the search for physical types that caused crime was taken up by Ernest A. Hooton, a Harvard anthropologist. He began with an extensive critique of Goring's research methods and proceeded to a detailed analysis of the measurements of more than 17,000 criminals and noncriminals from eight different states (Hooton, 1939). In his three-volume study he argued that "criminals are inferior to civilians in nearly all of their bodily measurements" (Hooton, 1939, Vol. 1, p. 329). He also reported that low foreheads indicated inferiority and that "a depressed physical and social environment determines Negro and Negroid delinquency to a much greater extent than it does in the case of Whites" (p. 388).

These and similar conclusions generated severe criticism of Hooton's work, especially the racist overtones and his failure to recognize that the prisoners he studied did not represent criminal offenders who had not been caught or offenders who had been guilty but not convicted. His control group was criticized also for not being representative of any known population of people. They consisted of Nashville firefighters and members of the militia, each of whom could be expected to have passed rigorous physical examinations that would distinguish them from average males. He also included in his control group beachgoers, mental patients, and college students. He offered no explanation as to why these disparate categories of people represented normal physical types. Hooton was criticized also for treating some small difference in measurement as greatly significant and for ignoring other differences that were found.

It is important to notice that despite the stinging criticism received by Hooton and by others who were searching for biological explanations, the search nevertheless continued and expanded into the 1940s and 1950s. The work by William H. Sheldon (1949), for instance, shifted attention away from adults to delinquent male youths. He studied 200 males between 15 and 21 years of age in an effort to link physiques to temperament, intelligence, and delinquency. By relying on intense physical and psychological examinations, Sheldon produced an "Index to Delinquency" that was used to give a quick and easy profile of each male's problems. A total score of 10 meant a lad's case was severe enough to require total institutionalization; a score of 7 meant the case was borderline, while a score of 6 was interpreted as favoring adjustment and independent living outside of an institution.

Sheldon (1949) classified the boys' physiques by measuring the degree to which they possessed a combination of three different body components. The three components were endomorphy, mesomorphy, and ectomorphy. Each could dominate a physique. Endomorphs tended to be soft, fat people; mesomorphs had muscular and athletic builds; ectomorphs had skinny, flat, and fragile physiques. Sheldon also rated each of the 200 youths' physiques by assigning a score of 1 to 7 for each component. For example, the average physique score for the 200 males was 3.5-4.6-2.7, a rather husky male (p. 727). Overall, Sheldon concluded that because youths came from parents who were delinquent in very much the same way that the boys were delinquent, the factors that produce delinquency were inherited.

Sheldon's findings were given considerable support by Sheldon Glueck and Eleanor Glueck's (1950) comparative study of male delinquents and nondelinquents. As a group, the delinquents were found to have narrower faces, wider chests, larger and broader waists, and bigger forearms and upper arms than the nondelinquents. An examination of the overall ratings of the boys indicated that approximately 60% of the delinquents and

31% of the nondelinquents were predominantly mesomorphic. They included this finding in their list of outstanding factors associated with male delinquency. As with each of the previous scholars who have attempted to explain criminal behavior by relying primarily on biological factors, their findings neglected the importance of sociological phenomena. It is unclear, for instance, if the Gluecks' mesomorphs were delinquents because of their builds and dispositions or because their physiques and dispositions are conceived socially as being associated with delinquency. This in turn could create expectations about illegal activities that males might feel pressured to perform.

Psychogenic causes of crime. At this point we turn our attention to another form of positivism, one that places no emphasis on types of physiques as causes of crime. Here the search for the causes of crime is directed to the mind. Often these theories are referred to as the "psychogenic school" because they seek to explain crime by focusing attention on the personality and how it was produced. In this way, the analysis is "dynamic" rather than "constitutional," as was the emphasis from biological positivism. This school of thought developed along two distinct lines: One stressed psychoanalysis; the other placed emphasis on personality traits. We begin with Freud and the psychoanalytical approach.

Sigmund Freud (1859-1939), a physician, did not address directly the question of what caused criminal behavior. He was interested in explaining all behavior, including crime. If an explanation could be found for normal behavior, surely, he reasoned, it also could explain crime.

At the core of his and his colleagues' theories is the argument that all behavior is motivated and purposive. However, not all desires and behavior are socially acceptable, so they must be repressed into the unconsciousness of the mind for the sake of morality and social order. The result is that tensions exist between the unconscious id, which is a great reservoir of aggressive biological and psychological urges, and the conscious ego, which controls and molds the individual. The superego, according to Freud (1920, 1927, 1930), is the force of self-criticism that reflects the basic behavioral requirements of a particular culture. Crime, therefore, is a symbolic expression of inner tensions that each person has but fails to control. It is an "acted out" expression of having learned self-control improperly.

Franz Alexander, a psychoanalyst, and William Healy, a physician, both applied Freud's principles in their study of criminal behavior (Alexander & Healy, 1935). For example, they explained one male criminal's behavior as the result of four unconscious needs: (a) overcompensation for a sense of inferiority, (b) the attempt to relieve a sense of guilt, (c) spite reactions toward his mother, and (d) gratification of his dependent tendencies by living a carefree existence in prison.

Freud's colleague, August Aichhorn (1936), wrote that many children continued to act infantile because they failed to develop an ego and superego that would permit them to conform to the expectations of childhood, adolescence, and adulthood. Such children, Aichhorn contended, continued to operate on the "pleasure principle," having failed to adapt to the "reality principle" of adulthood. Kate Friedlander (1949), a student of Freud and Aichhorn, also focused on the behavior of children and argued that some children develop antisocial behavior or faulty character that makes them prone to delinquency. Redl and Wineman (1951) advanced a similar argument that stated that some children develop a delinquent ego. The result is a hostile attitude toward adults and aggression toward authority because the child has not developed a good ego and superego.

The search for personality traits, the second tradition of investigation that attempted to locate the cause of crime within the mind, was started by attempting to explain mental faculties biologically. Feeblemindedness, insanity, stupidity, and dull-wittedness were thought to be inherited. This view was part of the efforts in the late 19th century to explain crime constitutionally. It became a popular explanation in the United States after *The Jukes* was published (Dugdale, 1877). It described a family as being involved in crime because they suffered from "degeneracy and innate depravity."

Interest in explaining family-based mental deficiencies by heredity continued through the end of the 19th century and well into the first quarter of the 20th century. H. H. Goddard, for example, published *The Kallikak Family* in 1912, and a follow-up study on the Jukes by Estrabrook appeared in 1916. Unfortunately, these studies were very general, each avoiding advanced and comparative statistics.

More exacting studies of the mind came from European research on the measurement of intelligence. French psychologist Alfred Binet (1857-1911), for example, first pursued intelligence testing in laboratory settings and later applied his findings in an effort to solve the problem of retardation in Paris's schools. Aided by his assistant, Theodore Simon, Binet revised his IQ tests in 1905, 1908, and 1911, and when the scale appeared in the United States it was revised once again. Common to each revision was the idea that individuals should have a mental age that could be identified with an intelligence quotient, or IQ score.

H. H. Goddard (1914, 1921), author of the famed Kallikak study, usually is credited as the first person to test the IQs of prison inmates. He concluded that although most inmates were feebleminded, the percentage of feeblemindedness ranged from 29% to 89%. However, his research was plagued by the difficult issue of determining what score(s) should be used to define feeblemindedness.

The legitimacy and practical value of IQ testing were given great support when the U.S. Army Psychological Corps decided to use this method to determine who was fit for military service in World War I (Goddard, 1927). The result was that at one point nearly a third of the draft army was thought to be feebleminded. This conclusion was modified later, but faith in IQ testing as a means of explaining crime continued well past World War I and into the 1920s and 1930s. However, the increasing use of sophisticated research methods began to produce results that indicated that when inmates were compared to the general population, only slight differences in feeblemindedness were found. Today very little if any research tries to explain crime as the result of feeblemindedness.

The Consequence of Theory:
Policy Implications

The Positivist School and
the Control of the Biological Criminal

The most obvious orientation displayed by positivists of the mid-19th century through the first quarter of the 20th century was their placement of the causes of crime primarily within individual offenders. This is not at all surprising once we recognize that the early positivists—especially Lombroso, Ferri, and Garofalo in Italy; Freud, Aichhorn, and Kretschmer in Austria and Germany; and Alexander and Healy in the United States— each were educated in medicine, in law, or in both fields. Each of these disciplines places great emphasis on individuals as the explanation of behavior. It is this flavor of emphasis that sheds much light on the policy consequences of their explanations of crime. But the disciplinary perspectives alone are inadequate for the purposes of understanding fully these consequences, because each discipline was influenced by the general temper of the times. For the positivists considered in this chapter, the temper of the times was Darwinism strongly flavored by Victorianism.

The magnitude of the impact of the Darwinian argument is difficult to describe in a few paragraphs or pages and, indeed, even in a score of books. Nevertheless, an effort must be attempted before we proceed. In the simplest of terms Darwin's evolutionary thesis represents one of the most profound theories of all times. It not only offered revolutionary new knowledge for the sciences, but it helped also to shatter many philosophies and practices in other areas. It commanded so much attention and prestige that the entire literate community felt "obliged to bring his world-outlook into harmony with their findings" (Hofstadter, 1955b, p. 3). According to Hofstadter, Darwin's impact is comparable in its magnitude to the work of Nicolaus Copernicus (1473-1543), the European astronomer; Isaac Newton (1642-1727), the English mathematician and physicist; and Sigmund Freud (1859-1939), the Austrian psychoanalyst. In effect, all of the Western world had to come to grips with Darwin's evolutionary scheme.

Although there was much discussion and controversy about the social meaning of Darwin's theory of the "struggle for survival" and the "survival of the fittest," social Darwinists generally agreed that the theory's policy implications were politically conservative. It was argued that any policies that advocated government-sponsored social change would, if executed, actually be an interference with nature. The best approach was minimum involvement. "Let nature take its course" became a frequent refrain uttered by social Darwinists. It carried the clear message that accelerated social change was undesirable. Policies designed to accomplish "equal treatment," for example, were opposed strongly. Social welfare programs, it was argued, would perpetuate the survival of people who were negligent, shiftless, silly, and immoral; at the same time it would retard individual and national economic development. Hard work, saving, and moral constraint were called on as the solutions to individual and collective social and economic good fortune.

It is important to note an irony regarding the social Darwinists. Although many of the nation's leaders in the late 19th and early 20th centuries were opposed to programs of social change because they feared these programs would threaten the nation's survival, they were often the same people who were changing our economy radically and plundering our natural resources through speculation, innovation, and daring. They were also the same leaders who were introducing "new economic forms, new types of organization, new techniques" (Hofstadter, 1955b, p. 9). Changes that benefited their interests were acceptable; changes for the less fortunate were not. The stage was set for "scientifically justified" forms of control that would contain or eliminate crime. This control came in the form of the genetics movement with the blessings of the Victorian concern for morality and purity (Pivar, 1973). Unfortunately the stage was set also for scientifically justified policies that in fact resulted in selective abuse and neglect.

When social Darwinism was used to formulate crime control policies, major themes appeared. On the one hand, the "born criminal" legacy from Lombroso and his students and especially Garofalo's policy of "elimination" for certain criminal offenders produced a penal philosophy that stressed incapacitation. Clearly the emphasis was on removing criminals from the community to prevent them from committing any additional biologically determined harm. It therefore was inappropriate to attempt to reform or rehabilitate criminal offenders; warehousing convicted offenders was considered a sufficient socially responsible response to the problem of what to do with lawbreakers.

On the other hand, the second means of controlling crime allowed for a type of rehabilitation. It was based on medical reasoning that viewed individuals as biological objects that needed treatment and allowed some of the most repressive state policies in the history of American penology. The worst of these policies were justified by the study of genetics and what has been called the eugenics movement (Beckwith, 1985).

As a science in the early 1900s, the study of eugenics claimed that inheritance could explain the presence of simple and complex human behavioral characteristics. It thus reinforced the ideas of biological determinism and contributed greatly to the argument that many of the social problems of the late 19th century, such as the conflicts over wages and working conditions, could be traced to the genetic inferiority of foreigners who were working in the United States. The 1886 Haymarket bombings and riots in Chicago, for example, were thought to be caused by "inferior foreigners." This theme was advanced by industrialists and newspapers such as the *New York Times*, which described labor demonstrations as "always composed of foreign scum, beer-smelling Germans, ignorant Bohemians, uncouth Poles and wild-eyed Russians" (Beckwith, 1985, p. 317).

With the support of leading industrialists such as the Carnegies and leading education institutions such as Harvard, centers for the study of eugenics soon were established, and efforts were undertaken to study the nation's "stock." Accordingly, many states passed laws designed to permit the application of the eugenicists' arguments. Between 1911 and 1930, for example, more than 30 states established laws requiring sterilization for behavioral traits thought to be determined genetically (Beckwith, 1985, p. 318). The laws targeted such behavior as criminality, alcoholism, sodomy, bestiality, feeblemindedness, and the tendency to commit rape. The result was the sterilization of at least 64,000 people. Many of the same states also passed laws permitting psychosurgeries, including the now infamous frontal lobotomy. The total number of these types of operations is unknown.

The laws passed under the influence of the eugenics movement were not restricted to sterilization and psychosurgery, although these were the two most brutal and repressive measures they sponsored. They also endorsed miscegenation laws in 34 states that made it illegal for Blacks and Whites to marry each other; some states also forbade marriage between Whites and Orientals (Provine, 1973). They also called vigorously for the passage of immigration laws to be based on a quota system calculated on the proportion of people living in the United States from a specific country in 1890. And in 1924 the United States Congress, after hearing leading eugenicists testify that our stock was being weakened by the influx of people from southern and eastern European countries, passed the Immigration Restriction Act of 1924. It was directed explicitly to a population of people who were thought to be biologically inferior. As such, it was a racist law and a forerunner of the 1930s and 1940s eugenic policies of Nazi Germany.

Despite the clear implications of eugenic policies for repressing a targeted population, the practice of sterilization and psychosurgery continued in the United States until well into the 1970s. Between 1927 and 1972 in Virginia alone, more than 8,000 individuals were sterilized because they were identified as feebleminded (Katz & Abel, 1984, p. 232); more than 20,000 people were sterilized in California. However, as Katz and Abel pointed out, the real reason for sterilization was not feeblemindedness: It was class. "The one characteristic that did have to be demonstrated was indigency. . . . Commitment papers had to certify that the individual was both without means of support and without any acquaintance who would give bond" (p. 233). To allow the poor to propagate, it was claimed, would increase the number of feebleminded offspring, the poor, alcoholics, criminals, and prostitutes.

The Positivist School and Criminal Justice Reform

In pointing out the worst effects of biologically oriented theories, we are not unmindful that the positivist school also helped to usher in an approach to policy that was reformative rather than punitive in impulse. To be sure, the conclusion that offenders are characterized by unchangeable bodily or psychological characteristics leads logically to the conclusion that offenders should be either eliminated, caged indefinitely (incapacitation), or altered physically through intrusive measures. And "crime prevention," as we have seen, becomes a matter of not allowing the "defectives" to multiply. However, if one assumes that the causes determining crime are *changeable*—for example, unemployment or the emotional turmoil from family conflict—then the policy implications are much more optimistic. The challenge becomes diagnosing the forces that moved a person to break the law and then developing a strategy—perhaps job training, perhaps family counseling—to help the person overcome these criminogenic factors. In short, the challenge is to rehabilitate offenders so that they might rejoin society as "normal" citizens.

Notably, as America pushed into the 20th century, the appeal of biologically oriented theories eventually began to diminish. In their place, more optimistic positivist theories emerged, which drew their images of offenders from psychology and especially from sociology. These newer approaches argued that the troubles of criminals could be rectified through counseling or by fixing the social environments in which they lived.

This new way of thinking about crime had a large effect on policy. Indeed, in the first two decades of this century, this thinking helped shape a campaign that renovated the criminal justice system. Reformers, called Progressives, argued that the system should not be arranged to punish offenders, but to rehabilitate them. Across the nation, state after state established a separate juvenile court to "save" children from a life in crime (Platt, 1969). Similarly, efforts were undertaken to make release from prison based on the extent to which a person had been rehabilitated, not on the nature of the crime (as the classical school would mandate). Accordingly, states passed laws that made sentencing more indeterminate (offenders were given sentences, for example, that might range from 1 to 5 years) and created parole boards to decide which offenders had been "cured" and should be returned to the community. Probation, a practice through which offenders were to be both supervised and helped by an officer of the court, also was implemented widely. More generally, criminal justice officials were given great discretion to effect the individualized treatment of offenders (Rothman, 1980).

We will return to these themes in the next chapter and later in the book as well. Even so, we need to emphasize two points. First, controversy still exists today on whether the policies instituted in the name of rehabilitation made criminal justice systems more humane or more repressive. Some criminologists believe that the discretion given to criminal justice officials allowed offenders to be abused (Rothman, 1980), although other criminologists insist that rehabilitation has helped to humanize a system that is punitive by nature (Cullen & Gilbert, 1982). Second, although the ideas of the early positivist theorists declined in popularity—though certainly they did not disappear as the Virginia sterilization example shows—we now are seeing a renewed interest in the idea that the origins of crime lie in unchangeable characteristics of individuals. As Chapter 8 will discuss, the 1980s brought a revitalization of the view that criminals are wicked by nature, a view that has had questionable, if not disquieting, policy implications.

Conclusion

It should be clear that in order to understand the policies that are created to address the problems of crime, we must realize that they are influenced greatly by the theories that guide them. We must remember also to examine the social context in which theories and policies are constructed. This lesson is important because it points out that theories are neither value-free nor free from the times in which they are advocated. Theories also have an impact on people. Sometimes the scientifically justified policies are allowed to do great harm because the social context in which they are advocated and implemented is ignored. The consequences are often irrevocable.

3

REJECTING INDIVIDUALISM
The Social Roots of Crime

Although exceptions exist, most early theories located the sources of crime *within* the individual. These theories differed markedly on where precisely the source of waywardness lay: Was it in the soul? The mind? The body's very biological makeup? Even so, they shared the assumption that little insight on crime's origins could be gained by studying the social environment or context external to individuals. In one form or another, these early theories blamed individual offenders, not society, for the crime problem.

As the United States turned into the 20th century, however, a competing and powerful vision of crime emerged: a vision suggesting that crime, like other behavior, was a social product. The earlier theories did not vanish immediately or completely—indeed, in important ways, they continue to inform current-day thinking—but they did suffer a stiff intellectual challenge that thinned greatly the ranks of their supporters. But this major theoretical shift—one that rejected individualistic explanations of crime in favor of social explanations—might have been expected. Society was undergoing significant changes, and people's experiences were changing as well. The time was ripe for a new understanding of why some citizens break the law.

By the end of the 1930s, two major criminological traditions had been articulated that sought, in David Matza's (1969) words, to "relocate pathology; it was moved from the personal to the social plane" (p. 47). The first of these traditions—the Chicago school of criminology—argued that one aspect of American society, the city, contained potent criminogenic forces. The other tradition—Robert K. Merton's (1938) strain theory—contended that the pathology lay not in one ecological location, such as the city, but in the broader cultural and structural arrangements that constitute America's social fabric. Although they differed in how they believed that society created lawbreakers, these theories agreed that the key to unlocking the mystery of crime was in understanding its social roots. Taken together, therefore, they offered a strong counterpoint to explanations that blamed individuals for their criminality.

The effects of these two schools of thought have been long-lasting. Even today, a half century after their initial formulation, the Chicago school and strain theories continue to be of interest to criminologists and to shape correctional policies. They deserve careful consideration.

The Chicago School of Criminology

Theory in Context

What made it seem reasonable—why did it make sense—to blame cities for the nation's crime problem? Why would such a vision become popular in the 1920s to 1930s and, moreover, find special attention in Chicago?

In part the answers to these questions can be found in the enormous changes that transformed the face of the United States and made the city—not the "little house on the prairie"—the nation's focal point. In the last half of the 1800s, cities grew at a rapid pace and became, as J. John Palen (1981) observed, "a controlling factor in national life" (p. 63). Between 1790 and 1890, for example, the urban population grew 139-fold; by 1900, 50 cities existed with populations in excess of 100,000 (p. 63).

Chicago's growth, however, was particularly remarkable. When the city incorporated in 1833, it had 4,100 residents; by 1890 its population had risen to 1 million, and by 1910 the count surpassed 2 million (Palen, 1981, p. 63). But such rapid expansion had a bleaker side. Many of those settling in Chicago (and in other urban areas) carried little with them; there were waves of immigrants, displaced farm workers, and Blacks fleeing the rural

South. For most newcomers, the city—originally a source of much hope—brought little economic relief. They faced a harsh reality: pitiful wages; working 12-hour days, 6 days a week, in factories that jeopardized their health and safety; living in tenements, which "slumlords built jaw-to-jaw ... on every available space" (p. 64). Writing on the meat-packing industry in Chicago, Upton Sinclair (1905) gave this environment a disquieting label: "the jungle."

As did other citizens, criminologists in the 1920s and 1930s witnessed—indeed lived through and experienced—these changes that created bulging populations and teaming slum areas. It was only a short leap for them to believe that growing up in the city, particularly in the slums, made a difference in people's lives. In this context crime could not be seen simply as an individual pathology, but made more sense when viewed as a social problem.

This conclusion, moreover, was reinforced by a broad liberal reform movement that arose early in the 1900s: the Progressive movement. Although they believed in the essential goodness of America and thus rejected calls for radical change, Progressives were critical of the human costs wrought by America's unbridled industrial growth. They were troubled particularly by the plight of the urban poor, a mushrooming population of the system's casualties who had few prospects of a stable or rewarding life. They worried, as David Rothman (1980) wrote, that the "promise" of the American system "did not extend evenly to all segments of the society; it did not penetrate the ghetto or the slum. Thus an understanding of the etiology of crime demanded a very close scrutiny of the conditions in these special enclaves" (p. 51).

Criminologists in the Chicago school would echo this conclusion. The Progressives rejected the social Darwinists' logic that the poor, and the criminals among them, were biologically inferior and had fallen to society's bottom rung because they were of lesser stock. They preferred a more optimistic interpretation: The poor were pushed by their environment, not born, into a life of crime. Accordingly, hope existed that changing the context that nurtures offenders would reverse the slum's negative effects and transform them into law-abiding citizens. In particular, the goal was to save the poor, particularly their children, by providing social services—schools, clinics, recreational facilities, settlement houses, foster homes, and reformatories if necessary—that would lessen the pains of poverty and teach the benefits of middle-class culture (Platt, 1969; Rothman, 1980).

The moral imperative, however, was to act on this belief—and the Progressives did, creating what came to be known as the "age of reform" (Hofstadter, 1955a, 1963). The linchpin of their agenda was the assumption that the government could be trusted to create and administer agencies that would effect needed social reform. The Progressives campaigned to have the state guide the nation toward the common good by controlling the greed of industry and by providing the assistance the poor needed to reach the middle class. In the area of criminal justice, their efforts led to the creation of policies and practices that were intended to allow the state to treat the individual needs and problems of offenders: the juvenile court, community supervision through probation and parole, and the indeterminate sentence (Rothman, 1980).

Thus in the first decades of the 1900s, the city became a dominant feature of American life, and a pervasive movement arose warning that the social fabric of urban slums bred crime. Still, the question remains as to why Chicago became a hotbed of criminological research. As suggested, part of the answer can be found in this city's status as an emerging economic and population center. But the other piece of the puzzle lies in the existence at the University of Chicago of the nation's oldest sociology program, established in 1892.

By the 1920s, "surrounded . . . with ever-present reminders of the massive changes that were occurring within American society," the department's faculty and students had embarked on efforts to study systematically all aspects of the urban laboratory that lay before them (Pfohl, 1985, p. 143). Robert E. Park, a newspaper reporter-turned-sociologist, was particularly influential in shaping the direction of this work. "I expect I have actually covered more ground," he commented, "tramping about in cities in different parts of the world, than any other living man" (Madge, 1962, p. 89). These journeys led Park to two important insights.

First, he concluded that like any ecological system, the city's development and organization were not random or idiosyncratic, but rather they were patterned and could be understood in terms of basic social processes such as invasion, conflict, accommodation, and assimilation. Second, he observed that the nature of these social processes and their impact on human behaviors, such as crime, could be ascertained only through careful study of city life. Accordingly, he urged students and colleagues to venture into Chicago and to observe firsthand its neighborhoods and diverse conglomeration of peoples (Madge, 1962). Several scholars, most notably Clifford R. Shaw and Henry D. McKay, embraced Park's agenda and explored how urban life shaped fundamentally the nature of criminal activity. In doing so, they laid the foundation for the Chicago school of criminology.

Shaw and McKay's Theory of Juvenile Delinquency

Shaw and McKay were not faculty members at the University of Chicago but rather were employed as researchers for a state-supported child guidance clinic. Even so, they enjoyed close relationships with the sociology department and were influenced profoundly by its theorizing. In particular, they were persuaded that a model of the city formulated by Ernest Burgess, Park's colleague and collaborator, provided a framework for understanding the social roots of crime. Indeed, it was Burgess's model that led them to the conclusion that neighborhood organization was instrumental in preventing or permitting delinquent careers (Gibbons, 1979; Pfohl, 1985). Next we will review this general model of urban growth and then consider how it guided Shaw and McKay's approach to studying delinquency in Chicago.

Burgess's concentric zone theory. As cities expand in size, how do they grow? One answer is that the growth is haphazard, not according to any set pattern. Like Park, however, Burgess rejected this view in favor of the hypothesis that urban development is patterned socially. He contended that cities "grow radially in a series of concentric zones or rings" (Palen, 1981, p. 107).

As Figure 3.1 shows, Burgess delineated five zones. Competition decided how people were distributed spatially among these zones. Thus commercial enterprises were situated in the "loop" or central business district, a location that afforded access to valuable transportation resources (e.g., railroads and waterways). In contrast, most high-priced residential areas were in the outer zones, away from the bustle of the downtown, away from the pollution of factories, and away from the residences of the poor.

The zone in transition, however, was a particular cause for concern and study. This zone contained rows of deteriorating tenements, often built in the shadow of aging factories. The push outward of the business district, moreover, led to the constant displacement of residents. As the least

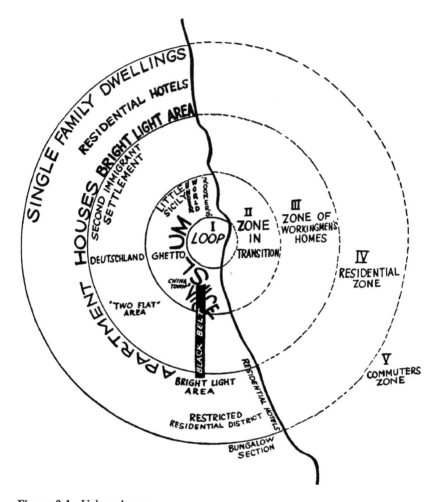

Figure 3.1. Urban Areas

SOURCE: Burgess (1925/1967, p. 55). Copyright © 1925/1967 by The University of Chicago. All rights reserved. Used by permission.

desirable living area, the zone had to weather the influx of waves of immigrants and other migrants who were too poor to reside elsewhere.

These social patterns, Burgess observed, were not without consequences: They weakened the family and communal ties that bound people together and resulted in *social disorganization*. This disorganization, Burgess and the other Chicago sociologists believed, was the source of a range of social pathologies, including crime.

Disorganization and delinquency. Burgess's model was parsimonious and persuasive, but did it really offer a fruitful approach to the study of crime? Would it stand up to empirical test?

Shaw and McKay took it on themselves to answer these questions. As a first step, they sought to determine if crime rates would conform to the predictions suggested by Burgess's model: highest rates in the zone in transition, with this rate declining progressively as one moved outward to the more affluent communities. Through painstaking research, they used juvenile court statistics to map the spatial distribution of delinquency throughout Chicago.

Their data analysis confirmed the hypothesis that delinquency flourished in the zone in transition and was inversely related to the zone's affluence and corresponding distance from the central business district. By studying Chicago's court records over several decades, they also were able to show that crime was highest in slum neighborhoods regardless of which racial or ethnic group resided there and that as groups moved to other zones, their rates decreased commensurately. This observation led to the inescapable conclusion that it was the nature of the neighborhoods—not the nature of the individuals within the neighborhood—that regulated involvement in crime.

But what social process could account for this persistent spatial distribution of delinquency? Borrowing heavily from Burgess and the other Chicago sociologists, Shaw and McKay emphasized the importance of neighborhood organization in preventing or permitting juvenile waywardness. In more affluent communities, families fulfilled youths' needs, and parents carefully supervised their offspring. In the zone in transition, however, families and other conventional institutions (schools, churches, and voluntary associations) were strained, if not broken apart, by rapid urban growth, migration, and poverty; social disorganization prevailed. As a consequence, juveniles received neither the support nor the supervision required for wholesome development. Left to their own devices, slum youths were freed from the type of social controls operative in more affluent areas; no guiding force existed to stop them from seeking excitement and friends in the streets of the city.

Shaw and McKay's focus on how weakening controls make possible a delinquent career allowed them to anticipate a criminological school that would become known eventually as *control* or *social bond* theory (see Chapter 4). As Ruth Rosner Kornhauser (1978) observed, however, they felt that another social circumstance also helped to make slum neighborhoods especially criminogenic. We turn next to this aspect of their thinking.

Transmission of criminal values. Shaw and McKay did not confine their research to the epidemiology of delinquency. Following Robert Park's admonition, they too "tramped" about Chicago. As we will see, they were activists who were involved in efforts to prevent delinquency. They also attempted to learn more about why youths become deviant by interviewing delinquents and compiling their autobiographies in a format called a life history. These efforts led to the publication of titles such as *The Jack-Roller: A Delinquent Boy's Own Story, The Natural History of a Delinquent Career,* and *Brothers in Crime* (Shaw, 1930, 1931, 1938; see also Shaw & McKay, 1972).

These life histories contained an important revelation: Juveniles often were drawn into crime through their association with older siblings or gang members. This observation led Shaw and McKay (1972) to the more general conclusion that disorganized neighborhoods helped produce and sustain "criminal traditions," which competed with conventional values and could be "transmitted down through successive generations of boys, much the same way that language and other social forms are transmitted" (p. 174). Thus slum youths grew up in neighborhoods characterized by "the existence of a coherent system of values supporting delinquent acts" (p. 173) and could learn readily these values in their daily interactions with older juveniles. In contrast, youths in organized neighborhoods—where the dominance of conventional institutions had precluded the development of criminal traditions—remained insulated from deviant values and peers; accordingly, for them a delinquent career was an unlikely option.

Summary. Shaw and McKay believed that juvenile delinquency could be understood only by considering the social context in which youths lived—a context that itself was a product of major societal transformations wrought by rapid urbanization, unbridled industrialization, and massive population shifts. Youths with the misfortune of residing in the socially disorganized zone in transition were especially vulnerable to the temptations of crime. As conventional institutions disintegrated around them, they were given little supervision and were free to roam the streets where they likely would become the next generation of carriers for the neighborhood's criminal tradition.

Later in this chapter, we will see how this vision of crime led Shaw and McKay to assert that delinquency prevention programs must be directed at reforming communities, not simply individuals. First, however, we will consider how their work laid the groundwork for Edwin Sutherland's classic theory of *differential association*.

Sutherland's Theory of Differential Association

In 1906 Edwin H. Sutherland departed his native Nebraska and traveled to the University of Chicago, where he enrolled in several courses in the divinity school. He was persuaded to register also for Charles R. Henderson's course, "Social Treatment of Crime." Henderson took an interest in his new student—an interest that proved mutual. It was not long before Sutherland decided to enter the sociology program; he would devote the remainder of his career to exploring the social roots of criminal behavior (Geis & Goff, 1983, 1986; Schuessler, 1973).

After receiving his doctorate in 1913, Sutherland held a series of academic positions at midwestern institutions, including the University of Illinois and the University of Minnesota. In 1930, however, he was offered and accepted a professorship at the University of Chicago. His stay in Chicago proved short-lived. Apparently disenchanted with his position— he cited "certain distractions" as reason for his departure—Sutherland left 5 years later to join the sociology department at Indiana University, a post he held until his death in 1950. Even so, he maintained contact with his friends in Chicago, including, it should be added, Henry D. McKay (Geis & Goff, 1983, p. xxviii; Schuessler, 1973, pp. xi-xii).

Although Sutherland spent most of his career away from the city and its university, the Chicago brand of sociology shaped intimately his thinking about crime. Indeed, as we will see next, much of his theorizing represented an attempt to extend and to formalize the insights found in the writings of Shaw and McKay and of other Chicago school scholars (see, for example, Thrasher, 1927/1963).

Differential Social Organization

Like most Chicago criminologists, Sutherland (1939) rejected individualistic explanations of crime. "The Neo-Lombrosian theory that crime is an expression of psychopathology," he claimed, "is no more justified than was the Lombrosian theory that criminals constitute a distinct physical type" (p. 116). Instead, he was convinced that social organization—the context in which individuals are embedded—regulates criminal involvement.

Shaw and McKay had used the term *social disorganization* to describe neighborhoods in which controls had weakened and criminal traditions rivaled conventional institutions. At the suggestion of Albert Cohen, however, Sutherland substituted for social *disorganization* the concept of *differential social organization,* a term that he felt was less value laden and captured more accurately the nature of criminal areas. Thus Sutherland (1942/1973) contended that social groups are arranged differently: Some are organized in support of criminal activity; others are organized against such behavior. In turn, he followed Shaw and McKay's logic in proposing that lawlessness would be more prevalent in those areas in which criminal organization had taken hold and on a daily basis shaped people's values and actions.

Differential Association

Although Sutherland incorporated into his thinking the thesis that community or group organization regulates rates of crime, he built more systematically on Shaw and McKay's observation that delinquent values are transmitted from one generation to the next. For Sutherland, to say that the preference for crime was "culturally transmitted" was, in effect, to say that criminal behavior is learned through social interactions. To describe this learning process, Sutherland coined the concept of *differential association.* Any person, he contended, may come into contact with "definitions favorable to violation of law" or with "definitions unfavorable to violation of law." The ratio of these definitions or views of crime—whether criminal or conventional influences are stronger in a person's life—determines if the person embraces crime as an acceptable way of life.

Sutherland held that the concepts of differential association and differential social organization were compatible and allowed for a complete explanation of criminal activity. As a social psychological theory, differential association explained why any given individual was drawn into crime. As a structural theory, differential social organization explained why rates of crime were higher in certain sectors of American society: Where groups are organized for crime (such as in slums), definitions favoring legal violations flourish and thus more individuals are likely to learn—to differentially associate with—criminal values.

Sutherland's theory of differential association went through various stages of development, but by 1947 he was able to articulate in final form a set of nine propositions. These propositions compose one of the most influential statements in criminological history on the causes of crime:

1. Criminal behavior is learned.
2. Criminal behavior is learned in interaction with other persons in a process of communication.
3. The principal part of the learning of criminal behavior occurs within intimate personal groups.
4. When criminal behavior is learned, the learning includes (a) techniques of committing the crime, which are sometimes very complicated, sometimes very simple; (b) the specific direction of motives, drives, rationalizations, and attitudes.
5. The specific direction of motives and drives is learned from definitions of legal codes as favorable and unfavorable.
6. A person becomes delinquent because of an excess of definitions favorable to violation of law over definitions unfavorable to violation of law. This is the principle of differential association.
7. Differential associations may vary in frequency, duration, priority, and intensity.
8. The process of learning criminal behavior by association with criminal and anticriminal patterns involves all the mechanisms that are involved in any other learning.
9. While criminal behavior is an expression of general needs and values, it is not explained by those general needs and values since noncriminal behavior is an expression of the same needs and values (Sutherland & Cressey, 1970, pp. 75-76).

Theoretical Applications

Taken together, these propositions convey an image of offenders that departs radically from the idea that criminals are pathological creatures driven to waywardness by demons, feeble minds, deep-seated psychopathology, or faulty constitutions. Instead, Sutherland was suggesting that the distinction between lawbreakers and the law-abiding lies not in their personal fiber but in the content of what they have learned. Those with the good fortune of growing up in a conventional neighborhood will learn to play baseball and to attend church services; those with the misfortune of growing up in a slum will learn to rob drunks and to roam the streets looking to do mischief.

But could the theory of differential association account for all forms of crime? Sutherland believed he had formulated a general explanation that could be applied to very divergent types of illegal activity. Unlike Shaw and McKay, therefore, he did not confine his investigations to the delinquency of slum youths. He compiled, for example, his famous life history of Chic Conwell, a "professional thief" (Sutherland, 1937). This study showed convincingly that differential association with thieves was the critical factor in determining whether a person could become a pickpocket, a shoplifter of high-priced items, or a confidence man or woman. Such contact was essential because it provided aspiring professional thieves with the tutelage, values, and colleagues needed to learn and perform sophisticated criminal roles.

More provocative, however, was Sutherland's (1949) claim that differential association could account for the offenses "committed by a person of respectability and high social status in the course of his [or her] occupation" (p. 9)—illegal acts for which Sutherland (1940) coined the term "white-collar crimes." His investigations revealed that lawlessness is widespread in the worlds of business, politics, and the professions. "Persons in the upper socioeconomic class," as he put it, "engage in much criminal behavior" (Sutherland, 1949/1983, p. 7). Indeed, his own research into the illegal acts by large American corporations revealed that they violated legal standards frequently and that most could be termed "habitual criminals" (Sutherland, 1949).

This empirical reality, Sutherland (1940) observed, presented special problems for most theories of his day, which assumed that "criminal behavior in general is due either to poverty or to the psychopathic and sociopathic conditions associated with poverty." After all, most "white-collar criminals . . . are not in poverty, were not reared in slums or badly deteriorated families, and are not feebleminded or psychopathic" (pp. 9-10). In contrast, the principle of differential association can explain the criminality of the affluent.

Thus, in many occupations, illegal practices are accepted widely as a way of doing business. White-collar workers, Sutherland (1940) noted, may "start their careers in good neighborhoods and good homes, [and] graduate from colleges with some idealism." At that point, however, they enter "particular business situations in which criminality is practically a folkway, and are inducted into that system of behavior just as into any other folkway" (p. 11). Similar to slum youths and offenders who become professional thieves, therefore, their association with definitions favorable to violation of law eventually shapes their orientations and transforms them from white-collar workers into white-collar criminals. In effect, a criminal tradition has been transmitted.

The Chicago School's Criminological Legacy

The Chicago school has not escaped the critical eye of subsequent scholars. One limitation critics often note, for example, is that the Chicago criminologists emphasized the causal importance of the transmission of a "criminal culture," but offered much less detail on the precise origins of this culture. Similarly, although deploring the negative consequences of urban growth—such as crime and delinquency—the Chicago theorists tended to see the spatial distribution of groups in the city as a "natural" social process. This perspective diverted their attention from the role that power and class domination can play in creating and perpetuating slums and the enormous economic inequality that pervades urban areas.

Scholars have questioned also whether the Chicago school can account adequately for all forms of crime. The theory seems best able to explain involvement in stable criminal roles and in group-based delinquency but is less persuasive in providing insights on the cause of "crimes of passion" or other impulsive offenses by people who have had little contact with deviant values. Sutherland's theory of differential association, moreover, has received special criticism. The formulation is plausible and perhaps correct, but can it be tested scientifically? Would it ever be possible to measure accurately whether, over the course of a lifetime, a person's association with criminal definitions outweighed his or her association with conventional definitions (Empey, 1982; Pfohl, 1985; Vold & Bernard, 1986)?

Despite these limitations, few scholars would dispute that the Chicago school has had a profound influence on criminology. On the broadest level, the Chicago criminologists leveled a powerful challenge—backed by a wealth of statistics—to explanations that saw crime as evidence of individual pathology. They captured the truth that where people grow up and with whom they associate cannot be overlooked in the search for the origins of crime.

The Chicago school also laid the groundwork for the development of two perspectives that remain vital to this day. On the one hand, as indicated previously, Shaw and McKay's premise that weakening social controls permit delinquency to take place was an early version of what has become known since as *control* or *social bond* theory (see Chapter 4). On the other hand, the Chicago criminologists' thesis that criminal behavior occurs as a consequence of cultural transmission or differential association gave rise to *cultural deviance* theory—a perspective that assumes that people become criminal by learning deviant values in the course of social interactions (Empey, 1982).

Cultural deviance theory has evolved along a number of paths, but we can identify four particularly influential versions. First, a number of criminologists have explored how "delinquent subcultures" arise in particular sectors of society (urban, lower-class areas). These subcultures are, in effect, relatively coherent sets of antisocial norms, values, and expectations that, when transmitted or learned, motivate criminal behavior (Cloward & Ohlin, 1960; Cohen, 1955). We will return later in the chapter to this line of analysis.

Second, other researchers have developed a similar theme in arguing for the existence of "subcultures of violence." Wolfgang and Ferracuti (1982), for example, noted that in areas in which such a subculture has taken hold (e.g., urban slums), people acquire "favorable attitudes toward . . . the use of violence" through a "process of differential learning, association, or identification." As a result, "the use of violence . . . is not necessarily viewed as illicit conduct, and the users do not have to deal with feelings of guilt about their aggression" (p. 314). In this regard, a raging theoretical and empirical debate is whether high rates of homicide in the South can be attributed to a regionally based subculture of violence (Hawley & Messner, 1989).

Third, some criminologists have asserted that lower-class culture as a whole—not subcultures within lower-class areas—is responsible for generating much criminality in urban areas. Walter Miller (1958/1979) has offered perhaps the clearest and most controversial of these theories. According to Miller, urban gang delinquency is not a product of intergenerational poverty per se, but of a distinct lower-class culture whose "focal concerns" encourages not conformity but deviance. If the focal concerns of middle-class culture are achievement, delayed gratification, and hard work, then the lower-class counterparts are trouble, smartness, toughness, fate, and autonomy. As a result, middle-class youths are oriented toward good grades, college, and career; lower-class youths are oriented toward physical prowess, freedom from any authority, and excitement on the street. Not surprisingly, Miller contended, youths who adhere to such "cultural practices which comprise essential elements of the total life pattern of lower class culture automatically violate legal norms" (p. 166).

Finally, Ronald Akers and his associates have been instrumental in exploring the mechanisms through which criminal learning takes place (see, for example, Akers, 1977; Akers, Krohn, Lanza-Kaduce, & Radosevich,

1979; Burgess & Akers, 1966). The Chicago theorists, such as Sutherland, emphasized that criminal values are learned through associations but had little to say about how precisely this occurred. In his *social learning* theory, Akers addressed this issue. Borrowing from operant psychology, he proposed that social reinforcements—rewards and punishments—determine whether any behavior is repeated. Involvement in crime, therefore, depends on exposure to social reinforcements that reward this activity. The stronger and more persistent these reinforcements, the greater the likelihood that criminal behavior will occur and persist. As a result, crime rates will be highest in those groups characterized by associations that reinforce deviant rather than prosocial behavior (Pfohl, 1985).

The Consequences of Theory: Policy Implications

As we have noted, the Chicago criminologists rejected individualistic explanations in favor of elucidating crime's social roots. Consistent with this theoretical perspective, they offered the "first systematic challenge to the dominance of psychology and psychiatry in public and private programs for the prevention and treatment of juvenile delinquency" (Schlossman, Zellman, & Shavelson, 1984, p. 2). The solution to youthful waywardness, they contended, was not in eradicating the pathologies that lie within individuals; rather the challenge was to eradicate the pathologies that lie within the very fabric of disorganized *communities*.

Beginning in the early 1930s, Clifford Shaw embarked on efforts to put his theory into practice, establishing the Chicago Area Project (CAP). Shaw's strategy was for CAP to serve as a catalyst for the creation of neighborhood committees in Chicago's disorganized slum areas. Committee leaders and the project's staff would be recruited not from the ranks of professional social workers but from the local community. The intention was to allow local residents the autonomy to organize against crime; unless the program developed from the "bottom up," Shaw felt, it would neither win the community's support nor have realistic prospects for successful implementation (Kobrin, 1959; Schlossman et al., 1984).

The Chicago Area Project took several approaches to delinquency prevention. First, a strong emphasis was placed on the creation of recreational programs that would attract youths into a prosocial environment. Second, efforts were made to have residents take pride in their community by improving the neighborhood's physical appearance. Third, CAP staff members would attempt to mediate on behalf of juveniles in trouble. This might involve discussions with school officials on how they might reduce a youth's truancy, or it might involve appealing to court officials to divert a youth into a CAP program. Fourth, CAP used staff indigenous to the area to provide "curbside counseling." In informal conversations as opposed to formal treatment sessions, these streetwise workers would attempt to persuade youths that education and a conventional lifestyle were in their best interest. "They served," observed Schlossman et al. (1984), "as both model and translator of conventional social values with which youths . . . had had little previous contact" (p. 15).

Was Shaw's project effective? Unfortunately, the lack of a careful evaluation using a randomized control group precludes a definitive answer. Even so, in 1984 Schlossman and his associates provided a "fifty-year assessment of the Chicago Area Project." They concluded that the different kinds of evidence they amassed, "while hardly foolproof, justify a strong hypothesis that CAP has long been effective in reducing rates of reported juvenile delinquency" (Kobrin, 1959, p. 28; Schlossman et al., 1984, p. 46). CAP reminds us, they added, "that despite never-ending hard times and political powerlessness, some lower-class, minority neighborhoods still retain a remarkable capacity for pride, civility, and the exercise of a modicum of self-governance" (Schlossman et al., 1984, p. 47).

Although Shaw and McKay's social disorganization theory called for efforts to reorganize communities, the Chicago school's emphasis on cultural learning suggested that crime can be countered by treatment programs that attempt to reverse offenders' criminal learning. In general, the requirement is to place offenders in settings where they will receive prosocial reinforcement. This might involve, for example, placing youths in a program that uses positive peer counseling or in a residential facility that uses a "token economy" in which conformist behavior earns juveniles points that allow them to purchase privileges (e.g., home visits, ice cream, late curfew).

Merton's Strain Theory

In 1938 Robert K. Merton published "Social Structure and Anomie." The original article extended only 10 pages—other elaborations by Merton (1957, 1964, 1968) followed—but it succeeded in defining an approach that captured the imagination of criminologists. As we will see, Merton's paradigm became particularly influential in the 1960s, shaping both theory and policy in important ways. Even today, however, his theorizing occupies a prominent place in criminological writings (Bernard, 1984; Cullen, 1984; Messner, 1988).

Below we begin by reviewing Merton's main theoretical assertions. We follow this discussion by considering the context that shaped strain theory over the years, the criminological legacy of Merton's work, and the impact of the perspective on criminal justice policy.

America as a Criminogenic Society

The Chicago school believed that the roots of crime were embedded predominantly in one area of American society—city slums—and that people became criminal by learning deviant cultural values. Although Merton never rejected this formulation, he outlined a very different social process—one that involved *conformity* to conventional cultural values—that he felt produced high rates of crime and deviance.

Structurally induced strain. The United States, in Merton's eyes, was an unusual society, not simply because the culture places an extraordinary emphasis on economic success but also because this goal is universal, held up for all to want and achieve. Poor people are not taught to be satisfied with their lot but rather are instructed to pursue the "American dream"; through hard work, it is said, even the lowliest among us can rise from rags to riches.

This widespread aspiration for success, however, has an ironic and unanticipated consequence, for the "cardinal American virtue, 'ambition,' " Merton (1968) cautioned, ultimately "promotes a cardinal American vice, 'deviant behavior' " (p. 200). But why should the desire for social mobility lead to deviance? The problem, Merton observed, is that the social structure limits access to the goal of success through legitimate means (e.g., college education, corporate employment, family connections). Members of the lower class are particularly burdened because they start far behind in the race for success and must be exceptionally talented or fortunate to catch up. The disjunction between what the culture extols—universal striving for success—and what the social structure makes possible—limited legitimate opportunities—thus places large segments of the American population in the strain-engendering position of desiring a goal that they cannot reach through conventional means. This situation, Merton concluded, is not without important social consequences: It "produces intense pressure for deviation" (p. 199).

Typology of adaptations. Merton (1968) proposed that different ways existed for people to resolve the strains generated from the inability to attain success. To conceptualize these possible responses, he developed his classic typology, which, as Table 3.1 shows, outlined five possible modes of adaptation.

Merton realized that most people, even if they found their social ascent limited, did not deviate. Instead, the modal response was for people to conform, to continue to ascribe to the cultural success goal, and to believe in the legitimacy of the conventional or institutionalized means through which success was to be attained. But for many others the strain of their situation proved intolerable. Because the means-goal disjunction was the source of their problem, a requisite for alleviating strain was changing their cultural goal and/or withdrawing their allegiance to institutionalized means. In following either or both courses, however, they were deviating from norms prescribing what should be desired (success) or how this should be achieved (legitimate means such as education or employment).

Thus Merton (1957, 1968) delineated four deviant modes of adaptation. Much criminal behavior, he felt, could be categorized as *innovation,* because this adaptation encompasses those who continue to embrace as a worthy end pecuniary success but who turn to illegitimate means when they find blocked their legitimate prospects for economic gain. The behavior of the robber barons, of white-collar criminals, and of scientists who report discoveries based on fraudulent research are examples of how the intense desire for success can produce innovation among the more affluent. Even so, this adaptation appears prevalent particularly in the lower strata. Faced with the "absence of realistic opportunities for advancement," the disadvantaged, Merton (1968) felt, are especially vulnerable to the "promises of power and high income from organized vice, rackets, and crime" (p. 199).

In contrast, *ritualists* maintain outward conformity to the norms governing institutionalized means. They mitigate their strain, however, by scaling down their aspirations to the point where these ends can be reached comfortably. Despite cultural mandates to pursue the goal of success, they are content to avoid taking risks and to live within the confines of their daily routines.

TABLE 3.1 Merton's Typology of Modes of Individual Adaptation

Modes of Adaptation	Culture Goals	Institutionalized Means
I. Conformity	+	+
II. Innovation	+	−
III. Ritualism	−	+
IV. Retreatism	−	−
V. Rebellion	±	±

SOURCE: Merton (1968, p. 140). Reprinted with the permission of The Free Press, an imprint of Simon & Schuster from SOCIAL THEORY AND SOCIAL STRUCTURE, Revised & Enlarged Edition by Robert K. Merton. Copyright © 1967, 1968 by Robert K. Merton.
+ signifies acceptance; − signifies rejection; ± signifies rejection of prevailing values and substitution of new values.

Retreatists, however, make a more dramatic response. Strained by expectations of social ascent through conventional lifestyles, they relinquish allegiance to both the cultural success goal and the norms prescribing acceptable ways of climbing the economic ladder. These are people who "are in society but not of it," and they escape society's requirements through various deviant means: alcoholism, drug addiction, psychosis, or vagrancy (Merton, 1968, p. 207). Suicide, of course, is the ultimate retreat.

Finally, Merton described as *rebellious* citizens who not only reject but also wish to change the existing system. Alienated from prevailing ends and normative standards, they propose to substitute a new set of goals and means. In American society, an example of a rebel might be a socialist who argues for group rather than individual success and for norms mandating the distribution of wealth equally and according to need rather than unequally and according to the outcome of ruthless competition.

Anomie. Because much of Merton's analysis details the social sources of strains potent enough to generate high rates of nonconformity, scholars often have referred to his perspective as *strain theory* (Empey, 1982; Hirschi, 1969; Kornhauser, 1978; Vold & Bernard, 1986). We can recall, however, that Merton (1938) labeled his classic article "Social Structure and *Anomie*" (emphasis added). What role does *anomie* play in the genesis of crime?

Merton borrowed the notion of anomie—normlessness or deregulation, as it usually is defined—from Emile Durkheim, the French sociologist. In his classic work, *Suicide,* Durkheim (1897/1951) used the concept to describe a social condition in which institutionalized norms lost their power to regulate human needs and action. He argued further that as Western society modernized, a great emphasis was placed on "achieving industrial prosperity" without a corresponding attention to restraining people's appetites for success. This development, he observed, had left the economic sphere in a "chronic state" of anomie. People now were free, if not encouraged, to seek seemingly limitless economic success. But disquieting consequences befell those who succumbed to these temptations. "Overweening ambition," warned Durkheim, "always exceeds the results obtained, great as they may be, since there is no warning to pause here. Nothing gives satisfaction and all this agitation is uninterruptedly maintained without appeasement" (p. 60). For many, suicide posed the only means of escape from the pain of "being thrown back." We will return to Durkheim's theorizing in the next chapter.

Merton did not buy Durkheim's framework whole cloth, but he did borrow selectively from it (Cullen, 1984; Vold & Bernard, 1986). Most important, perhaps, he learned that institutionalized norms will weaken—anomie will take hold—in societies placing an intense value on economic success. When this occurs, the pursuit of success is guided no longer by normative standards of right and wrong; instead, "the sole significant question becomes: Which of the available procedures is most efficient in netting the culturally approved value?" (Merton, 1968, pp. 189, 211). The Wall Street insider trading scandals seemingly provide one example of how the widespread preoccupation with amassing fortunes results in a breakdown of institutionalized norms—anomie sets in—and fosters the unbridled pursuit of pecuniary rewards.

We should add also that innovative conduct becomes especially prevalent as anomie intensifies. In contrast to ritualism (or conformity), this adaptation requires an ability to relinquish commitment to institutionalized means in favor of illegitimate means. Fluctuations in levels of anomie, whether over time or within certain sectors of society at any given time, can be expected to determine not only overall rates of deviance but also rates of particular kinds of deviance, including crime, the prototypical innovative response.

Anomie and deviance, moreover, are mutually reinforcing. The weakening of institutionalized norms initially allows a limited number of people to violate socially approved standards. But such deviance, once completed successfully and observed by others, poses a concrete challenge to the norms' legitimacy. This process, Merton (1968) noted, "enlarges the extent of anomie within the system" (p. 234), which in turn heightens the chance that waywardness will become more pervasive.

The escalating use of marijuana perhaps illustrates this phenomenon. As norms prohibiting its use lost strength in the 1960s—claims of "reefer madness" were ridiculed—increasing numbers of youths experimented with the substance, typically in social situations. This widely observed, if not flaunted, deviant behavior undermined the legitimacy of institutionalized norms, even to the point that in some locales police and courts refused to enforce existing laws and recreational use was decriminalized. Anomie thus became pervasive and restraints against "smoking pot" were vitiated greatly—a development that made marijuana use even more pervasive.

Rejecting individualism. In sum, Merton contended that the very nature of American society generates considerable crime and deviance. The disjunction between the cultural and social structures places many citizens, but particularly the disadvantaged, in the position of desiring unreachable goals. Tremendous strains are engendered that move many people to find deviant ways to resolve this situation. The cultural emphasis on success, moreover, diminishes the power of institutional norms to regulate behavior. As anomie becomes prevalent, people are free to pursue success goals with whatever means are available, legitimate or illegitimate. In this situation, innovation—an adaptation encompassing many forms of crime—becomes possible, if not likely.

Like the Chicago theorists, Merton located the roots of crime and deviance within the very fabric of American society. Again, the Chicago school stressed the criminogenic role of the city and of conformity to a *criminal culture*, although Merton stressed the criminogenic role of conformity to the universal and *conventional* cultural goal of pecuniary success. This difference aside, however, both perspectives rejected the notion that crime's origins lay within individuals' minds or bodies.

Indeed, Merton was especially vociferous in his attack on the individualistic explanations that prevailed in the 1930s (Merton & Montagu, 1940). Most of these theories, he explained, were based on the fallacious premise that the primary impulse for evil lay within human nature. In contrast, Merton (1968) argued for a perspective that "considers socially deviant behavior just as much a product of social structure as conformist behavior" and that "conceives of the social structure as active, as producing fresh motivations which cannot be predicted on the basis of knowledge about man's native drives" (p. 175).

Strain Theory in Context

Robert K. Merton was 28 and teaching at Harvard University when "Social Structure and Anomie" was published in 1938; eventually he would become a professor at Columbia University (1941) and would be elected as president of the American Sociological Association. His origins, however, were more modest. He was born in the slums of South Philadelphia and attended college only by winning a scholarship to Temple University and then a graduate assistantship to Harvard University (Hunt, 1961; Persell, 1984).

In a very real sense, Merton's travels from city slum to elite institution meant that he had lived the American dream. We are limited to speculation, but this personal journey may have helped to focus Merton's attention on the prominent role in the national culture of social ascent. It seems reasonable as well to suggest that this social context shaped the theoretical emphasis he placed on the structural limitations to social mobility. As Stephen Pfohl (1985) noted, "most of Merton's slum neighbors did not fare so well . . . a lesson of slum life which Merton never forgot" (p. 211). He also had experienced the Depression era and witnessed the consequence of large numbers of people deprived of the opportunity to reach what they had been taught to desire.

Regardless of how Merton came to formulate his paradigm, one point is clear: His article on "Social Structure and Anomie" is perhaps the most cited article not only in criminology but in sociology as a whole (Pfohl, 1985). Even so, the article did not receive widespread attention until nearly two decades after its 1938 publication (Pfohl, 1985; see also Cole, 1975). In part, the sudden interest in his work in the late 1950s and early 1960s was prompted by the appearance of two important books on juvenile gangs that drew heavily from Merton's theorizing: Albert K. Cohen's *Delinquent Boys* (1955) and Richard A. Cloward and Lloyd E. Ohlin's *Delinquency and Opportunity* (1960). We can point also to the effects of Merton's (1957, 1959, 1964, 1968) own renewed interest in elaborating his earlier article.

By themselves, however, these observations do not offer a complete explanation of why, as the United States turned into the 1960s, criminologists became fascinated so intensely by this particular way of thinking about crime, as opposed to some other set of ideas. The social context of the time, we believe, must be considered also.

As Charles Murray (1984) noted, prior to 1960 poverty was not viewed, in political circles at least, as a major social problem rooted in the very structure of American society. By the early part of the 1960s, however, a fundamental transformation in thinking had occurred. An increasing consensus had emerged, Murray argued, that poverty "was not the just deserts of people who didn't try hard enough. It was produced by conditions that had nothing to do with individual virtue and effort. *Poverty was not the fault of the individual but of the system*" (p. 29; emphasis in original). The civil rights movement, moreover, provided a language for conceptualizing this issue: Minorities and other disadvantaged citizens were being denied "equal opportunity."

This view of the world was embraced increasingly by government officials, journalists, and academics (Murray, 1984). Criminologists, too, were influenced profoundly by the legitimacy now given to the idea that large segments of the U.S. population were denied access to the American dream. In this context it becomes understandable why Merton's theory and offshoots such as the delinquency books by Cohen and by Cloward and Ohlin suddenly gained attention. For at the core of Merton's paradigm was the lesson that the United States was a society in which all were expected to ascend economically but whose very structure denied equal opportunity to attain this cherished goal. To criminologists of the 1960s, this premise rang true; it made sense that crime and deviance would be a consequence of a system that was to blame for holding back unfairly many of its citizens.

Status Discontent and Delinquency

As indicated, the writings of Albert Cohen and of Richard Cloward and Lloyd Ohlin represented important extensions of Merton's deviance approach. Although these scholars offered different variants of strain theory, they shared common themes. First, they investigated how the theory could be applied to the study of juvenile gangs in urban areas. Second, they focused on the origins and effects of delinquent subcultural norms. Third, they drew not only from Merton's structural tradition but also from the Chicago school.

Delinquent Boys

While still an undergraduate at Harvard University, Albert K. Cohen enrolled in a senior course instructed by a young professor, Robert K.

Merton. A year later, Cohen was off to Indiana University, where he took a seminar run by Edwin H. Sutherland. As might be expected, this fortuitous encounter with two influential and persuasive scholars prompted Cohen to ponder how notions of cultural transmission and structurally induced strain might be reconciled.

Sutherland had convinced Cohen that differential association with a criminal culture would lead youths into legal trouble. Yet Cohen felt also that this thesis of cultural transmission begged more fundamental questions. Where, Cohen wondered, did the criminal culture come from? Why did such subcultures have a specific social distribution, locating themselves in slum areas? Why did the subcultures have a particular normative content? And why did these values persist from generation to generation?

Returning to Harvard for his doctorate, Cohen addressed these questions in his dissertation; a much revised version was published in 1955 carrying the title *Delinquent Boys: The Culture of the Gang.* He began by making several important observations. Delinquent gangs and the subcultural values they embrace are concentrated in urban slums. Moreover, the content of these subcultures not simply is supportive of crime but rather is "nonutilitarian, malicious and negativistic" (p. 25). Because slum youths learn and act on the basis of these values, they engage in delinquency that is contemptuous of authority and is irrational to conventional citizens; seemingly, the only guide for their conduct is that they do things for "the hell of it."

To account for these patterns, Cohen (1955) proposed that delinquent subcultures—like all subcultures—arise in response to the special problems people face. Following Merton's insights, he noted that lower-class youths are disadvantaged in their efforts to be successful and achieve status in conventional institutions. Schools, which embody middle-class values, present a particular obstacle; poor kids lack the early socialization and resources to compete successfully with their counterparts from more affluent families. Consequently, they are "denied status in the respectable society because they cannot meet the criteria of the respectable status system" (p. 121).

How can these status problems be solved? "The delinquent subculture," Cohen (1955) contended, "deals with these problems by providing criteria of status which these children can meet" (p. 121). In a process approximating a reaction formation, lower-class youths reject the middle-class goals and norms that they have been taught to desire but by which they are judged inadequate. In place of middle-class standards, they substitute a set of oppositional values; if conventional society values ambition, responsibility, rationality, courtesy, control of physical aggression, and respect for authority, these youths will place a premium on behavior that violates these principles. Accordingly, status will be accorded to compatriots who are truant, flout authority, fight, and vandalize property for "kicks" (Cohen, 1955).

In short, Cohen (1955) suggested that the strains of class-based status discontent are conducive to the emergence of subcultural values supportive of delinquency. Lower-class youths, thrown together in high-density urban neighborhoods and saddled with a common problem, find a common solution in embracing values that provide both the chance to gain status and the psychic satisfaction of rejecting respectable values that lie beyond their reach. Because American society continues to present each new generation of urban youths with status problems, a structural basis exists for the persistence of these delinquent norms and the gang organization they nourish. Moreover, once in existence, the subculture assumes a reality of its own. As the Chicago theorists taught, this criminal culture can be transmitted to youths in the neighborhood. Even juveniles whose status discontent is insufficient in itself to motivate delinquency, Cohen cautioned, can be attracted by the lure of the gang and its offer of friendship, excitement, or protection.

Delinquency and Opportunity

Like Cohen's work, Richard Cloward and Lloyd Ohlin's work brought together the traditions of the Chicago school and strain theory. As with Cohen, personal circumstance ostensibly played a role in making possible this attempt at a theoretical merger. Thus Ohlin had studied under Sutherland and later received his doctorate from the University of Chicago; Cloward, on the other hand, had been Merton's student at Columbia University. Eventually, they became colleagues on Columbia's social work faculty (Laub, 1983) and entered into a collaboration that bore the important fruit of *opportunity theory* (Cloward & Ohlin, 1960; see also Cloward, 1959).

From Merton, Cloward and Ohlin learned that the social structure generates pressures for deviance, pressures experienced most intensely in the lower class. Similar to Cohen's extension of Merton's work, they argued that slum youths face the problem of lacking the legitimate means—the opportunity—to be successful and earn status. In American society, where success in school and in career are valued and rewarded so greatly, this failure presents a special problem: the strain of status discontentment. "The disparity between what lower-class youths are led to want and what is actually available to them," as Cloward and Ohlin (1960) put it, "is the source of a major problem of adjustment." It causes "intense frustrations" and the "exploration of nonconformist alternatives may be the result" (p. 86).

But Cloward and Ohlin also drew an important lesson from the writings of the Chicago theorists. In reading works such as the *The Professional Thief* (Sutherland, 1937) and *The Jack-Roller* (Shaw, 1930) that elucidated how criminal roles are learned through cultural transmission, they were led to the conclusion that people are not free to become any type of criminal or deviant they like. To become a doctor or lawyer, one must, of course, have access to the requisite legitimate means (education, financial resources); this logic, they reasoned, could be extended to the criminal world: To become a professional thief or jack-roller, one must have access to the requisite *illegitimate* means (contact with thieves, residence in a slum neighborhood).

This lesson from the Chicago school helped to resolve a shortcoming of Merton's paradigm. As discussed, Merton noted that strain could be adapted to through innovation, ritualism, retreatism, or rebellion. He provided only rudimentary insights, however, on the conditions under which a person would choose one, rather than another, adaptation. The Chicago school, Cloward and Ohlin proposed, furnished an answer to this question: The selection of adaptations is regulated by the availability throughout the social structure of illegitimate means. Thus affluent people may have access to the financial positions needed to embezzle or to embark on an insider trading scheme; in contrast, although precluded from white-collar crime, lower-class residents might have access to friends who would help them rob or teach them how to fence stolen goods.

Now Cloward and Ohlin believed that the concept of illegitimate means could illuminate why delinquent subcultures existed in slum areas and why they took a particular form. One relevant consideration was that lower-class youths experienced high levels of strain. But in itself this factor explains only why youths might be motivated to violate the law, not why subcultural responses of a particular type emerge. "To account for the development of pressures toward deviance," Cloward and Ohlin (1960) cautioned, "does not sufficiently explain why these pressures result in one deviant solution rather than another" (p. 34).

Accordingly, they proposed that delinquent subcultures could emerge and persist only in areas where enough youths were concentrated to band together and to support one another's alienation from conventional values. They observed further, however, that the type of collective response the youths could make would be shaped intimately by the neighborhood in which they resided (Cloward & Ohlin, 1960). In organized slum areas, for example, criminal subcultures are possible because older offenders serve as role models for a stable criminal life and train youths in the performance of illegal enterprises (e.g., through fencing stolen merchandise).

In more disorganized neighborhoods, on the other hand, access to such organized criminal apprenticeships is absent. Lacking the opportunity to embark on more lucrative, utilitarian illegal careers, youths turn to violence as a way of establishing "rep" or social status. Conditions are ripe, therefore, for the emergence of a "conflict" or fighting-oriented subculture.

Cloward and Ohlin (1960) also identified a third subcultural form: the "retreatist" or drug-using subculture. These groupings arise when sufficient numbers of youths exist who have been "double-failures": people who have failed to achieve status through either legitimate or illegitimate means. Thus these lower-class juveniles not only have been unsuccessful in conventional settings such as the school, but also "have failed to find a place for themselves in criminal or conflict subcultures." As a result, they look to "drugs as a solution" to their "status dilemma" (p. 183).

One final point warrants emphasis. Although Cloward and Ohlin focused their substantive analysis on delinquent subcultures, they believed that their opportunity theory—a consolidation of the cultural transmission and strain traditions—offered a *general* framework for studying crime and deviance (Cloward, 1959; Cloward & Piven, 1979). Again, they were persuaded that Merton had identified a major source of pressures for deviance—denial of legitimate opportunity—but that strain theory was incomplete without a systematic explanation of why people solve their status problems in one way and not another. The issue of the selection of adaptations, they felt, could be answered only by focusing on how the illegitimate opportunity structure regulated access to different forms of crime/deviance for people located at different points in society (Cullen, 1984). Thus white-collar crime and mugging represent two possible innovative methods to acquire financial resources; even so, participation in one, rather than the other, of these offenses is determined not by strain but by social class differentials in the availability of illegitimate opportunities.

The Criminological Legacy of Strain Theory

Criticisms

As strain theory emerged in the early 1960s as the most prominent criminological explanation, it won considerable attention not only from adherents but also from opponents (Cole, 1975). The perspective's critics developed a variety of lines of attack (for summaries, see Empey, 1982; Pfohl, 1985; Vold & Bernard, 1986).

Some scholars, for example, questioned whether in a society as diverse as the United States, all citizens ascribed to the goal of pecuniary success. At the very least, possible variations in the degree to which different groups were socialized effectively into the American dream would have to be investigated. Other scholars have disparaged strain theory for assuming that strain and deviance were more prevalent in the lower classes. This class-biased assumption is said to ignore white-collar crime and to convey the impression that lawlessness is exclusively a lower-class problem (but see Merton, 1957, 1968). Still other more radical scholars have expressed concern over Merton's failure to offer a broader, more penetrating analysis (Taylor, Walton, & Young, 1973). In this view, Merton succeeded in identifying a contradiction central to U.S. society—an open-class ideology and a restricted class structure—but stopped short of asking why this condition originated and persists unabated. The answer, as Pfohl (1985) and others argued, is that "the political-economic structure of capitalism must be seen as a basic source of the contradictions which produce high rates of deviance" (p. 234).

The attempts of Cohen and of Cloward and Ohlin to explain delinquent subcultures have been criticized also. Most frequently, commentators have questioned whether these theorists described accurately the content of subcultures. Cohen portrayed delinquents as embracing "non-utilitarian, malicious, and negativistic" values, but some youths' criminality is consumption oriented and ostensibly utilitarian. Similarly, Cloward and Ohlin delineated three distinct subcultural forms (criminal, conflict, retreatist), but delinquents appear to mix these activities. "Delinquent boys," LaMar Empey (1982) observed, "drink, steal, burglarize, damage property, smoke pot, or even experiment with heroin and pills, but rarely do they limit themselves to any single one of these activities" (p. 250; see, for example, Short & Strodtbeck, 1965).

Although these observations have merit, it is important to distinguish between the theorists' substantive analysis of subcultures (which may be in need of revision) and the general framework that they suggest for the study of crime. Cohen and Cloward and Ohlin not only identified potentially important sources of youthful disaffiliation from conventional norms but also raised the critical theoretical question of why certain forms of crime (delinquent gangs, white-collar criminality) are distributed differentially throughout the social structure. Thus, if their description of juvenile subcultures did not prove fully satisfactory, their challenge to criminologists to explain the emergence, persistence, and differential selection of criminal adaptations remains valid.

Last, an empirical critique has been leveled against strain theory. Contrary to the perspective's predictions that frustrated ambitions push people outside the law, some researchers have reported that high aspirations are associated with conformity and low aspirations are associated with delinquent involvement (Hirschi, 1969; Kornhauser, 1978). Thomas Bernard's (1984) assessment of available research studies, however, showed that empirical data exist that clearly support strain theory (see also Burton & Cullen, 1992; Cole, 1975). Moreover, studies that claim to falsify the perspective's premises often use questionable measures of key concepts, overlook supportive findings, and do not assess systematically all of the theory's components (Bernard, 1984; Messner, 1988). Bernard (1984) also noted that strain theory offers perhaps the most promising approach to understanding serious urban male delinquency. "The data on serious gang delinquency," he concluded, "virtually demand a strain type explanation" (p. 366).

Even so, it must be admitted that after dominating criminologists' attention in the 1960s, strain theory's popularity lessened. Some scholars were critical for purely intellectual reasons. But as we have cautioned, the popularity of criminological theories is shaped also, perhaps more profoundly, by changes in the social context that make previously cherished ideas seem odd and new ideas seem a matter of common sense. Particularly as we discuss the labeling and conflict perspectives (Chapters 5 and 6), we will see how events in the late 1960s and early 1970s caused many criminologists to shift their allegiance to theories that emphasized the role of the state and of power in defining what is crime and why people engage in it.

Recent Developments

All this is not to imply, however, that strain theory was relegated to the criminological scrap heap; quite the contrary. Although the paradigm's appeal diminished, over the past two decades it remained required reading for criminologists and served as a standard against which newer theories often were compared and tested (Burton & Cullen, 1992). More important, in recent years, a renewed interest in strain theory has cropped up (see, for example, Agnew, 1992; Cullen, 1988; Messner, 1988; Passas, 1990; Rosenfeld, 1989). Particularly significant are efforts that build on and revise the insights of traditional strain theory. Two promising lines of inquiry warrant our attention: Agnew's general strain theory and Messner and Rosenfeld's analysis of crime and the American dream.

General strain theory. Robert Agnew suggested that theorizing in the Mertonian school of strain theory is not so much wrong as it is limited. According to Agnew (1992), Merton and status frustration theorists identify one type of criminogenic strain: "relationships in which others prevent the individual from achieving positively valued goals" (p. 50), such as economic success or status in a high school. However, there may be other kinds of negative relations or situations that create strain and prompt people to break the law. The time has come, observed Agnew, to move beyond Merton's paradigm and to explore these other sources of criminogenic strain; in short, the challenge is to develop a general strain theory of crime.

Toward this end, Agnew delineated two other types of strain. First, although Merton focused on blockage of a desired goal, Agnew (1992) argued that strain can be generated from the "actual or anticipated removal (loss) of positively valued stimuli from an individual" (p. 57). This strain might occur, for example, when parents take away privileges such as use of the family automobile, when a student is kicked off an athletic team, when a dating relationship is terminated, when an individual's job is eliminated, or when a loved one dies. In these situations, people might take drugs to manage the stress, or they might resort to illegal means to replace what was taken away (e.g., steal a car) or to seek revenge against those who caused their strain (e.g., assault a parent, coach, or boss).

Second, strain can be induced by the "actual or anticipated presentation of negative or noxious stimuli" (Agnew, 1992, p. 58). These adverse situations might include exposure to a sexually or physically abusive relationship, living in a family wracked by conflict, attending a dangerous school, and being supervised by a boss who is unfair or harassing. As Agnew pointed out, crime and delinquency may take place when people respond to this adversity by seeking to escape (e.g., running away from home), to eliminate or obtain revenge against the source of the stress (e.g., murder an abuser), or to dull the psychic pain by taking drugs.

Agnew (1985, 1989; Agnew & White, 1992) has presented empirical data showing the utility of general strain theory. Further support for broadening the focus of strain theory has come from Bill McCarthy and John Hagan's (1992) research on delinquency among youths who have left home and are living on the streets. Building on Agnew's work, McCarthy and Hagan's analysis revealed how adverse or noxious conditions can result in delinquent involvement both directly and indirectly.

Youths who leave home, observed McCarthy and Hagan, often live on "mean streets," where they experience hunger, unemployment, and a lack of shelter. In a direct attempt to alleviate these adverse situations, they steal food and obtain money by pilfering property and by prostitution. Other adverse conditions influence delinquency indirectly by causing youths to take to the streets in the first place. Thus youths who find themselves in homes in which they are sexually and physically abused are more likely to escape this adversity by leaving home—only to find themselves facing the pressures for crime inherent in the deprivations of street life.

Crime and the American dream. Steven Messner and Richard Rosenfeld (1994) have argued that much is to be gained by revisiting and revising Merton's paradigm of social structure and anomie. The United States, they noted, has a higher rate of serious crime than any other industrial nation (see also Currie, 1985). Why is this so? They doubt that the rampant lawlessness can be traced to individual traits, such as Americans having a disproportionate number of defective personalities or bodies. Instead, taking a macrolevel perspective, they argue for the need to discern what is distinctive about the very culture and structure of American *society.*

The special contribution of Robert Merton's paradigm, contended Messner and Rosenfeld, is that it identifies the central role that the American dream plays in generating criminal behavior (see also Messner, 1988; Rosenfeld, 1989). Messner and Rosenfeld (1994) defined the American dream as "a commitment to the goal of material success, to be pursued by everyone in society, under conditions of open, individual competition" (p. 69). Like Merton, they noted that the American dream's strong cultural prescription for each individual to achieve monetary success, regardless of personal circumstance or the competition, erodes the power of norms to regulate the use of legitimate or legal means to obtain this success. In short, the American dream fosters anomie or the breakdown of normative control.

In this anomic context, there is a tendency for people to use the "technically most efficient means" to achieve desired goals. On the positive side, the prevailing normative flexibility creates space for innovation and for moving beyond outmoded ways of doing things. But there is a darker side as well: The most efficient means to monetary gain often is to break the law, to rob with a gun, or to defraud the stock market through insider trading. Anomie thus is criminogenic, and widespread anomie—as there is in American society—creates widespread lawlessness.

Although Messner and Rosenfeld embraced Merton's analysis of American culture, they found his structural analysis lacking. As may be recalled, Merton emphasized the role of America's stratification system in restricting opportunities for advancement and thus in creating criminogenic strains for individuals and anomie in society. Messner and Rosenfeld (1994), however, believe that Merton's approach misses what is distinctive about structural arrangements in the United States: the extent to which the "institutional balance of power is tilted toward the economy" (p. 76).

A capitalist economic system is conducive to producing individual pursuit of self-interest, competition, and innovation, but other developed nations with capitalist economies are not wracked by high rates of serious crimes. What is different about the United States? Messner and Rosenfeld answered that it is the economic institution that dominates other social, noneconomic institutions—the family, educational system, and politics— far more than in other countries. Indeed, U.S. social institutions are arranged to be subservient to and to support the economy. Education, for example, is seen as a means to higher paying employment; students who major in esoteric academic fields merely to learn or to foster personal development risk being ridiculed as "wasting their time" and "hurting their future." Family values are touted frequently, but corporate executives are expected to uproot their families if a promotion requires moving to another location. And politicians' reelection frequently hinges on little more than the strength of the nation's economy.

In other developed nations, however, social institutions counterbalance the capitalist economy's demand to pursue success at all costs and thus exert greater control over people's conduct. As Messner and Rosenfeld (1994) have pointed out, these social institutions "inculcate beliefs, values, and commitments other than those of the marketplace" (p. 86), and they tend to demand a level of involvement that constrains behavior. In the United States, however, noneconomic institutions are less successful in socializing, in securing the allegiance of, and thus in controlling the citizenry. Instead, "the cultural message that comes through with greatest force is the one most compatible with the logic of the economy: the competitive, individualistic, and materialistic message of the American Dream" (p. 86). The result is a context conducive to the spread of anomie and, in turn, of lawlessness.

In summary, Messner and Rosenfeld (1994) argued that the United States' high rate of serious crime is caused by the nation's distinctive, mutually reinforcing culture and institutional structure. The American dream serves as a powerful cultural force that generates anomie by motivating the pursuit of money "through any means necessary." It not only fosters but also receives continued legitimacy from the dominance of the economic institution. The intersection of culture and structure thus creates a society in which anomie is pervasive and controls are weak. Predictably, the United States' crime problem seems intractable and immune to the many "wars" waged against it.

The future of strain theory. It is difficult to determine whether Agnew's general strain theory and Messner and Rosenfeld's analysis of crime and the American dream are harbingers of strain theory's reemergence as a dominant criminological theory. At minimum, the intrinsic scholarly merit of these works will contribute to the revitalization of strain theory: Many criminologists will read these revisions of strain theory, and more than a few will publish articles testing the various propositions put forth by Agnew and by Messner and Rosenfeld. As America advances toward the 21st century, however, it also is possible that the prevailing social context will be conducive to renewed interest in the strain perspective. Two conditions seem particularly relevant.

First, in response to the excessive individualism and emphasis on greed in the 1980s, there are clear signs that the United States is beginning a cultural self-examination. Although many different voices are contributing to this discussion, they share the common theme that the core elements of the American dream—the pursuit of individual self-interest, competitiveness, and materialism—neither bring personal satisfaction nor create a good society. Instead, there is a call for Americans to think more about community, about the obligations of citizenship, and about helping others (Bellah, Madsen, Sullivan, Swindler, & Tipton, 1985, 1991; Coles, 1993; Etzioni, 1993; Reich, 1988; Wuthnow, 1991). Of course, as the American dream comes under critical scrutiny—as its darker side is unmasked—the relevance of strain theory is heightened.

Second, we also may be entering a period in which we no longer can ignore the complicity of U.S. society in a range of social ills, including crime. The Los Angeles riot of 1992, triggered by the acquittal of police officers charged with beating Rodney King, was a vivid reminder that the neglect of underlying problems eventually results in a day of reckoning (see also Currie, 1993). Messner and Rosenfeld (1994) make this point more broadly. "Given the growing awareness of vexing contemporary social problems—such as homelessness, the urban underclass, persistent economic stagnation accompanied by glaring social inequalities, and urban decay in general," they noted, "explanations of social behavior cast in terms of fundamental characteristics of society, rather than individual deficiencies, are likely once again to 'make sense' to many criminologists" (pp. 14-15). If so, strain theory—with its focus on the criminogenic costs of blocking opportunities for advancement and of placing people in adverse social circumstances—will receive its fair share of adherents in the criminological community.

The Consequences of Theory:
Policy Implications

If denial of opportunity generates criminogenic strains, then logic demands that the solution to crime lies in expanding legitimate opportunities. Most broadly, therefore, strain theory justifies programs that attempt to provide the disadvantaged with educational resources (e.g., Head Start), job training, and equal access to occupations. The perspective also would support efforts to introduce into prisons rehabilitation programs that allow offenders to earn educational degrees and to acquire marketable employment skills.

Apart from these general policy implications, it is noteworthy that strain theory has served as the basis for a variety of delinquency prevention programs (see Empey & Erickson, 1972; Empey & Lubeck, 1971), the most famous of which was Mobilization for Youth (Empey, 1982; Moynihan, 1969; Pfohl, 1985). MFY, as the program was known, was based directly on

Cloward and Ohlin's opportunity theory. The two scholars, in fact, played an integral role in seeing their ideas put into practice.

In 1959 they had been asked by a coalition of settlement houses located in New York's Lower East Side community to develop a theoretical framework for a proposal to secure government funds to provide youths with social services (Laub, 1983). *Delinquency and Opportunity* (Cloward & Ohlin, 1960) was one by-product of this collaboration; the other product was a 617-page report carrying the title *A Proposal for the Prevention and Control of Delinquency by Expanding Opportunities* (Empey, 1982, p. 241).

In different social times this proposal might have found a home on a dusty shelf, but in the early 1960s it offered a blueprint for social engineering that made eminent sense. The Kennedy administration had taken office recently with hopes of creating a "New Frontier of equal opportunity" and was ready to fulfill a long-standing family commitment to dealing with the problems of young Americans (Pfohl, 1985, pp. 224-225). In 1961 the administration created the President's Committee on Juvenile Delinquency and Youth Crime. David Hackett headed the committee.

In looking for promising strategies to address delinquency problems, Hackett learned of Cloward and Ohlin's work. As Stephen Pfohl (1985) noted, their opportunity theory "resonated well with the liberal domestic politics of John F. Kennedy" (p. 224) and particularly with the president's call for equal opportunity. Indeed, the fit between strain theory and the prevailing political context was so close that Lloyd Ohlin was invited to Washington, D.C., to assume a Health, Education, and Welfare (HEW) post and to assist in formulating delinquency policy. By May 1962 Mobilization for Youth had received a grant of $12.5 million, with over half of that amount coming from the federal government. Richard Cloward, meanwhile, was chosen as MFY's director of research.

MFY drew heavily from Merton's strain theory, setting up programs that extended youths' educational and employment support. But this reform also drew insights from the Chicago school, particularly Shaw and McKay's admonition that community organization was a prerequisite for delinquency prevention. One philosophical difference, however, existed between MFY and Shaw's Chicago Area Project. Although both programs were committed to community self-help, the leaders of MFY also felt the need to change the political structures that sustained inequities in opportunity. They agreed, for example, that the problem with employment was not simply that minorities lacked skills but that they were excluded from union apprenticeships; the problem of poor educational opportunities was a matter not simply of youths lacking books in the home but also of policies that assigned the newest and least talented teachers to schools in slum neighborhoods. What was needed to overcome such formidable barriers to opportunity, therefore, was not community organization but community *action* that attacked entrenched political interests. Accordingly, MFY promoted boycotts against schools, protests against welfare policies, rent strikes against slum landlords, lawsuits to ensure poor people's rights, and voter registration.

Commentators have disputed the wisdom of moving from the more focused agenda of providing youths educational and employment training to a broader attempt to reform the opportunity structure by empowering slum residents (Moynihan, 1969). The choice of strategy soon brought MFY into a political struggle with city officials dismayed by threats of lawsuits and other efforts by the poor to get their share of the pie. In the ensuing conflict, MFY was subjected to FBI investigations on suspicions of misappropriated funds and to claims by the *New York Daily News* that the staff was infested with "Commies and Commie sympathizers." Although exonerated of these kinds of charges, the swirl of controversy led to the resignation of key MFY leaders, including Cloward, and ultimately to the disappearance of much of the program (Liska, 1981, p. 52). In Washington, meanwhile, the President's Committee on Juvenile Delinquency and Youth Crime was allowed to wither away. "Influential members of Congress made it clear," LaMar Empey (1982) noted, "that the mandate of the President's Committee was to reduce delinquency, not to reform urban society or to try out sociological theories on American youths" (p. 243).

Thus attempts to reduce delinquency by changing fundamentally the nature of the opportunity structure met with much opposition. But should MFY be judged a failure? A less ambitious and confrontational reform might have succeeded in gaining more sustained political acceptance and support for programs. Two qualifications, however, must be added.

First, MFY must be credited for its attempt to attack the root causes of crime that most criminal reforms leave untouched. MFY's failure to avoid boisterous and powerful opposition says less about the correctness of the approach taken and more about the political interests that buttress America's structure of inequality. Second, although MFY's impact on delinquency has not been established definitively (Liska, 1981), it did serve as a model for similar community action programs across the nation. Daniel Moynihan (1969), a noted critic of the program, has nonetheless given MFY the credit it is due:

> MFY did lose in its battle with City Hall, but it set a pattern for the community action programs that were to spring up across the land at the very moment its own came under fire. . . . Preschool education, legal aid for the poor (not just to defend them, but to serve as plaintiffs), a theory of community organization, an emphasis on research and evaluation, and most especially the insistence on the involvement of the poor, all these were the legacy of Mobilization for Youth. It was no small achievement. (p. 123)

Conclusion

The Chicago school and Merton's strain theory represent early, yet bold and influential, efforts to show how the very fabric of American society—its slums, the contradictions between its cultural prescriptions and social structure—generates high rates of crime. They rejected as simplistic, if not as incorrect, previous theories that had sought to locate the causes of crime within individuals. Instead, they warned that the social organization of society constrains what people learn to become and what they might be pressured into doing. This is a lesson that cannot be overlooked casually, for it suggests, in a sense, that a society gets the crime it deserves.

The Chicago school and strain theory also illustrate the themes of this book. First, changes in the social context made each of these perspectives make sense to a good number of criminologists. For the Chicago school, the rapid growth and increasing diversity of urban society gave legitimacy to a theory that linked crime to these social transformations; for strain theory, the emergence of equal opportunity as a sociopolitical agenda provided an ideal context in which opportunity theory could win followers.

Second, the history of these perspectives shows how criminological theory can direct, or at least justify, criminal justice policy. The Chicago Area Project and Mobilization for Youth cannot be understood apart from the theories that provided the logic for their development and were convincing enough to prompt financial support. The writings of Shaw and McKay and of Cloward and Ohlin, therefore, clearly made a difference; ideas, as we have observed, have consequences.

4

SOCIETY AS INSULATION

Control Theory

The most important step in the solution to a problem, theoretical or otherwise, lies in asking the right questions about it. The proper formulation of the problem often may make the answer obvious. At the very least, asking the right question in the right way will contribute greatly to a solution. Asking the wrong question, or asking the right question in the wrong way, will result in no progress at all, although there may be an illusion of getting somewhere.

Unfortunately, the first step is also usually the most difficult. Not only does it require a thorough understanding of the nature of the situation with which one is faced, but it also demands the capacity to think about it in new and creative ways. Because we are not likely to ask questions about aspects of the situation that we take for granted, different criminologists have been led to see very different questions as the key to an understanding of crime and delinquency. What one takes for granted needs no explanation, but what one takes for granted depends on assumptions, in this case assumptions about human nature and social order.

Most criminologists have taken conformity for granted as part of the natural order of things and have concentrated on trying to explain the "crime problem." As we have seen, they have found their explanations in spirits and demons, in theories tracing the nonconformity to individual factors such as biological abnormalities or personality defects, or in theories tracing the nonconformity to social factors such as social disorganization, subcultural traditions, or inequality of opportunity, all of these being factors presumed to operate so as to distort the natural order of conformity. But is conformity really the natural order of things? To what extent should it be taken for granted?

By the time a person is a certain age, he or she speaks a certain language shared by others, drives a car in general obedience to traffic regulations, avoids urination or defecation in public, and in most other ways "goes along." All this tends to be taken for granted, but the evidence indicates that it is not at all "natural" (Davis, 1948). In fact, great effort is expended by parents, teachers, and the individual involved in a concerted effort to produce these results. Viewed in this way, all this conformity is a striking thing much in need of explanation. That is the focus of *control theory*, which takes the position that because conformity cannot be taken for granted, *nonconformity such as crime and delinquency is to be expected when social controls are less than completely effective.*

In this sense, control theory is not so much a theory of deviance as a theory of conformity. It does not ask the question, "Why do people commit crimes and acts of delinquency?" It suggests that crime and delinquency are going to occur unless people conform to all the social demands placed on them and then asks, "Why do people conform?" From this perspective on human nature and social order, crime and delinquency can be *expected* unless the sociocultural controls are operating effectively to prevent such behavior.

Below we will review several of the more prominent examples of control theory as they have emerged within the general context of criminological theory. These include Reiss's theory of personal and social controls, Nye's family-focused theory of social controls, Reckless's containment theory, the neutralization theory developed by Sykes and Matza as later modified by Matza's drift theory, Hirschi's control theory with its focus on social bonds, Gottfredson and Hirschi's self-control theory, and Hagan's power-control theory. First, however, we will examine some forerunners of contemporary control theory. As in the previous chapter, we will stress the significance of the work of Durkheim and the Chicago school. Both bodies of work remain rich sources of ideas about both human nature and social order. It is not surprising to find that they also contributed much to the reconsideration of the basic assumptions about the relationship between human nature and social order. This marked the development of control theory.

Forerunners of Control Theory

Durkheim's Anomie Theory

The origins of contemporary control theories of crime and delinquency are to be found in part in the work of French sociologist Emile Durkheim, in the same body of theory that inspired Merton's analysis of anomie as a source of crime (see Chapter 3). Durkheim's work was a product of the late 19th century, a period that had seen dramatic social change in the wake of the industrial revolution, and he described anomie not simply as "normlessness" but as the more or less complete collapse of social solidarity itself, the destruction of the fundamental bonds uniting individuals in a collective social order so that each person is forced to go it alone. Technological change had combined with the rise of capitalism, and the old world of agrarian society, in which farmers and herders lived simply in face-to-face relationships with interests in common, was rapidly giving way to a more complex, urban, technologically sophisticated social system. The sense of community was being eroded; the large, extended family consisting of many relatives working together was being torn apart and replaced with the new, nuclear family of parents alone with their children, and the pace of life was accelerating with an increasing division of labor separating different individuals into occupational specialties.

Describing London in 1844, Karl Marx's friend and collaborator Friedrich Engels (Josephson & Josephson, 1962) painted the picture as follows:

> The restless and noisy activity of the crowded streets is highly distasteful, and is surely abhorrent to human nature itself. Hundreds of thousands of men and women drawn from all classes and ranks of society pack the streets of London. . . . Yet they rush past each other as if they had nothing in common. They are tacitly agreed on one thing only—that everyone should keep to the right of the pavement so as not to collide with the stream of people moving in the opposite direction. No one even thinks of sparing a glance for his neighbors in the streets. . . . We know well enough that this isolation of the individual—this narrow-minded egotism—is everywhere the fundamental principle of modern society. (p. 32)

As we shall see in Chapter 6, Marx and Engels saw this situation as a consequence of the underlying economic shifts that had generated capitalism. Writing in France later in the century, Durkheim disagreed. For him, the moral order was more fundamental than the economic order. The idea of social solidarity can be said to represent almost a religion to Durkheim (1933). "Everything which is a source of solidarity is moral, everything which forces man to take account of other men is moral, everything which forces him to regulate his conduct through something other than the striving of his ego is moral, and morality is as solid as these ties are numerous and strong" (p. 398).

The importance of integration and regulation. In Durkheim's (1897/1951) view, social solidarity was maintained by two distinct sets of social functions: those involving *integration* and those involving *regulation.* Integration was described as a state of cohesion amounting to a common "faith" sustained by collective belief and practices leading to strong social bonds and the subordination of self to a common cause. For Durkheim, collective activity was what gave purpose and meaning to life. When integrative functions failed, the "collective force of society" was weakened, "mutual moral support" was eroded, and there was a "relaxation of social bonds" leading to extreme individualism (pp. 209-214).

Although Durkheim (1897/1951) saw *integration* as the sum of various social forces of *attraction* that drew people together, *regulation* was considered the sum of those forces of *constraint* that bound individuals to norms. Durkheim argued that the constraining regulative functions become more important in an urban society with a complex division of labor. Here different individuals may be attracted to a common goal and may be very willing to submit to the authority of the social system, but their efforts must be coordinated properly if society is to function smoothly. It is especially important that the regulative norms "deliver the goods," that they maintain their legitimacy by demonstrated effectiveness. Even if an individual wished to work with others toward a common social purpose, he or she might turn in a deviant direction if the norms regulating the common effort were perceived as unnecessary, overly burdensome, or otherwise questionable.

The nature of "man." Durkheim's (1897/1951) viewpoint was affected deeply by his conception of human nature. According to his *homo duplex* conception, any person was a blend of two aspects. On the one side there was the social self, the aspect of self that looks to society and is a product of socialization and cultivation of human potentials—the "civilized" member of a community. On the other side there was the egoistic self, the primal self that is incomplete without society and that is full of impulses knowing no natural limits. This conception of the primal aspect is somewhat similar to Freud's notion of the id. In Durkheim's view, conditions of social solidarity based on highly developed functions of social integration and social regulation allowed the more primal self to become humanized fully in a life shared with others on a moral common ground. One implication is that *unless* such social solidarity is developed and maintained, we may *expect* crime and delinquency.

The Influence of the Chicago School

As described in Chapter 3, the social upheaval that so concerned Durkheim in France was repeated even more dramatically in the United States a few decades later. During the early years of the 20th century and especially after World War I, the forces of technological change, increased industrialization combined with the rise of the large corporation, and rapid urbanization were accompanied by massive waves of immigration. Chapter 3 already has described the development of the Chicago school with its emphasis on immigration and especially urbanization as the major forces of social change that were leading to crime through social disorganization. But the Chicago school mined a rich vein of ideas about human nature and the social order, ideas that led some criminological theorists not toward a search for criminogenic forces in society that might be pulling or pressuring people away from their normal conformity but toward control theories that refused to take conformity for granted as the natural order of things.

Like some of the criminological theories discussed earlier, these control theories were influenced also by the social disorganization perspective, some explicitly and some implicitly. Although the accent was somewhat different among the various control theorists, two related Chicago school themes remained central. The first had to do with the interpretations of the nature of *human nature*. The second had to do with the nature of *community*.

Conceptions of human nature. As to human nature, the Chicago school developed the line of thought that explained the *self* as a blending of a primal self and a social self, but the focus was on showing just *how* the social self, so important to Durkheim, was formed. Although not at the University of Chicago himself, Charles H. Cooley can be considered part of "what came to be known as the Chicago School of Social Psychology" (Hinkle & Hinkle, 1954, p. 30). Cooley's work influenced George Herbert Mead of the University of Chicago, and Mead carried forward this and other contributions. Both Cooley and Mead considered the common notion of *imitation* insufficient to explain social behavior and sought to understand the process by which something like the primal self became the social self.

Cooley (1922) pointed out that the human offspring is dependent on other human beings in the family setting for a prolonged period. The family was treated as an example of what Cooley called a *primary group* in which interaction is of an intimate, face-to-face character leading to a "we-feeling" or sense of belonging and identification with the group. The child would not even develop a sense of self without the feedback provided by others serving as a mirror. According to Cooley's concept of the "looking-glass self," the child develops a concept of who he or she "really is" by imagining how he or she appears to others and how others interpret and evaluate what they perceive and then by forming a sense of self based on that process (Cooley, 1902, 1909). Without interaction in primary groups, a person would not be fully human. For Cooley (1909), human nature itself, defined as "those sentiments and impulses that are human in being superior to those of lower animals," was essentially the same throughout the world because the intense experience in primary groups was considered to be basically the same everywhere (p. 28).

Mead's (1934) social psychology was reminiscent of Durkheim's *homo duplex* in dividing the individual into an "I" and a "me." He did little to describe the "I" except to suggest that this represents a process of fundamental awareness that becomes focused in different ways leading to the development of the social self or "me." The focusing was said to occur though a process of "taking the role of the other" and seeing things from that perspective, with certain "significant others" being especially important and society representing a "generalized other" (pp. 82-92). It was through this process that socialization occurred.

If successful, such socialization was considered to lead to personally integrated social beings who would see the world not through the narrow and unstable perspective of the shifting "I" (to the extent that the "I" can be said to be capable of organized perception at all) but through a social "me" that included others' perspectives and interests as part of oneself. One implication was that *unsuccessful* socialization might lead to *personal disorganization*, to a self lacking in integration and consistency or to a self that was integrated internally but not integrated into society—or both.

The study of community. The second related Chicago school theme, the study of community, was reflected in the work of Park and Burgess and in the studies of the spatial distribution of natural areas and conflicting cultural traditions undertaken by Shaw and McKay as outlined in Chapter 3. There the stress was on the idea of *social disorganization*. In addition to this approach, much of the social psychological emphasis in the work of different members of the Chicago school had to do with the possibility of such social disorganization through the collapse of community as a consequence of increasing "social distance" among individuals who refused to get close to one another (Hinkle & Hinkle, 1954). Wirth (1938) described it as a problem of *segmentation* that separated people and made it impossible for them to relate to one another as total personalities. This theme emphasized the impersonality and anonymity of life in urban, industrialized societies in which people in the community did not know or care about one another and preferred it that way. The descriptions sounded like Durkheim's discussion of anomie or Engels's picture of London in 1844, only more so.

Beyond the concern with the apparent decline of community at a municipal or neighborhood level, some working within the tradition of the Chicago school focused attention on an even more ominous trend—the apparent decline in the moral integration of the basic primary groups themselves. Even the family, the most primary of all groups, seemed to be losing its influence over its members. If this proved true, it suggested not only social disorganization but also personal disorganization resulting from fundamental problems in the formation of the personal self. It was out of this context of social transformation and sociological thought that control theory was to emerge in criminology.

Varieties of Control Theory in Context

The concept of social disorganization led different criminological theorists in different directions. As suggested in Chapter 3, ideas of social disorganization could be seen in terms of severe pressures that themselves *produce* crime and delinquency, as in the strain theories, or in terms of a weakening of social controls that simply makes crime and delinquency more *possible*. The latter approach was taken by control theorists such as Reiss, Nye, Reckless, Sykes and Matza, Hirschi, Gottfredson and Hirschi, and Hagan. Each of these theorists, as we will see, tended to take the position that crime and delinquency could be *expected* in conditions where controls were not effective.

Reiss's Theory of Personal and Social Controls

In the late 1940s Albert J. Reiss (1949) completed a doctoral dissertation at the University of Chicago in which he attempted to develop an instrument for the prediction of juvenile delinquency. Two years later, he summarized part of his project in an article describing "Delinquency as the Failure of Personal and Social Controls" (1951). *Personal control* was defined as "the ability of the individual to refrain from meeting needs in ways which conflict with the norms and rules of the community" (p. 196). *Social control* was defined as "the ability of social groups or institutions to make norms or rules effective" (p. 196). According to Reiss, "Delinquency results when there is a relative absence of internalized norms and rules governing behavior in conformity with the norms of the social system to which legal penalties are attached, a breakdown in previously established controls, and/or a relative absence of or conflict in social rules or techniques for enforcing such behavior in the social groups or institutions of which the person is a member" (p. 196). This approach was influenced clearly by the social disorganization tradition, but it had a control theory emphasis.

Reiss (1951) maintained that conformity might result either from the individual's *acceptance* of rules and roles or from mere *submission* to them. Such a distinction ran parallel to Durkheim's division of social solidarity forces into those representing *integration* and those representing *regulation*. Personal controls were said to include both "(a) mature ego ideals or non-delinquent social roles, i.e., internalized controls of social groups governing behavior in conformity with non-delinquent group expectations, and (b) appropriate and flexible rational controls over behavior which permits conscious guidance of action in accordance with non-delinquent group expectations" (p. 203). Considered from the "perspective of the person," social control was held to lie "in the acceptance of or submission to the authority of the institution and the reinforcement of existing personal controls by institutional controls" (p. 201). Considered "from the standpoint of the group," it was said to lie "in the nature and strength of the norms of the institutions and the effectiveness of the institutional rules in obtaining behavior in conformity with the norms" (p. 201).

In an obvious reference to Chicago school work in the tradition of Shaw and McKay, Reiss (1951) took pains to stress that "this formulation is not in contradiction with the formulations which view certain types of delinquency as a consequence of social control in the delinquent gang" (pp. 196-197). He was not concerned with the way in which delinquency might be fostered through cultural transmission of norms that conflicted with those of the larger society but rather with underlying processes that seemed (a) to occur *prior* to any later processes such as conflicting cultural transmissions and (b) to be *necessary* before any such subsequent processes (whatever they might be) could ever take place. Being both antecedent and necessary, the processes involving loss of personal and social control might be considered more basic. As Reiss himself put it, "The delinquent peer group is here viewed as a *functional consequence* of the failure of personal and social controls" (p. 197; emphasis added).

It is important to remember that Reiss's goal was to develop a prediction instrument. As one reviewer pointed out at the time, Reiss was not seeking to explain what caused delinquency but to pin down those factors that had to occur before any such causes could be expected to produce their effects. "The chief concern as a predictor was failure to submit to social controls, the 'why' of such action being less important" (Symons, 1951, p. 208).

Following that tendency of the Chicago school tradition that stressed the *social psychological* dimension, Reiss (1951) began with the assumption that "primary groups are the basic institutions for the development of personal controls and the exercise of social control over the child" (p. 198). It followed that "delinquency and delinquent recidivism may be viewed as a consequence of the failure of primary groups to provide the child with appropriate non-delinquent roles and to exercise social control over the child so these roles are accepted or submitted to in accordance with needs" (p. 198). The key primary groups were identified as the family, the neighborhood, and the school.

Speaking of the family, for example, Reiss (1951) maintained that there is "social control over the child's behavior when the family milieu is structured so that the child *identifies* with family members . . . and *accepts* the norms" (pp. 198-199). On the other hand, acceptance of or submission to such social control may decline if the family fails to "meet the needs of its members" and "provide for members' needs through the purchase of material goods and services" (p. 198). Control might be lost also if the family exercised either "over-control or under-control" of the child's behavior (p. 199).

Nye's Family-Focused Theory of Social Controls

One of the leading figures in the sociology of the family, F. Ivan Nye was a product of Michigan State University and very much under the influence of the Chicago school. In the late 1950s he set forth a more systematic version of control theory, making explicit the formulation of the problem as one of explaining conformity rather than nonconformity. According to Nye (1958), "It is our position, therefore, that in general behavior prescribed as delinquent or criminal need not be explained in any positive sense, since it usually results in quicker and easier achievement of goals than the normative behavior" (p. 5). Thus the problem for the theorist was not to find an explanation for delinquent or criminal behavior; rather it was to explain why delinquent and criminal behavior is not more common.

In this view, it was not necessary to find some "positive" factor(s) of a biological, psychological, or sociological nature that operates to "cause" crime and delinquency. The problem was to locate the social control factor(s) that inhibited such nonconformity, the implication being that when the factor(s) was operating ineffectively for some reason, crime and delinquency became a *possibility* available to an individual. Nye's theoretical and research focus was on adolescents, and he considered the family to be the most important agent of social control over them. As the major primary group representing society, the family could generate *direct control, internalized control, indirect control,* and *control through alternative means of need satisfaction.* The same patterns of social control could be generated by other social institutions, although perhaps less powerfully.

These four modes of social control were also reminiscent of Durkheim's concepts of a combination of integration and regulation. Direct control was considered to be imposed on the individual by external forces such as parents, teachers, and the police through direct restraints accompanied by punishment for violation. Internalized control was considered to occur when the individual regulated his or her own behavior, even in the absence of direct, external regulation, through some process such as "conscience" or superego capable of restraining egoistic impulses. Indirect control had to do with the extent of affection and identification integrating the individual with authority figures in general and parents in particular. Such integration might serve to keep the person in line when regulation through either direct control or internalized self-control was minimal. Finally, a social system that made available various means of achieving satisfaction rather than demanding that everyone pursue exactly the same goal in exactly the same manner was held to exert social control by "delivering the goods" in such a variety of legitimate ways that the temptation to nonconformity was reduced.

Although these different modes of social control were held to operate somewhat independently, with one being more important in a particular situation and another in a different context, Nye (1958) pointed out that they were mutually reinforcing. The sense of identification with and affection for parents should, to use Reiss's (1951) terms, facilitate both an *acceptance* of and a *submission* to their direct controls. The same integration into the family unit should result in deeper internalization of parental expectations and regulations through an internal conscience that regulated behavior from within the individual. The fact that the family prepared the individual for the pursuit of alternative goals in life through a variety of means and that the larger society made this possible was a major force for the integration of the individual into the social order. Thus integration and regulation combined to reinforce one another and to reduce the likelihood of nonconforming behavior such as crime and delinquency.

Reckless's Containment Theory

Walter C. Reckless obtained his doctorate at the University of Chicago in the late 1920s, at the point of theoretical dominance for the Chicago school. He became especially interested in social psychology and in the social psychological aspects of criminology, asserting in the early 1940s that the central problem lay in explaining "differential responses" (1943, p. 51). By this he meant that criminology ought to pursue a search for "self-factors" that would explain why some individuals succumbed to social pressures leading to crime and delinquency although others remained relatively law-abiding in the same circumstances. Partly as a result of his search for self-factors during the 1940s and 1950s, Reckless (1961) was able to present what he called his *containment theory* in some detail at the beginning of the 1960s.

The social psychology of the self. Like Durkheim and the members of the Chicago school in general, Reckless argued that the great social transformation from life in fairly simple, integrated agrarian societies to life in complex, technologically sophisticated and highly industrialized urban environments placed a different set of pressures on the individual and the social order. As he revised his theory during the 1960s, Reckless (1967) became more explicit about the way in which the historical transformation represented in social psychological terms a "new pitch":

> The new situation or "pitch" may be described as follows. In a fluid, mobile society which has emphasized freedom of action for its individuals, the person is able to soar like a balloon without the ballast of social relationships. He can readily aggrandize himself at the expense of others. His society does not easily contain him. He no longer fits into expected roles. . . . He plays his major themes in life without agreed-upon ground rules. (p. 21)

Turning specifically to an examination of "crime in the modern world," Reckless (1967) focused attention on the "individualization of the self" (pp. 10-12).

> As an entity in personal development, the self seems to have had a sort of natural history. It appears to be relatively unimportant in primitive, isolated societies in which individuals very seldom break away from the undifferentiated uniformity of kin, village, and tribe. When human society in the course of evolution becomes differentiated, develops an increasing division of labor, and presents alternate choices to its members, the selves of certain persons begin to individualize and take on separate and distinct identities, departing from the mass of the people. (p. 11)

Pushes and pulls. As a control theorist, Reckless did not purport to offer a theory of crime causation. Indeed, he suggested that a variety of factors—including biophysical forces, psychological pressures, and social conditions such as poverty—might "push" a person toward crime or delinquency, and other factors—such as illegitimate opportunities—may "pull" one toward misbehavior. He recognized that the leading sociological theories in particular seemed to have analyzed effectively many of the central pushes and pulls. One of his more graphic analogies (1967) compared the etiology of crime and delinquency to that of malaria, insisting that the sociological theories stressing social structural forces be complemented by social psychological concepts emphasizing differential response.

> Sociological theories that do not account for a self factor to explain differential response are akin to explaining malaria on the basis of the lady mosquito, the swamp, or the lack of screens on houses. But everybody does not get malaria, even under conditions of extreme exposure. Some get a light touch. Some get a very severe attack. Some remain relatively immune. The

resistance is within the person—his blood, his chemistry, his differential immunity. (p. 469)

Reckless's containment theory was meant to explain why *in spite of* the various criminogenic pushes and pulls, *whatever they may be,* conformity remains the general state of affairs. He argued that to commit crime or delinquency requires the individual to break through a combination of outer containment and inner containment that together tend to insulate the person from both the pushes and pulls. With rare exceptions, only when these powerful containing forces were weakened could deviance occur. And even then, it was not assured, because containment theory was considered a *risk theory,* dealing in probabilities. Every weakening of containment was seen as tending to increase the odds for nonconformity by opening a breach in the armor provided by external social control and internal self-control.

Factors in outer containment. The listing of factors involved in outer containment differed somewhat in various statements of containment theory, as Reckless (1967) attempted to refine his theoretical position. He pointed out that the key factors binding the individual to the group might vary across different types of societies. Concentrating on "the external containment model for modern, urban, industrial, mobile society," he stressed (a) reasonable limits, (b) meaningful roles and activities, and (c) "several complementary variables such as reinforcement by groups and significant, supportive relationships, acceptance, the creation of a sense of belonging and identity" (pp. 470-471). Durkheimian themes were clear here, although not spelled out in detail. Thus, for example, although the containing limits reflected effective regulation, the latter set of variables "can also be called incorporation or integration of the individual" (p. 471). Translated into Durkheimian terms, it is clear that the containing force of "meaningful roles and activities" involved a combination of regulation and integration.

> Groups, organizations, associations, bureaucracies, to operate, or stay in existence . . . must expect reasonable conformity. . . . If a group or organization can get its members to internalize their rules, it would be doing an excellent job of containing. If a group or organization can get its members to comply (although they have not internalized the regulations), they are doing an excellent job. If they can minimize the number of infractions or hold the violations to tolerable proportions (where members are effective, if not enthusiastic conformists), they are doing a fair job. (Reckless, 1967, p. 470)

Factors in inner containment. For Reckless, however, the emphasis was on inner containment. In contemporary society, the individual who at one point might be operating in a context of powerful outer containment provided by regulating limits, meaningful roles, and a sense of integration into a particular family, organization, or community might in a short time be operating in another context with few regulations, meaningless activities, and a sense of alienation. Inner containment, on the other hand, would tend to control the individual to some extent no matter how the external environment changed. Reckless (1967) identified the key factors here as including *self-concept, goal orientation, frustration tolerance,* and *norm retention.*

The importance assigned to *self-concept* echoed Cooley's insistence on the significance of the "looking-glass self." As indicated in Chapter 3, members of the Chicago school such as Shaw and McKay focused attention on the manner in which certain natural areas of high delinquency tended to produce "bad boys." As a control theorist concerned with differential response, Reckless asked the *opposite question:* Why were there still so many "good boys" in these "swamps" of high delinquency? In a series of studies focusing on this question, Reckless and his associates concluded that such boys were "insulated" by a "favorable self-concept" (Dinitz, Reckless, & Kay, 1958; Dinitz, Scarpitti, & Reckless, 1962; Reckless, 1967; Reckless & Dinitz, 1967; Reckless, Dinitz, & Kay, 1957; Reckless, Dinitz, & Murray, 1956; Scarpitti, Murray, Dinitz, & Reckless, 1960). These studies suggested that an image of oneself as a law-abiding person of a sort not headed for trouble served to keep potential delinquents in relative conformity in spite of the pushes and pulls described previously. The research suggested that parents were the most influential sources of favorable self-concepts, with teachers and other authority figures also having some influence.

Reckless (1967) maintained that inner containment was greatly dependent also on *goal orientation,* defined as a sense of direction in life involving an orientation toward legitimate goals and an aspiration level "synchronized with approved and realistically obtainable goals" (p. 476). This approach ran directly opposite to the strain theory notion that social aspirations tended to become a major source of crime and delinquency because they were so frequently frustrated due to inadequate opportunity to achieve the goals in question. Instead, containment theory treated such goal orientation as providing a sense of direction that would keep the individual on the straight and narrow path of conformity. Such a perspective implied either (a) the assumption that opportunities were actually more widely available than was assumed by strain theory so that reasonable success goals were indeed "realistically obtainable," (b) the assumption that realistic goal orientations would involve a scaling down of aspirations on the part of many individuals, or (c) both assumptions.

Considering *frustration tolerance* as a major factor in inner containment, containment theory accepted the possibility that the control of biophysical urges toward deviance may be very frustrating and that contemporary society indeed may generate considerable frustration as a result of such facts as differential opportunity. It did not argue against efforts to deal with the sources of crime and delinquency by movement toward greater equality of opportunity, but it suggested that part of the differential response to familial, economic, political, and sexual frustrations can be accounted for by the fact that different individuals have developed different capacities for coping with frustration and that contemporary individualism generally is characterized by low frustration tolerance and consequent lack of self-control. Thus Reckless (1967) maintained that the contemporary individual "develops a very low frustration tolerance to the ordinary upsets, failures, and disappointments in life," and that this may result in "the inability to exert self-control, to tolerate frustration, to recognize limits, to relate to others" (pp. 20-21).

The fourth key component of inner containment, *norm retention,* referred to the "adherence to, commitment to, acceptance of, identification with, legitimation of, defense of values, norms, laws, codes, institutions, and customs" (Reckless, 1967, p. 476). Although the emphasis on goal orientation stressed the integration of the individual through the containing power of direction toward legitimate ends, the emphasis on norm retention stressed the integration of the individual through identification with acceptable means. For containment theory the key problem here was not, however, norm retention but rather *norm erosion,* of understanding the processes by which this containing factor sometimes was eroded to allow for the possibility of crime and delinquency. Norm erosion was described as including "alienation from, emancipation from, withdrawal of legitimacy from, and neutralization of *formerly internalized* ethics, morals, laws, and values" (p. 476; emphasis added).

Summary. It is apparent that containment theory followed the Chicago school approach in a way that was very Durkheimian. It took a historical focus, seeing what was apparently an increase in crime and delinquency as a product of the modern world. Unlike strain theories, it did not stress economic inequality and argue that crime and delinquency must be dealt with primarily through a liberal political agenda stressing equality of opportunity. Like the Durkheimian tradition, it regarded the moral order as more fundamental than the economic order and concerned itself to a considerable extent with what it took to be the problem of the individual in a complex society who increasingly is cast adrift with boundless desires, little capacity to tolerate denial, and no real sense of direction or commitment to the traditional rules of social life.

Sykes and Matza: Neutralization and Drift Theory

As we have seen, control theorists such as Reckless considered many of the sociological theories of crime and delinquency to be overly deterministic. If these problems were caused by slums, criminal traditions, lack of economic opportunity, and the like, why was it that many if not most of those suffering from such pressures in fact did not become criminals or delinquent at all? In the late 1950s Gresham Sykes and David Matza had turned attention to a related issue. If the social pressures causing delinquency, for example, were so powerful, then why was it that even the worst of delinquents seemed to be fairly conventional people, actually conforming in so many other ways? And why was it that although they continued to live in areas of crime and delinquency and continued to be faced with lack of economic opportunity, most of them did *not* continue law-violating behavior beyond a certain age but rather settled down in law-abiding lives? Could it be that the delinquency that took up so small a part of their lives for so short a time was really some sort of aberration, a temporary, albeit occasionally dramatic, quirk rather than a basic characteristic?

Techniques of neutralization. According to Sykes and Matza's (1957) original statement, the delinquent really had not rejected the larger social order as suggested by notions such as that of a delinquent subculture. In their view, such theories overemphasized the difference between delinquents and nondelinquents. But how was it possible for them to violate the conventional morality if they in fact had not rejected it, if they remained essentially integrated into the society and generally respectful of its regulations? Sykes and Matza explained the possibility by arguing that part of the process through which one learned the conventional social norms consisted of the learning of excuses or *techniques of neutralization* by which those norms could be neutralized temporarily, thus permitting violations *in certain cases* without the necessity of rejecting the norms themselves.

Specific techniques of neutralization were listed as (a) denial of responsibility, (b) denial of injury, (c) denial of the victim, (d) condemnation of the condemners, and (e) appeal to higher loyalties. *Denial of responsibility* is exemplified by the excuse that "a lot of the trouble I get into is not my fault." *Denial of injury* is exemplified by such excuses as "they've got so much, they'll never miss it," while an excuse such as "I only steal from drunks ('queers,' 'rednecks,' 'outsiders,' etc.)" represents *denial of the victim. Condemnation of the condemners* amounts to an insistence that certain people have no right to condemn certain violations because, for example, "They're worse than we are" and "We have to do it to protect our turf" represent excuses by *appeal to higher loyalties.* Sykes and Matza argued that it was the use of these techniques of neutralization that allowed delinquents to violate occasionally laws that they actually accepted and obeyed most of the time.

Drift theory. This explanation of delinquency in terms of techniques of neutralization represented a control perspective in that their use was treated as neutralizing the existing social control, thereby *allowing the possibility* of delinquency. In fact, Ball (1966) has argued that the concept of techniques of neutralization is not developed sufficiently to constitute a theory in its own right and might be integrated into Reckless's more systematic containment theory by considering the various techniques as examples of the more general process of norm erosion posited by Reckless.

In any case, Matza (1964) himself developed the notion further in the middle 1960s, arguing that delinquents in general were no more committed to their delinquency than to conventional enterprises, but that the delinquency was a matter of "drift" facilitated by the existence of a "subterranean convergence" between their own techniques of neutralization and certain ideologies of the authorities who represented the official moral order. By this he meant that the authorities themselves often excused violations by blaming parents, citing provocation on the part of the victim, or accepting explanations defining the infraction as involving self-defense or "accident" in a way that reinforced the norm neutralization of the juveniles. In this double-edged way the controlling power of conventional norms might either be weakened by all sorts of qualifications built into them or be eroded through time as attempts to apply them met with objections, excuses, and vacillations.

Still, neutralization merely makes delinquency *possible.* In Matza's (1964) language, "Those who have been granted the potentiality for freedom through the loosening of social controls but who lack the position, capacity, or inclination to become agents in their own behalf, I call drifters, and it is in this category that I place the juvenile delinquent" (p. 29). Dealing with the argument against control theory that holds that "delinquency . . . cannot be assumed to be a potentiality of human nature which automatically erupts when the lid is off" (Cohen & Short, 1958, p. 30) but must involve at least some triggering factors(s), Matza made a concession that many other control theorists would not accept: He agreed that because delinquency may involve unfamiliar and dangerous behaviors, something more than loss of control is necessary to explain it. He held that the triggering factors consisted of a combination of *preparation* and *desperation.*

For Matza, preparation involved a process by which the person discovered that a given infraction could be pulled off by *someone,* that the individual had the ability to do it *himself or herself,* and that fear or *apprehension* could be managed. Even if a delinquent infraction had become possible, it might not occur unless someone learned that it was possible, felt confident that he or she could do it, and was courageous or stupid enough to minimize the dangers. Otherwise the possibility would fail to become a reality. As for the element of desperation, Matza argued that the central force there was a profound sense of fatalism, a feeling that the self was overwhelmed, with a consequent need to violate rules of the system to reassert individuality. Unlike Reckless, Matza did not criticize such a need for individuality as amounting often to a misplaced egoism.

The Context of the 1950s

When Reiss (1951) published his article treating delinquency as a failure of personal and social controls at the beginning of the 1950s, the social disorganization themes of the Chicago school as developed in the Roaring 20s were still in fashion, having been reinforced by the experiences of the Great Depression, World War II, and the rapid social change following the war. But almost as if Americans collectively were exhausted by these upheavals and were determined to have peace and quiet, the 1950s became a time of relative social conformity, at least on the surface. Such television shows as *Lassie* and *Leave It to Beaver* were almost caricatures of the era, with the (stereotypical) middle-class American father coming home from the office to greet the (stereotypical) happy if slightly mischievous children at their lemonade stand before inquiring of his (stereotypical) wife (clad in her stereotypical housedress and apron), "What's for dinner, honey?" Conformity, conventionality, and complacency were the order of the day.

Given this pervasive atmosphere, approaches such as Nye's theory tracing delinquency to departures from the model of the ideal family with all its conventional controls over the young seemed almost like common sense. Social critics were more alarmed by the atmosphere of stifling over-conformity than by concern over general social disorganization. By the close of the 1950s and even into the early 1960s, Americans were being criticized as a "nation of sheep" (Lederer, 1961), in which the mother was trapped at home in a set of stereotypes about women amounting to a "feminine mystique" (Friedan, 1963) and the father went off to work only to submit meekly as an "organization man" (Whyte, 1957). Despite the fascination with the apparent wildness of the big-city gangs, the young in general were being criticized as a mass of pop-culture conformists, and traditionally unruly college students were being castigated as so lacking in any willingness to question things as to constitute a "silent generation" (Starr, 1985, p. 238). Throughout the 1950s society as a whole seemed to be sleeping through the American dream.

Of course, not everyone was satisfied. As indicated in Chapter 3, there was concern in some quarters about continuing social inequality and differential opportunity, as evidenced by the renewal of interest in Merton's (1938) anomie theory. The general public was fascinated with and strangely alarmed by the apparently senseless behavior of highly publicized adolescent male, working-class gangs in the large cities, exotic groups that in some strange way failed to fit into the dream. Cohen's (1955) delinquent subculture theory represented an effort to explain some of this, although Sykes and Matza (1957) maintained that delinquents were not as different as they might appear. By and large, opportunity theory fit the 1950s, stressing as it did the importance of everyone having access to full participation in the American way of life.

The tendency to stress the strain theory aspect of Merton's approach tells a great deal about the preoccupations of the time. Although he himself used Durkheim's term and described the way in which the amorality coming with intense emphasis on economic success weakened social control through a deemphasis on traditional normative standards of right and wrong, it was the idea of a discontinuity between success goals and the institutionalized means for their achievement that captured most of the attention. Many paid little attention to the powerful Durkheimian theme of moral erosion in their excitement over the theme that traced much of the nonconformity that did exist to a lack of access to legitimate opportunities to achieve those conventional economic aspirations so central to the dream.

Although the potentials for social change were seething under the surface of all this apparent tranquillity and were already beginning to be felt here and there, this general atmosphere still prevailed in large part when Reckless (1961) first set forth his containment theory at the beginning of the 1960s. The formulation had somewhat less impact than might have been expected from a major theoretical statement by one of the nation's leading criminologists. In some ways his containment theory seemed to reflect more of the social climate of the post-World War I years of the 1920s, when Reckless was a graduate student at the University of Chicago and concerns over social disorganization filled the air, than of the complacent 1950s. But the onslaught of the 1960s was to make control theory much more popular.

The Context of the 1960s

The massive social changes that took place in America of the 1960s, including the rising tide of protest over discrimination, the development of a youth counterculture, and the reaction to the war in Vietnam, not only shook American society but also had a considerable impact on criminological theory. Although Martin Luther King's Southern Christian Leadership Conference (SCLC) had begun its work in the middle 1950s, the civil rights movement had not exploded into public consciousness until its rapid acceleration with the dramatic lunch counter sit-in by Black students in Greensboro, North Carolina, in 1960 (Zinn, 1964; Starr, 1985). The coming of the civil rights movement shattered much of the complacency of the 1950s, and its reliance on a nonviolent strategy of civil disobedience entailing the deliberate violation of segregation laws represented a direct repudiation of conventional social control in the name of a higher morality. But this was only the beginning.

The so-called Beats, representing part of the avant garde literary world of the 1950s, had made a special point of defying conventionality by flaunting drug use, and the latter part of the decade had seen the birth of a strange new brand of rebellious music called "rock and roll." Even so, neither of these had shaken the Establishment. But between 1960 and

1966 the number of U.S. students enrolling in college more than doubled, topping 7.3 million (Starr, 1985). Early in the 1960s, widely publicized student protests at such respectable and prestigious institutions as the University of California at Berkeley attacked the impersonality and complacency of the bureaucracies of higher education and demanded a place for individuality and greater freedom of expression. This developing counterculture tended to reject many of the conventional aspects of the American dream, including the characteristic overconformity, the model of the middle-class family, and the ruthless pursuit of material success. The search for an "authentic self" became a priority; "the perception of the banality of existence became the core of the youth revolt of the 1960s" (Aronowitz, 1973, p. 331).

Changes such as these, as well as dramatic events such as the assassination of President Kennedy in 1963 and growing uneasiness over the slow escalation of military involvement in Southeast Asia, meant that Matza's theory positing drift associated with a decline in moral consensus and a combination of preparation and desperation could find a more receptive audience. As the decade moved on, the continuing drama of the civil rights movement, the coming of militant feminism, the Vietnam protests, the appearance of the hippies, the advocacy of psychedelic drug use on the part of respected Harvard professors, and a host of other dramatic social and cultural shifts seemed to many to signal the complete collapse of personal and social control.

By the middle of the 1960s the civil rights movement had taken on a different and more radical tone. The movement for Black separatism, demanding that several states be set apart for Blacks within the United States, had gained considerable strength. The Black Muslim movement had led many Black Americans to reject Christianity as a "White man's religion," to change their names, and to embrace a variation of the Islamic faith. For many Black Americans, much of the machinery of personal and social control seemed to be designed to ensure their continued social and emotional bondage.

As the escalation of U.S. involvement in Vietnam accelerated under President Johnson, protests became more frequent and more violent. News media increasingly referred to the nation as being "torn apart" by the war. Social consensus appeared to have evaporated. The 1950s began to seem like an era in another and very different society.

As for the feminist movement of the 1960s, it represented in large part an attack on the revered institution of the conventional family as a deceptive front for the political, economic, and sexual oppression of women. The counterculture of hippies and others—which grew up among the new breed of college students and spread to include both students and non-students, youths and adults—seemed to mock the staid buttoned-down mentality of the 1950s as many clean-cut, middle-class young men took to beards, sandals, beads, and shoulder-length hair and previously demure young ladies adopted similar attire, minus the beards. Drugs, especially marijuana, seemed to be everywhere among them, and they were most united in their rejection of the middle-class preachments regarding conventional family life and dedication to the economic rat race.

Hirschi's Control Theory

To many observers, the 1960s seemed to be characterized by loss of self-control on the part of the individual and of social control on the part of organized religion, the family, educational institutions, the economic order, and the political state. It sometimes appeared that everything was being called into question and that all the conventional institutions were crumbling. When at the close of the decade Travis Hirschi, himself working at Berkeley, set forth his own highly refined version of control theory (1969), the times were ripe for acceptance of such a perspective if it could be formulated in appropriate theoretical terms.

Hirschi's forerunners. Hirschi's (1969) theoretical position was expressed with special clarity through a critique of alternative perspectives, an exploration of the differences between his own formulation and those of his predecessors in the development of control theory, and an examination of his position in the light of empirical data. A review of his approach will provide not only a clear example of the way in which criminological theories reflect contexts of time and place, but also of the manner in which they are shaped by special considerations aside from the orientations of the particular theorists. Hirschi himself has shown an appreciation of this and unusual candor in admitting just how certain considerations affected the way in which he set forth his position. These included the nature of the data available to him and the current unpopularity of one specific tradition through which he might have expressed his ideas—the social disorganization theme of the Chicago school.

Hirschi has pointed out the significance of the data factor in a recent interview:

Control theory as I stated it cannot really be understood unless one takes into account the fact that I was attached to a particular method of research. When I was working on the theory, I knew that my data were going to be survey data; therefore I knew that I was going to have mainly the perceptions, attitudes, and values of individuals as reported by them. . . . Had I data on other people, or on the structure of the community, I would have had to state the theory *in a quite different way*. (Bartollas, 1985, p. 190; emphasis added)

The problem with the social disorganization theme was that it had lost a great deal of its popularity as an explanation of social problems in general and crime in particular (Rubington & Weinberg, 1971). Like the older concept of *social pathology*, it had come under intense criticism as a matter of vague generalities masking a lack of value-neutrality. As criminologist Marshall Clinard (1957) commented:

There are a number of objections to this frame of reference. (1) Disorganization is too subjective and vague a concept for analyzing a general society . . . (2) Social disorganization implies the disruption of a previously existing condition of organization, a situation which generally cannot be established . . . (3) Social disorganization is usually thought of as something "bad," and what is "bad" is often the value judgment of the observer and the members of his social class or other social groups . . . (4) The existence of forms of deviant behavior does not necessarily constitute a major threat to the central values of a society . . . (5) What seems like disorganization actually may often be highly organized systems of competing norms . . . (6) Finally, as several sociologists have suggested, it is possible that a variety of subcultures may contribute, through their diversity, to the unity or integration of a society rather than weakening it by constituting a situation of social disorganization. (p. 41)

These and other criticisms of the concept of social disorganization were widely accepted in the 1960s, and Hirschi has been equally candid in describing how he deliberately avoided linking his theory to the social disorganization tradition because of its unpopularity at the time:

For example, I was aware at the time I wrote my theory that it was well within the social disorganization tradition. I knew that, but you have to remember the status of social disorganization as a concept in the middle 1960s when I was writing. I felt I was swimming against the current in stating a social control theory at the individual level. Had I tried to sell social disorganization at the same time, I would have been in deep trouble. So I shied away from that tradition. As a result, I did not give social disorganization its due. I went back to Durkheim and Hobbes and ignored an entire American tradition that was directly relevant to what I was saying. But I was aware of it and took comfort in it. I said the same things the social disorganization people had said, but since they had fallen into disfavor I had to disassociate myself from them. Further, as Ruth Kornhauser so acutely points out, social disorganization theories had been associated with the cultural tradition. That was the tradition I was working hardest against; so in that sense, I have compromised my own position or I would have introduced a lot of debate I didn't want to get into had I dealt explicitly with social disorganization theory. Now, with people like Kornhauser on my side, and social disorganization back in vogue, I would emphasize my roots in this illustrious tradition. (Bartollas, 1985, p. 190)

So Hirschi (1969) was especially careful to avoid working explicitly out of the social disorganization tradition and to ground his position instead in the thought of other forerunners such as Durkheim and Hobbes. Concentrating on a search for the essential variables providing control through bonds to conventional society, he developed his own position and presented a body of systematic research in support of it. This combination seemed to represent the epitome of tightly reasoned and empirically grounded control theory.

Hirschi's sociological perspective. The control theorists examined to this point tended to distinguish between control exerted from sources external to the individual and control exerted from within the individual. Indeed, Reckless (1961) had argued that the individual is so isolated in contemporary society, so free to move from one context of external control to another or even to escape from most of it, that internal control is the more basic factor in conformity. Hirschi's position was much more sociological in nature. The characteristics that other control theorists took to be aspects of the personality he considered to be factors sustained by ongoing social relationships, which he termed *social bonds*.

Other control theorists gave great weight to the notion of *internalization*, the process by which social norms are taken so deeply into the self as to become a fundamental part of the personality structure. Citing Wrong's (1961) critique of this "oversocialized conception of man," Hirschi (1969, p. 4) insisted instead that what seems to be deeply rooted internalization of social expectations is actually much too superficial to guarantee conformity. First, he rescued Durkheim from the strain theorists. Pointing out that "because Merton traces his intellectual history to Durkheim, strain theories are often called 'anomie' theories," he showed that "actually, Durkheim's theory is one of the purest examples of control theory" (Hirschi, 1969, p. 3). Next he turned to the question posed by Hobbes—"Why do men obey the rules of society?"—observing that an assumption of internalization was used commonly as a means of avoiding Hobbes's own conclusion that conformity was based essentially on fear. Here there was an echo of Reiss's distinction between conformity resulting from acceptance of the rules and conformity based on mere *submission*.

This willingness to acknowledge that conformity might be based on simple submission to the forces of social regulation without internalized acceptance of the norms became fairly clear in Hirschi's first citation of Durkheim as a control theorist. Hirschi (1969) remarked that "both anomie and egoism are conditions of 'deregulation,' and the 'aberrant' behavior that follows is an automatic consequence of such deregulation" (p. 3), without noting Durkheim's complementary stress on integration as a factor in conformity. Turning immediately to Hobbes, he put the matter with stark clarity as follows:

> Although the Hobbesian question is granted a central place in the history of sociological theory, few have accepted the Hobbesian answer. . . . It is not so, the sociologist argued: There is more to conformity than fear. Man has an "attitude of respect" toward the rules of society; he "internalizes the norms." Since man has a conscience, he is not free simply to calculate the costs of illegal or deviant behavior. . . .
>
> Having thus established that man is a moral animal who desires to obey the rules, the sociologist was then faced with the problem of explaining his deviance. (Hirschi, 1969, p. 5)

For Hirschi (1969), then, the problem of explaining deviance was a false problem based on the mistaken assumption that people are fundamentally moral as a result of having internalized norms during socialization. He insisted, however, that it was an "oversimplification" to say that "strain theory assumes a moral man while control theory assumes an amoral man," because the latter "merely assumes variation in morality: For some men, considerations of morality are important, for others they are not" (p. 11). Unlike Matza, who felt it necessary to suggest forces of preparation and desperation as a way of explaining why the mere loss of control might result in delinquency, Hirschi suggested no motivational factors and simply noted that loss of control sets the individual free to calculate the costs of crime. "Because his perspective allows him to free some men from moral sensitivities, the control theorist is likely to shift to a second line of social control—to the rational, calculational component in conformity and deviation" (p. 11).

Social control by social bonds. To explain conformity Hirschi (1969) stressed four control variables, each of which represented a major social bond: *attachment, commitment, involvement,* and *belief.* These terms have been the source of some confusion, primarily because Hirschi employed them in a sociological sense rather than in the primarily psychological sense that had become commonplace in the age of the individual preoccupied with allegedly internal states. He resisted the assumption that traced so much of human behavior to alleged internalization of attitudes and norms on the part of individuals.

By *attachment,* for example, Hirschi (1969) did not mean the strength of an internal, emotional bond so subjective that it might grow even stronger in the absence of interaction, such as in the old adage, "Absence makes the heart grow fonder" (e.g., more attached to the distant other), but the very opposite. By *commitment* he did not mean some deep, internal dedication of self to others even to the extent of self-sacrifice, as when people speak of a loving mother being committed to her child or of two adults making a genuine commitment to one another, but the very opposite. By *involvement* he meant something quite different from the psychological notion of emotional entanglements, of being "bound up in one another" or emotionally "part of each other." And, finally, by *belief* he did not mean profound inner faith or even deep belief in someone or something, but a bond much less internalized. Perhaps human relationships had become more superficial, or perhaps individuals really had never internalized as deeply as had been assumed by some theorists.

Importance of the family and school. Hirschi felt that the two conventional systems through which the adolescent could be expected to form the key bonds with society were the family and the school. *Attachment* was used to signify *continuing intimacy of interaction* as evidenced by the extent to which parents or teachers exerted supervision, the intimacy of communication with them, the extent to which the adolescent felt competent in and performed well in school settings, and the degree of concern felt for the opinions of parents and teachers. *Attachment* used in this sense is close, for example, to Sutherland's concept of differential association, except that it stresses the idea that the very bond formed by the attachment is more important than the specific content of the learning that may result. For Hirschi (1969) such an approach had the advantage of avoiding "the problem of explaining changes over time by locating the 'conscience' in the bond to others rather than making it part of the personality" (p. 19). The

bond was considered to lie in the sociological nature of the ongoing association with conventional groups rather than in some subjective, psychological attachment independent of this ongoing association.

Commitment was defined not in terms of a surrender of self-interest but,
on the contrary, as *the degree to which the individual's self-interest has been
invested* in a given set of activities. For Hirschi (1969) this was the "rational
component of conformity," essentially a matter of the rational calculation
of potential gains and losses, so that the individual contemplating a deviant
act "must consider the costs of this deviant behavior, the risk he runs of
losing the investment he has made in conventional behavior" (p. 20). In
this sense a youth who has invested much time and energy in conforming
to the expectations of parents and teachers, working hard and perhaps
graduating with honors, has a tighter bond with society because he or she
has a powerful "stake in conformity" and much to lose by getting out of
line. Of course, "in order for such a built-in system of regulation to be
effective, actors in the system must perceive the connections between
deviation and reward and must value the rewards society proposes to
withhold as punishment for deviation" (p. 162). Thus Hirschi went on to
point out that "the stance taken toward aspirations here is virtually opposite to that taken in strain theories," because in control theory "such
aspirations are viewed as constraints on delinquency" (p. 162). Although
strain theory tended to see high aspirations as leading to frustration and
consequent deviance, Hirschi, like Reckless, maintained that the opposite
was true: Legitimate aspirations gave a "stake in conformity" that tied one
to the conventional social order, at least when the individual had invested
in the pursuit of such goals instead of merely wishing for them.

As for *involvement* as a factor in social control, Hirschi (1969) stressed
not the psychological theme of emotional entanglement but the sociological observation that "many persons undoubtedly owe a life of virtue to a lack
of opportunity to do otherwise" (p. 21). Acknowledging that the old thesis
"idle hands are the devil's workshop" and the commonsense suggestion that
delinquency could be prevented by keeping the young people busy and
off the streets had so far found little support in research, he went on to
examine the possibility that involvement defined in terms of sheer *amount
of time and energy devoted to a given set of activities* might represent a key factor
in social control. Aside from such findings as those relating time spent on
homework to extent of delinquency, however, Hirschi's data failed to lend
much support to the hypothesis that involvement, as he conceptualized it,
represented a variable crucial to preventing wayward behavior.

Finally, Hirschi's (1969) use of the term *belief* was also much more sociological than psychological. He did not use the term to indicate deeply held convictions but to suggest approbation in the sense of assent to certain values and norms with some degree of approval. Used in this way, beliefs are not seen as profoundly internalized personal creeds but as impressions and opinions that are highly dependent on constant social reinforcement. If the degree of approbation is slight, the belief becomes a matter of simple assent, of a willingness to submit and "go along," at least for the present. If the degree of approbation is greater, it may amount to a belief to which the individual gives eager approval and wholehearted cooperation. The point is that such beliefs were not taken to be inner states independent of circumstances but somewhat precarious moral positions much in need of social support based on the ongoing attachment to conventional social systems described earlier.

Hirschi (1969) was careful to point out that he was not accepting that approach to control theory in which "beliefs are treated as mere words that mean little or nothing if the other forms of control are missing" (p. 24). He was equally careful to reject the other extreme represented by Sykes and Matza's (1957) insistence that delinquents "believe" in the conventional morality to the extent that techniques of neutralization become necessary before violations can occur. Hirschi (1969) took the position that individuals differ considerably in the depth and power of their belief and that this variation is dependent on the degree of attachment to systems representing the beliefs in question. As he put it, "The chain of causation is thus from attachment to parents, through concern for the approval of persons in positions of authority, to belief that the rules of society are binding on one's conduct" (p. 200). In this view, it is not that people lack consciences, that they are in truth totally amoral beings who simply babble on about how much they think they "believe in" things. It is rather that "attachment to a system and belief in the moral validity of its rules are not independent"; what is called "belief" depends on the strength of attachment and will decline with it (p. 200).

Gottfredson and Hirschi's Self-Control Theory

Control theory has continued as a major criminological perspective well into the 1990s (Cullen & Burton, 1994). Two newly formulated paradigms have been particularly influential in sustaining interest in control explanations of criminal behavior: Gottfredson and Hirschi's (1990) *self-control theory of crime,* which we review here, and Hagan's (1989) *power-control theory,* which we consider in the next section.

Self-control and crime. In *A General Theory of Crime,* Michael Gottfredson and Travis Hirschi (1990) crafted an explanation of crime that departs significantly from Hirschi's earlier work. As noted previously, social bond theory rejected the attempt to explain crime through internalized control. Instead, taking a distinctively sociological approach, Hirschi (1969) emphasized that control is sustained by individuals' continuing relationship with the conventional order, that is, by their bonds to family, school, work, everyday activities, and beliefs. Now, Gottfredson and Hirschi abandoned the idea that continuing social bonds insulate against illegal involvement in favor of the proposition that self-control, internalized early in life, determines who will fall prey to the seductions of crime.

It is perhaps instructive that Gottfredson and Hirschi's conception of control as a permanent internal state rather than an ongoing sociological product reflects a broader trend in criminological theory, encouraged by the context of the 1980s, to revitalize individual theories of crime (see Chapter 8). In any case, Gottfredson and Hirschi contended that their approach was formulated for a more important reason: It explains what we know about the nature of crime.

Gottfredson and Hirschi have claimed that much criminological theorizing pays virtually no attention to the facts about the nature of crime uncovered by empirical research: Crime provides short-term gratifications, such as excitement, small amounts of money, and relief from situational aggravations. People who engage in crime also engage in analogous behaviors that furnish short-term gratifications, such as smoking, substance abuse, speeding in automobiles, gambling, and irresponsible sexual relations. Criminals do not plan their conduct. Their crimes are not specialized or sophisticated but responses to whatever easy, illegal opportunity that presents itself. Similarly, offenders fail in social domains—school, work, and marriage—that require planning, sustained effort, and delayed gratification. Last—and important—involvement in crime appears to be stable: Children manifesting behavioral problems tend to grow into juvenile delinquents and eventually into adult offenders.

Gottfredson and Hirschi derived their theory from these facts about crime. If crime and analogous behaviors provide easy gratifications, why does not everyone engage in these acts? Logic suggests that something must be restraining law-abiding citizens from taking advantage of the ubiquitous temptations they confront in their daily routines. Further, if crime is stable and its roots planted early in life, this restraint must be inculcated in childhood and be capable of operating across time and social situations.

Gottfredson and Hirschi (1990) proposed that self-control is the restraint that allows people to resist crime and other short-term gratifications. Because the path toward or away from crime starts early in life, they contended further that the inculcation of self-control depends on the quality of parenting in a child's early years. Those with the misfortune of having parents who are neglectful and ineffectual in child rearing will "tend to be impulsive, insensitive, physical (as opposed to mental), risk-taking, short-sighted, and nonverbal, and they will tend therefore to engage in criminal and analogous acts" (p. 90). In fact, their futures are bleak: Lacking self-control, they not only will be attracted to crime but also are likely to fail in and drop out of school, to lose jobs, and to be unable to sustain a meaningful intimate relationship. In contrast, children with parents with enough caring and resources to supervise and punish their misconduct will develop the self-control needed to resist the easy temptations offered by crime and to sustain the hard work necessary to succeed in school, work, and marriages.

Assessing self-control theory. Although recently proposed, Gottfredson and Hirschi's (1990) self-control theory already has been tested empirically. The early returns appear favorable: Studies generally support the theory's conclusion that low self-control is related to criminal involvement (Brownfield & Sorenson, 1993; Burton, Cullen, Evans, & Dunaway, in press; Grasmick, Tittle, Bursik, & Arneklev, 1993; Keane, Maxim, & Teevan, 1993; Nagin & Paternoster, 1993; Wood, Pfefferbaum, & Arneklev, 1993). Accordingly, it seems likely that this perspective will continue to influence criminological thinking in the time ahead.

At the same time, self-control theory appears to be overstated in places. Although self-control explains variation in criminal involvement, this does not mean that causes identified by rival theoretical models—differential association, for example—are unimportant (Brownfield & Sorenson, 1993; Burton et al., in press; Nagin & Paternoster, 1993). In particular, and contrary to the logic of self-control theory, Robert Sampson and John Laub (1993) presented longitudinal data showing that adult social bonds—such as stable employment and cohesive marriages—can redirect offenders into a pathway to conformity well beyond their childhood years. The relationship among self-control, crime, and analogous behaviors also seems problematic. It is doubtful that criminal and analogous (or deviant) behaviors will be correlated strongly among all offenders, including, for example, white-collar criminals who have evidenced delayed gratification in acquiring high-status occupational positions (Benson & Moore, 1992). And some evidence suggests that contrary to theoretical predictions, self-control is not related strongly to all types of analogous behaviors, such as smoking (Arneklev, Grasmick, Tittle, & Bursik, 1993).

Gottfredson and Hirschi (1990) also failed to resolve a hidden inconsistency in their thinking. On one hand, they implied that social class is an unimportant correlate of crime and that crime is found across the class structure. On the other hand, the logic of their model seemingly predicts a strong correlation between class and crime. Their image of the offender, we may recall, is as someone who is a social failure: Lacking self-control, offenders do poorly in school and poorly in the job market. They inevitably slide into the lower class. Further, offenders can be expected to be inadequate parents themselves, passing on low self-control and economic disadvantage to their offspring. Over generations, then, crime should be concentrated increasingly in the bottom rungs of society. In the future, this inconsistency will require systematic attention.

Finally, although Gottfredson and Hirschi may have identified a crucial link in the chain of conditions causing crime, they remained silent on the larger structural conditions that might affect family well-being, the ability to deliver quality parenting, and, in turn, the inculcation of self-control. Elliott Currie (1985) called this omission the "fallacy of autonomy—the belief that what goes on inside the family can usefully be separated from the forces that affect it from outside: the larger social context in which families are embedded for better or for worse" (p. 185). A more complete understanding of crime thus would place parents and children within the context of a changing American society. In particular, it seems essential to examine the structural forces and government policies that have shredded the social fabric of many inner-city neighborhoods, impeded the development of stable and nurturing families, and placed many youths at risk for early involvement in crime (Currie, 1985, 1989, 1993; Panel on High-Risk Youths, 1993).

Hagan's Power-Control Theory

John Hagan's (1989) power-control theory shares common aspects with Gottfredson and Hirschi's perspective. First, Hagan contended that delinquency is more likely when a person has a preference for taking risks—an orientation that Gottfredson and Hirschi saw as central to a lack of self-control. Second, both approaches believe that personal orientations, whether risk taking or self-control, are established by the nature of parenting. In short, families are incubators for or prophylactics against criminal involvement.

At this juncture, the two theories diverge. For Gottfredson and Hirschi, parenting was either good or bad, and this determines whether self-control is or is not inculcated. For Hagan, however, the critical issue was how the balance of power between parents affects the nature of parenting and, in turn, risk preferences and crime. That is, power relations between husbands and wives shape how children are controlled (hence "power-control" theory).

Hagan contended that in patriarchal families, parents exercise greater control over female than male children. The family, in effect, tries to reproduce gender relations in the next generation. Daughters are socialized to be feminine and to value domesticity—in short, to prepare for their future as homemakers; sons are encouraged to develop boldness and to experience the world—in short, to prepare for their future as breadwinners. The result is that boys have stronger preferences for risk taking that, in turn, increase their involvement in delinquency.

In egalitarian families, however, parents supervise female and male children more similarly. "In other words," observed Hagan (1989), "as mothers gain power relative to husbands, daughters gain freedom relative to sons" (p. 157). Again, parents tend to reproduce themselves. Daughters, not just sons, are seen as potentially entering the occupational arena and as being equal partners in future relationships. Unlike girls in patriarchal families, they are not socialized as fully into the "cult of domesticity" and are given more latitude to engage in risky activities. The result is that daughters' and sons' risk preferences become more alike, and thus their rate of involvement in delinquency converges.

Although power-control theory has not been without its critics and may be in need of some qualification, the perspective is amassing a fair amount of empirical support as a useful theory of delinquency (Hagan, 1989; Hagan, Gillis, & Simpson, 1990; Hagan & Kay, 1990; Hill & Atkinson, 1988; Jensen & Thompson, 1990; Singer & Levine, 1988). Further, the theory advances criminological thinking by illuminating the need to consider how gender-based power relations in society influence parental control and ultimately delinquent involvement. The theory's principal limitation, however, is that it remains largely silent on how other structural conditions affect the nature and effectiveness of parenting. In particular, the theory must address the intersection of class and gender and thus speak to issues such as parenting by single mothers within the context of impoverished, inner-city communities.

Conclusion

It is instructive to note that the control theories that focus on explaining juvenile delinquency tend to locate control influences primarily in the family and secondarily in the school, and that those that focus on adult crime tend to put greater emphasis on inner factors such as self-concept or self-control. Although juveniles might be influenced less by internal factors than by such social forces as peer pressures or parental control, internal factors might be more important in raising the odds of conformity on the part of an adult out of school and away from family supervision. In short, the adult is more on his or her own in the world, complete with a character structure that presumably is crystallized more fully.

Similarities and dissimilarities. There are certain similarities among these theories in addition to the fact that they all take the control perspective. Thus Reckless's stress on *goal orientation* sounds very much like the emphasis Hirschi placed on *commitment* in his earlier sociologically oriented social bonds theory. Both consider legitimate aspirations to be a crucial factor in insulating a potential deviant from nonconformity. Reckless's concept of *norm erosion* as the obverse of *norm retention* is closely related to Sykes and Matza's concept of *techniques of neutralization* in such a way that the latter can be subsumed easily as one aspect of the former (Ball, 1966). In much the same way, Reiss's distinction between conformity as a consequence of *acceptance* and conformity as a consequence of *submission* is quite similar to Nye's distinction between *internalized control* and *direct control.* Gottfredson and Hirschi's psychologically oriented self-control theory shows considerable similarity to Reckless's notion of *inner containment,* although with a much more systematic theory of how such control may fail to develop. Hagan's power-control theory reads in some ways like an update of Nye's perspective in terms of U.S. families in the late 1980s as compared with the more patriarchal families of the 1950s. All of these theories bear the Durkheimian stamp, but they vary somewhat in their stress on particular forces of integration and regulation and in their attachment to a social disorganization perspective in contrast to influences from sources such as the conflict theories to be discussed in Chapter 6.

Policy implications. Unlike some of the other theories examined in this book, control theory has tended to reinforce the sorts of prevention and intervention efforts that have been around for decades and that have become to many a matter of "common sense" (Empey, 1982, p. 268). It is worth noting, however, that the Durkheimian heritage has emphasized prevention through the strengthening of the institutions of socialization rather than through a policy of deterrence relying primarily on fear of getting caught. And it is important to stress that control theory has suggested that regulation of the individual must come through policies fostering integration into the social order rather than through policies of isolation and punishment.

The control theories we have examined have less to say about the prevention and control of professional crime, organized crime, and corporate and white-collar crime than about prevention and control of juvenile delinquency or ordinary street crime. With respect to prevention, they have provided considerable support for programs to strengthen families, particularly with respect to effective child rearing. Specific programs include Parents Anonymous, which has more than 150 chapters, and a variety of youth self-help groups (Bartollas, 1985). Many of these programs stress early training in parenting skills for high school students. Others emphasize efforts to overcome the family isolation that restricts the capacity of parents to develop good child-rearing strategies and that breeds child abuse and other forms of family violence by integrating families into a supportive network of kin and community resources.

To the extent that such programs focus on development of self-control, they stress the need for policies that assist the family in inculcating the favorable self-concepts, impulse control, and frustration tolerance that can keep a person out of trouble even in situations of weak external control. With respect to reintegration of delinquents and adult criminals, they make an effort to reestablish ties with conventional families and to strengthen these families through strategies ranging from counseling to financial assistance. Some even involve efforts to empower the women and children in high-risk families in such a way as to reduce the violence and destruction of self-esteem sometimes associated with the more patriarchal family forms.

School programs influenced by control theory have provided support for educational programs that facilitate involvement in school activities and greater identification with the school. Because teaching of conventional values is considered so important and because of considerable evidence suggesting that tracking systems that classify students according to different academic levels actually lead to a value system that rewards misbehavior rather than achievement, programs influenced by control theory (as well as labeling theory) have moved to abolish tracking in the schools (Bartollas, 1985). Control theory also has provided support for programs designed to integrate the schools more closely into the community, especially through developing closer ties to students' families, who seem to be the key to their academic success.

Control theory suggests prevention and reintegration policies moving adults into stable social networks of employment and community activities, but less has been done here than with programs for youth. It also suggests a search for policies capable of demonstrating the payoff of hard work toward conventional goals to draw both adolescents and adults into positions of personal commitment in which there is too much of a stake in conformity to lose by a return to delinquency or crime. Unfortunately, such programs have tended to become casualties of the shifting political climate of the 1980s and 1990s, where a "get tough" policy is more popular.

Control theories are most impressive to the extent that one accepts the larger social structure and conventional, middle-class values as things to be taken for granted. For control theory, the systems that are to accomplish the *regulation* of the individuals at risk for crime and delinquency through their *integration* are almost always systems defined in conventional, middle-class terms. Interestingly enough, this seems true even of approaches such as Hagan's power-control theory, in which the egalitarian family is really the new ideal of the middle class, although it is true that this approach faces up to the possibility that the freedom gained by daughters in such families may represent actually a weakening of control. The larger question is: What if all these systems themselves (i.e., families, schools, etc.), or at least some of them, are part of the problem rather than the solution? Integration into a "bad" system may be worse than no integration at all. As we will see in Chapters 5 and 6, some criminological theorists have argued that the major problems are located indeed in the conventional systems themselves and that these systems, rather than the particular criminals or delinquents, are the major sources of crime and delinquency. The labeling theorists insist that the conventional systems tend to aggravate crime and delinquency by overreacting to minor nonconformity, although the conflict theorists maintain that these systems are really covert instruments of oppression masquerading as helpful agencies of desirable socialization.

Even if one is convinced that conventional institutions such as the middle-class family and the school do not create major problems through a tendency to reject and stigmatize those who do not fit into them well and that they are not instruments of social oppression, it does not follow that successful integration and regulation functions will solve crime and delinquency problems. Speaking of impoverished Blacks, for example, Empey (1982) remarked that "it is not merely that underclass children are sometimes in conflict with their parents, or that their academic achievement is low, but that they are caught in an economic and political system in which they are superfluous" (p. 299). If the basic problem is located in the larger sociopolitical order, how can policies focused on strengthening families and schools do much to prevent and control crime and delinquency in the long run? Is the sociopolitical order to be accepted as it is, in which case policy must be directed toward inculcating values that support it? Or must more basic policies be developed—policies that challenge some of the assumptions on which the conventional order is based? The labeling theorists and conflict theorists to be examined in the next two chapters have directed our attention in just that direction.

5

THE IRONY OF STATE INTERVENTION

Labeling Theory

When people violate the law, we assume that the state's most prudent response is to make every effort to apprehend the culprits and to process them through the criminal justice system. Informing this assumption is the belief that state intervention reduces crime, whether by scaring offenders straight, by rehabilitating them, or by incapacitating them so they are no longer free to roam the streets victimizing citizens. Scholars embracing the labeling theory of crime, however, attack vigorously this line of reasoning. Rather than diminishing criminal involvement, they caution, state intervention—labeling and reacting to offenders as "criminals" and "ex-felons"—can have the unanticipated and ironic consequence of deepening the very behavior it was meant to halt.

Thus labeling theorists argue that the criminal justice system not only is limited in its capacity to restrain unlawful conduct, but also is a major factor in anchoring people in a criminal career. Pulling people into the system makes matters worse—not better. This contention takes on importance when we consider the width of the net cast by criminal justice officials. On any given day, more than one American in every hundred is under some form of state control. The statistical count breaks down in this way: over 1 million people in state and federal prisons, 400,000 in local jails, and 2 million offenders on either probation or parole supervision (Irwin & Austin, 1994).

In this chapter, we examine why labeling theorists believe that state intervention is dangerously criminogenic, particularly in light of the faith current policy makers have in the power of prisons to solve the crime problem. We also consider why, in the 1960s and early 1970s, labeling theory—or as it is known also, the "societal reaction" approach—grew rapidly in popularity and influenced markedly criminal justice policy. First, however, we will discuss how scholars in this school of thought rooted their work in a revisionist view of what crime is and of how its very nature is tied inextricably to the nature of societal reaction.

The Social Construction of Crime

Before the advent of labeling theory, most criminologists were content to define crime as "behavior that violates criminal laws." This definition was useful in guiding inquiry and in setting rough boundaries for criminology as a field of study. Too often, however, the easy acceptance of this definition led criminologists to take for granted that they knew what crime was and could get on with the business of finding its causes either in offenders or in their environments. This reification of conceptual definitions blinded many scholars from seeing that as a socially constructed phenomenon, what is, or is not, "criminal" changes over time, across societies, and even from one situation to the next. Without this insight, scholars failed to explore the social circumstances that determine which behaviors are made criminal, why some people have the label of criminal applied to them, and what consequences exist for those bearing a criminal label.

Labeling theorists sought to correct this oversight. As a starting point, they urged criminologists to surrender the idea that behaviors are somehow inherently criminal or deviant. To be sure, behaviors such as killing or raping another human being are injurious by nature. Even so, what makes an act criminal is not the harm it incurs, but whether this label is conferred on the act by the state. Thus it is the nature of the societal reaction and the reality it constructs, not the immutable nature of the act per se, that determines if a crime exists (Becker, 1963; Erikson, 1966). Stephen Pfohl's (1985) discussion of whether killing is "naturally deviant" illustrates nicely the essence of this position:

> Homicide is a way of categorizing the act of killing, such that taking another's life is viewed as totally reprehensible and devoid of any redeeming social

justification. Some types of killing are categorized as homicide. Others are not. What differs is not the behavior but the manner in which reactions to that behavior are socially organized. The behavior is essentially the same: killing a police officer or killing by a police officer; stabbing an old lady in the back or stabbing the unsuspecting wartime enemy; a black slave shooting a white master or a white master lynching a black slave; being run over by a drunken driver or slowly dying a painful cancer death caused by a polluting factory. Each is a type of killing. Some are labeled homicide. Others are excused, justified, or viewed, as in the case of dangerous industrial pollution, as environmental risks, necessary for the health of our economy, if not our bodies. The form and content of what is seen as homicide thus varies with social context and circumstance. This is hardly the characteristic of something which can be considered naturally or universally deviant. (p. 284)

Armed with this vision of crime as socially constructed, labeling theorists argued that criminologists could ill afford to neglect the nature and effects of societal reaction, particularly when the state was the labeling agent. One important area they investigated was the origins of criminal labels or categories. Howard Becker (1963), for example, explored how the commissioner of the Treasury Department's Federal Bureau of Narcotics served as a "moral entrepreneur" who led a campaign to outlaw marijuana through the Marijuana Tax Act of 1937. In Becker's view, this campaign, marked by attempts to arouse the public by claims that smoking pot caused youths to lose control and commit senseless crimes, was undertaken to advance the bureau's organizational interests. The bureau's success in securing passage of the act, Becker concluded, resulted in "the creation of a new fragment of the moral constitution of society, its code of right and wrong" (p. 145; see also Galliher & Walker, 1977).

Numerous other scholars provided explanations of attempts to criminalize other forms of behavior. Thus Anthony Platt (1969) studied how, at the turn of the century, affluent women "invented delinquency" through their successful campaign to create a court exclusively for juveniles. With the establishment of this court, juveniles were treated as a separate class of offenders, and the state was granted the power to intervene not only when youths committed criminal acts but also when they showed signs of a profligate lifestyle—acts such as truancy or promiscuity, which became known as "status offenses." This movement, Platt observed, was class biased because it was directed primarily at "saving" lower-class youths, reaffirmed middle-class values, and left unaddressed the structural roots of poverty.

In a like vein, Stephen Pfohl (1977) investigated the "discovery of child abuse," which prior to the 1960s largely had escaped criminal sanctioning.

Pfohl showed how pediatric radiologists, who read X rays in hospitals, were instrumental in bringing attention to the abuse of children. Their efforts, he claimed, were fueled by the incentive to demonstrate the importance of pediatric radiology and thereby to enhance the low prestige of this specialty in the medical community.

Kathleen Tierney (1982) focused on the "creation of the wife beating problem." She revealed how wife battering did not emerge as a salient social issue deserving of criminal justice intervention until the mid-1970s, when feminist organizations and networks were developed sufficiently to make domestic violence socially visible, to establish victim shelters, and to earn the passage of new laws. Also critical to the battered women's movement was the media, which dramatized wife beating because "it mixed elements of violence and social relevance . . . [and] provided a focal point for serious media discussion of such issues as feminism, inequality, and family life in the United States—without requiring a sacrifice of the entertainment value, action, and urgency on which the media typically depend" (pp. 213-214).

These and similar analyses showed, therefore, that what the state designated as criminal was not a constant, but the result of concrete efforts by men and women to construct a different reality, to transform how a particular type of behavior was defined officially. Moreover, it was not simply the extent or harmfulness of the behavior that determined its criminalization; after all, drug use, juvenile waywardness, child abuse, and wife battering long had escaped state criminal intervention despite their pervasiveness and injurious effects. These behaviors were criminalized only when the social context was ripe for change and groups existed that were sufficiently motivated and powerful to bring about legal reform.

But what occurs once a form of behavior is defined as unlawful and a criminal label is created? To whom will this label be applied? The common answer to this question is that those who engage in the proscribed activity will be labeled as criminals. Labeling theorists, however, were again quick to point out that such thinking implicitly assumes that societal reaction can be taken for granted and treated as nonproblematic. It ignores not only that the innocent occasionally are accused falsely, but also that only some rule breakers actually are arrested and processed through the criminal justice system (see Becker, 1963). A lawbreaker's behavior, therefore, is only one factor—and perhaps not the most important factor at that—in determining whether a criminal label is conferred.

A number of labeling theory studies illustrate this principle. In one experimental study conducted in Los Angeles, a racially mixed college student sample, all of whom had perfect driving records in the past year, had Black Panther bumper stickers affixed to their car bumpers. Within hours of the experiment's start, they began to accumulate numerous tickets for traffic violations (e.g., for improper lane change), thus suggesting that police officers were "labeling" differentially on the basis of the bumper stickers (Heusenstamm, 1975). Other researchers, interested in police encounters with juveniles, observed that officers' decisions to arrest wayward youths were based less on what law was violated and more on the juveniles' demeanor—whether they were respectful and cooperative or surly and uncooperative (Piliavin & Briar, 1964).

Still another researcher, William Chambliss (1984), examined one community's societal reaction to two groups of high school boys: a middle-class group he called the "Saints" and a working-class group known as the "Roughnecks." Although the two groups had a rate of delinquency that was "about equal," the "community, the school and the police react[ed] to the Saints as though they were good, upstanding, nondelinquent youths with bright futures but to the Roughnecks as though they were tough, young criminals who were headed for trouble" (pp. 126, 131). Why did this occur? In Chambliss's view, a major reason was the community's lower-class bias, which led police to define as pranks the Saints' behavior and to anticipate that the poorly dressed and poorly mannered Roughnecks were up to no good.

Through these and similar studies, labeling theorists revealed that the nature of state criminal intervention was not simply a matter of an objective response to illegal behavior but shaped intimately by a range of extralegal contingencies (Cullen & Cullen, 1978). Much attention was focused on how criminal justice decision making was influenced by individual characteristics, such as race, class, and gender. In addition, however, researchers explored how rates of labeling vary according to the resources available to and political demands placed on police and other criminal justice organizations. This body of research also highlighted how official measures of the extent of crime—such as arrest statistics reported each year by the FBI—depend not only on how many offenses are committed but also on the arrest practices of police. Accordingly, official crime statistics may be inaccurate to the extent that they reflect a systematic bias in enforcement against certain groups (e.g., the urban poor) or fluctuations in the willingness of police to enforce certain laws (e.g., rape laws).

In sum, labeling theorists elucidated the importance of considering the origins of criminal labels and the circumstances that affected their application. But they did not confine their attention to these concerns. They proceeded to put forward the more controversial proposition that labeling and reacting to people as criminals composed the major source of chronic involvement in illegal activity. State intervention, they claimed, created, rather than halted, crime. We consider this line of reasoning next.

Labeling as Criminogenic:
Creating Career Criminals

Where should the search for the cause of crime begin? As we have seen, scholars have argued traditionally that the starting point for criminological inquiry should be either individual offenders themselves or the social environments in which they reside. Labeling theorists, however, argued that causal analysis should not commence with offenders and their environs but with the societal reaction that *other* people—including state officials— have toward offenders. Again, their contention was based on the belief that labeling and treating lawbreakers as criminals have the unanticipated consequence of creating the very behavior they were meant to prevent.

Early Statements of Labeling Theory

The idea that criminal justice intervention can deepen criminality did not originate with the labeling theorists of the 1960s. A number of early criminologists, for example, noted that prisons—a severe form of societal reaction—were breeding grounds for crime. Jeremy Bentham, the classical school theorist, lamented that "an ordinary prison is a school in which wickedness is taught by surer means than can ever be employed for the inculcation of virtue. Weariness, revenge, and want preside over these academies of crime" (quoted in Hawkins, 1976, p. 57). In 1911 Lombroso echoed this theme in his observation that "the degrading influences of prison life and contact with vulgar criminals . . . cause criminaloids who have committed their initial offenses with repugnance and hesitation, to develop later into habitual criminals" (Lombroso-Ferrero, 1972, pp. 110-111). Willem Bonger (1916/1969), the Dutch Marxist scholar, noted similarly that in imprisoning "young people who have committed merely misdemeanors of minor importance . . . we are bringing up professional criminals" (p. 118). And Clifford Shaw (1930) felt compelled to title the chapter in the *Jack-Roller* on correctional institutions "The House of Corruption."

Although observations such as these anticipated the more developed views of later labeling theorists, Frank Tannenbaum (1938) was perhaps the earliest scholar to state in general terms the principle that state intervention is criminogenic because it "dramatizes evil." "Only some of the children [who break the law] are caught," he noted, "though all may be equally guilty." And this event is not without consequence. The youth is "singled out for specialized treatment" as the "arrest suddenly precipitates a series of institutions, attitudes, and experiences which other children do not share." Now the youth's world is changed fundamentally; people react differently, and the youth starts to reconsider his or her identity. "He is made conscious of himself as a different human being than he was before his arrest," observed Tannenbaum. "He becomes classified as a thief, perhaps, and the entire world about him has suddenly become a different place for him and will remain different for the rest of his life" (p. 19). This is true particularly if the youth is placed in prison, for here incipient, "uncrystallized" criminal attitudes are "hardened" through the "education" older offenders provide (pp. 66-81).

In the end, Tannenbaum (1938) cautioned, we would do well to weigh carefully taking the initial step of pulling a juvenile into the criminal justice system:

> The first dramatization of "evil" which separates the child out of his group for specialized treatment plays a greater role in making the criminal than perhaps any other experience. . . . He has been tagged. A new and hitherto nonexistent environment has been precipitated out of him. The process of making the criminal, therefore, is a process of tagging, defining, identifying, segregating, describing, emphasizing, making conscious and self-conscious; it becomes a way of stimulating, suggesting, emphasizing, and evoking the very traits that are complained of. . . . The person becomes the thing he is described as being. (pp. 19-20)

In 1951 Edwin Lemert formalized further these insights when he distinguished two types of deviance: primary and secondary. *Primary deviance*, he contended, arises from a variety of sociocultural and psychological sources. At this initial point, however, offenders often try to rationalize their behavior as a temporary aberration or see it as part of a socially acceptable role. They do not conceive of themselves as deviant or organize their life around this identity (p. 75).

In contrast, *secondary deviance* is precipitated by the responses of others to the initial proscribed conduct. As societal reaction intensifies progressively with each act of primary deviance, the offender becomes stigmatized through "name calling, labeling, or stereotyping" (Lemert, 1951, pp. 76-77). The original sources of waywardness lose their salience as others' reactions emerge as the overriding concern in the person's life and demand to be addressed. Most often, offenders solve this problem by accepting their "deviant status" and by organizing their "life and identity . . . around the facts of deviance." Accordingly, they become more, rather than less, embedded in nonconformity. As Lemert (1972) explained:

> Primary deviance is assumed to arise in a wide variety of social, cultural, and psychological contexts, and at best has only marginal implications for the psychic structure of the individual; it does not lead to symbolic reorganization at the level of self-regarding attitudes and social roles. Secondary deviation is deviant behavior, or social roles based upon it, which becomes means of defense, attack, or adaptation to overt and covert problems created by the societal reaction to primary deviation. In effect, the original "causes" of the deviation recede and give way to the central importance of the disapproving, degradational, and isolating reactions of society. (p. 48)

Labeling as a Self-Fulfilling Prophecy

Although Tannenbaum and Lemert stated fairly explicitly the theme that societal reaction can induce waywardness, this view of labeling did not win wide intellectual attention and become an identifiable school of thought in the criminological community until the mid- to late 1960s (Cole, 1975). As will be discussed later, the sudden, pervasive appeal of labeling theory can be traced largely to the social context in the 1960s that made it seem plausible that state intervention was the crime problem's cause and not its solution. Another circumstance, however, was important also in contributing to labeling theory's ascendancy: the existence of a group of scholars—Howard Becker (1963), Kai Erikson (1966), and John Kitsuse (1964) were perhaps the most influential among them—whose combined writings argued convincingly that societal reaction is integral to the creation of crime and deviance.

To show how societal reaction brings about more crime, these labeling theorists borrowed Robert K. Merton's (1968) concept of the "self-fulfilling prophecy." For Merton, "the self-fulfilling prophecy is, in the beginning, a *false* definition of the situation evoking a new behavior which makes the originally false conception come *true*" (p. 477; emphasis in original).

Consistent with this reasoning, labeling scholars argued that most offenders are defined falsely as criminal. In making this claim, they did not
mean to imply that offenders do not violate the law or that justice system
officials have no basis for intervening in people's lives. Instead, the false-
ness in definition is tied to the fact that criminal labels, once conferred,
do not simply provide a social judgment of offenders' behavior but also
publicly degrade their moral character (Garfinkel, 1956). That is, being
arrested and processed through the justice system means that citizens not
only define the offenders' lawbreaking *conduct* as bad but also assume that
the offenders as *people* are criminal and, as a consequence, are the "type"
that soon again would be in trouble. Yet as Lemert's (1951) work suggested, such predictions about personal character and future behavior are
likely to be incorrect. Much primary deviance—including initial experiments in crime and delinquency—is not rooted fundamentally in character or in lifestyle and thus is likely to be transitory, not stable (see Scheff,
1966).

In short, theorists observed that the meaning of the label "criminal" in
our society leads citizens to make assumptions about offenders that are
wrong or only partially accurate. These assumptions, moreover, are con-
sequential because they shape how people react to offenders. Equipped
with false definitions or stereotypes of criminals, citizens treat all offenders
as though they were of poor character and likely to recidivate. On one
level, these reactions are prudent, if not rational; after all, it seems safer
not to chance having one's child associate with the neighborhood's "juvenile delinquent" and not to employ a "convicted thief" to handle one's
cash register. Yet on another level, these reactions have the power to set in
motion processes that evoke the very behavior that was anticipated, that
transform an offender into the very type of criminal that was feared.

But how is the prophecy fulfilled? How are incipient criminals, who
might well have gone straight if left to their own devices, turned into
chronic offenders? Again, the conferring of a criminal label singles a
person out for special treatment. The offender becomes, in Becker's
(1963) words, "one who is different from the rest of us, who cannot or will
not act as a moral human being and therefore might break other important rules" (p. 34). As a result, being a "criminal" becomes the person's
"master status" or controlling public identification (pp. 33-34; see also
Hughes, 1945). In social encounters, citizens do not consider the offender's social status as a spouse, as a parent, or perhaps as a worker, but

instead focus first and foremost on the fact they are interacting with a criminal.

Admittedly, this public scrutiny might scare or shame some offenders into conformity. But for other offenders, the constant accentuation of their criminal status and the accompanying social rebuke has the unanticipated consequence of undermining the conforming influences in their lives and of pushing them into criminal careers. Thus, in the face of repeated designation as criminals, offenders are likely to forfeit their self-concept as conformists or "normal" persons and internalize increasingly their public definition as deviants. As this identity change takes place, the offender's self-concept loses its power to encourage conformity: The pressure to act consistently with one's self-concept now demands breaking the law.

Similarly, people who are stigmatized as criminal often are cut off from previous prosocial relationships. As one's reputation as a reprobate spreads, phone calls are not returned, invitations to social engagements are not extended, friends suddenly no longer can find time to meet, and intimate relationships terminate. One solution to being a social pariah is to bind together with those of a like status. Accordingly, conditions are conducive for offenders wearing a criminal label to differentially associate with other lawbreakers, thus forming criminal subcultural groupings. Such associations are likely to reinforce further antisocial values and to provide a ready supply of partners in crime.

The abrogation of ties to conventional society, labeling theorists warned, is most probable when state intervention involves institutionalization. Imprisonment entails the loss of existing employment and strains family relations to the point that they may not survive. It also mandates that offenders reside in a social setting where contact with other, more hardened criminals is enforced. Education in crime, as Tannenbaum (1938) and other early criminologists noted, is the likely result.

Finally, saddling offenders with an official criminal label—particularly when they have spent time in jail and carry the status of ex-convict—limits their employment opportunities. Through their sentences, offenders may "pay back" society for their illegal behavior, but they find it far more difficult to shake their definition as persons of bad character who may fall by the wayside at any time. Employers, therefore, see them as poor risks and hesitate to hire them or to place them in positions of trust. Most often, offenders are relegated to low-paying, dreary jobs with few prospects for advancement. In this context, crime emerges as a more profitable option and a lure that only the irrational choose to resist.

In sum, labeling theorists asserted that the false definition of offenders as permanently criminal and destined for a life of crime fulfills this very prophecy by evoking societal reactions that make conformity difficult and criminality necessary, if not attractive. The labeling process thus is a powerful criminogenic force that stabilizes participation in illegal roles and turns those marginally involved in crime into chronic or career offenders. It is an especially dangerous source of crime, moreover, because its effects are unanticipated and rarely observed. Indeed, the common response to escalating crime rates is not to minimize societal reaction but to arrest and imprison more people. From a labeling perspective, such "get tough" policies will prove ultimately self-defeating, for they will succeed only in subjecting increasing numbers of offenders to a self-fulfilling process that makes probable a life in crime.

Assessing Labeling Theory

Few criminologists would dispute that labeling theory succeeded in bringing attention to the issue of societal reaction or that this distinctive focus won the perspective many adherents. Even so, labeling theory's central propositions have not escaped considerable critical analysis (Gove, 1975, 1980). As we will see, this assessment suggests the need to temper some of the perspective's boldest claims but also indicates that it would be unwise to discount the insights set forth in the labeling tradition.

One line of criticism came from conflict or radical criminologists. Although they agreed that crime was socially constructed and labels differentially applied, they did not believe that labeling theorists went far enough in their analysis. Radical scholars argued that the origins and application of criminal labels were influenced fundamentally by inequities rooted in the very structure of capitalism. As the next chapter shows in greater detail, the radicals insisted that differences in power determined that the behaviors of the poor, but not those of the rich, would be criminalized. Labeling theorists understood that political interest and social disadvantage influenced societal reaction but, again, they did not make explicit the connection of the criminal justice system to the underlying economic order. As Taylor, Walton, and Young (1973) observed, they failed "to lay bare the structured inequalities in power and interest which underpin processes whereby laws are created and enforced," and thus they stopped short of exploring "the way in which deviancy and criminality are shaped by society's larger structure of power and institutions" (pp. 168-169).

A very different critique was leveled by criminologists of a traditional positivist bent, who maintained that labeling theory's major tenets wilted when subjected to empirical test. These critics contended—correctly, we believe—that the perspective's popularity had little to do with its empirical adequacy, but rather with its voicing a provocative message that meshed with the social times (Hagan, 1973; Hirschi, 1975). After all, in asserting that state intervention deepened criminality, none of the early labeling theorists had presented hard data supporting this thesis.

These positivist or empirically oriented criminologists brought data to bear on what were considered labeling theory's two principal propositions. First, they assessed the premise that extra-legal factors, such as an offender's race, class, and gender, are more important in regulating criminal justice labeling than legal factors, such as the seriousness of the illegality or the offender's past record. Contrary to the expectations of the labeling theorists, research studies found repeatedly that the seriousness of the crime, not the offender's social background, was the largest determinant of labeling by police and court officials (Sampson, 1986). Extra-legal variables, the critics concluded, exert only a weak effect on labeling (Gove, 1980; Hirschi, 1975; Tittle, 1975b).

Recent research by Robert Sampson (1986), however, forces a reconsideration of the critics' sweeping rejection of the idea that official reactions are influenced by a variety of contingencies. In perhaps the most systematic test to date, Sampson uncovered an "ecological bias" in police control of juveniles. Even when he took into account the seriousness of lawbreaking behavior, police were found to be more likely to make arrests in poor as opposed to more affluent neighborhoods. One possible explanation for this ecological pattern is that police resources are concentrated more heavily in lower-class areas, where it is assumed that anyone encountered is likely to have a character sufficiently disreputable to warrant close surveillance. In any case, Sampson has provided convincing evidence of an extralegal circumstance that causes differential selection into the criminal justice system.

Labeling theory's second major proposition is that state intervention through the justice system causes stable or career criminality. Phrased in these terms, however, the proposition is difficult to sustain. As critics point out, many offenders become deeply involved in crime *before* coming to the attention of criminal justice officials (Mankoff, 1971). Chronic delinquency, for example, seems far more tied to the criminogenic effects of spending years growing up in a slum neighborhood than to being arrested and hauled into juvenile court as a teenager. Similarly, we know that offenders become involved extensively in such illegalities as corporate crime, political corruption, wife battering, and sexual abuse without ever being subjected to criminal sanctioning.

Tests of labeling's causal effects have yielded mixed results (Bazemore, 1985; Klein, 1986; Morash, 1982; Palamara, Cullen, & Gersten, 1986; Shannon, 1982; Thomas & Bishop, 1984; Ward & Tittle, 1993). One interpretation of this finding is that criminal justice labeling has "no effects" (Hirschi, 1975, p. 198). If this view is accurate, it means that state intervention neither deepens criminality as the labeling theorists have claimed nor deters criminality as advocates of punishment have asserted (Thomas & Bishop, 1984). Alternatively, it suggests, as traditional criminologists have argued, that the sources of why people experiment with crime, become chronic offenders, or recidivate after incarceration are to be found not in the operation of the criminal justice system but in the social forces that impinge on offenders in their everyday lives.

Indeed, the complexity of labeling can be seen in recent experimental studies assessing how police officers' mandatory arrest of batterers influences subsequent episodes of domestic violence (Sherman, 1992). Although the finding and its interpretation still must be viewed tentatively, the research suggests that the impact of arrest—or labeling—varies according to whether batterers are employed. Perhaps because their economic well-being and "stake in conformity" are threatened, those who are working are less likely to recidivate after arrest. In contrast, arrest appears to escalate incidents of abuse among batterers who are unemployed and thus who have weak bonds to conventional society (Sherman, 1992).

Another interpretation is possible of the studies' mixed results. It well may be that labeling's overall effect remains unclear because researchers have yet to disentangle the conditions under which contact with the criminal justice system increases or diminishes commitment to crime (Palamara et al., 1986; Tittle, 1975a). At present, research has addressed in only a rudimentary way how vulnerability to criminal labels might vary by factors such as individual sociodemographic characteristics, stage in a criminal career, family strength, and neighborhood context. Until these empirical issues are settled, general statements about labeling effects remain premature.

In sum, critics have provided a necessary corrective to bold claims that extralegal variables dominate the discretionary decision making of criminal justice officials and that societal reaction is the major source of career criminality. Even so, it would be misguided to make the opposite error of assuming that labeling theory "points to processes that exist but their overall impact is small" (Gove, 1980, p. 268) and "appears off the mark on almost every aspect of delinquency it is asked to predict or explain" (Hirschi, 1975, p. 198). As research by Sampson (1986) and others (Link, Cullen, Frank, & Wozniak, 1987) cautions, societal reaction is a complex process and its effects have yet to be understood fully or established empirically (see also Paternoster & Iovanni, 1989; Sampson & Laub, 1993).

Extending Labeling Theory: Shame and Reintegration

In *Crime, Shame and Reintegration,* John Braithwaite (1989) took up the issue of the conditions under which societal reaction increases crime, as labeling theorists contend, or decreases crime, as advocates of punishment predict. Legal violations evoke formal attempts by the state and informal efforts by intimates and community members to control the misconduct. Central to social control is what Braithwaite called *shaming,* which he defined as "all processes of expressing disapproval which have the intention or effect of invoking remorse in the person being shamed and/or condemnation by others who become aware of the shaming" (p. 9).

Shaming, however, comes in two varieties—*reintegrative* and *disintegrative*—and each has a different impact on recidivism. Consistent with labeling theory, Braithwaite (1989) argued that disintegrative shaming stigmatizes and excludes, thus creating a "class of outcasts" (p. 55). The offender not only is castigated for his or her wrongdoing but also is branded as a criminal who is beyond forgiveness and unworthy of restoration to membership in the community. As labeling theory warns, the result is further entrenchment in crime: The offender is denied employment and other legitimate opportunities to bond with conventional society and consequently joins with other outcasts in creating and participating in criminal subcultures.

But shaming also can be reintegrative. In these instances, an illegal act initially evokes community disapproval but then is followed by attempts "to reintegrate the offender back into the community of law-abiding or respectable citizens through words or gestures of forgiveness or ceremonies to decertify the offender as deviant" (Braithwaite, 1989, pp. 100-101). There is a stick followed by a carrot, condemnation followed by community responses aimed at binding the offender to the social order. In this case, shaming has two faces: It makes certain that the inappropriateness of the misconduct is known to the offender and to all observers, and it presents an opportunity to restore the offender to membership in the group. This combination, argued Braithwaite, reduces crime by exerting greater control over offenders and by not setting in motion the criminogenic processes caused by stigmatization and social exclusion.

Braithwaite (1989) extended labeling theory not only by delineating types of shaming or societal reaction but also by observing that the underlying social context determines the degree to which shaming will be reintegrative or disintegrative. In communitarian societies such as Japan, "individuals are densely enmeshed in interdependencies which have the special qualities of mutual help and trust" (p. 100). As might be expected, in this context shaming is reintegrative and produces low crimes rates.

In the United States, however, communitarianism is weakened by urbanization, racial and ethnic heterogeneity, extensive residential mobility, and a strong ideology of individualism. As a consequence, America lacks the cultural and institutional basis that would encourage seeing offenders as part of an interdependent community. Social control thus has a strong disintegrative quality: Lawbreakers are marked indelibly as ex-offenders and provided few avenues to reestablish full societal membership. This stigmatization creates a class of outcasts who individually turn to crime and who collectively develop criminal subcultures and illegal opportunity structures. The result, claimed Braithwaite, is that America is burdened with a high rate of lawlessness.

In summary, Braithwaite enriched labeling theory by illuminating that shaming (or labeling) varies in its nature and effects and why this variation ultimately is contingent on the society in which shaming takes place. The empirical adequacy of Braithwaite's contentions remains to be demonstrated, but his theory of reintegrative shaming promises to earn much attention in the time ahead.

Labeling Theory in Context

A central theme informing this book has been that changes in society expose people to new experiences, which in turn prompt them to think differently about many issues, including crime. The 1960s was just such a period when social change gripped the United States and caused citizens and criminologists alike to take stock of their previous assumptions about criminal behavior (Sykes, 1974). We have seen in Chapter 4, for example, that the tumultuous context of the 1960s sensitized some scholars to the importance of controls in constraining human conduct; in Chapter 6 we will see how the decade's events radicalized other scholars and led them to assert that crime and criminal justice were shaped intimately by the conflict and inequities inherent in capitalism. More relevant to our present concerns, we can recall that the 1960s also proved fertile ground for the growth of labeling theory (Cole, 1975).

Why did many criminologists suddenly embrace the notion that state intervention through the criminal justice system was the principal cause of the crime problem? In the absence of strong empirical evidence, why did labeling propositions—voiced earlier by Tannenbaum (1938) and Lemert (1951)—suddenly strike a chord and seem sensible to so many scholars?

The key to answering these questions, we believe, lies in understanding how the prevailing context led many people to lose trust or confidence in the government. In the early 1960s, optimism ran high. As noted in Chapter 3, the Kennedy administration instilled the expectation that a "New Frontier of equal opportunity" was within reach; a "Great Society" was possible that would eliminate poverty and its associated ills, such as crime. Moreover, this agenda reaffirmed the Progressives' belief that the government should play a central role through social programs in effecting this change. The state could be trusted to do good.

But as the 1960s unfolded, this optimism declined, eventually turning to despair as the bold promises made at the decade's start went unfulfilled (Bayer, 1981; Empey, 1979). Thus the civil rights movement laid bare not only the existence of pernicious patterns of racism, sexism, and class inequality, but also revealed the inability, if not the unwillingness, of government officials to address these long-standing injustices. Vietnam raised other concerns. Although the use of U.S. troops was justified as necessary to protect democracy, this policy lost its moral value as many citizens perceived the United States as merely propping up a corrupt regime. More disquieting, however, was the government's response to political protest. The United States witnessed not only demonstrators being chased and beaten by police but also students being gunned down at Kent State. The Attica riot, in which troopers storming the prison fatally wounded 32 inmates and 10 guards being held hostage, confirmed the state's proclivity to abuse its power in the suppression of insurgency. The state's moral bankruptcy seemed complete with the disclosure of the Watergate scandal, which showed that corruption not simply penetrated to but rather pervaded the government's highest echelons (Cullen & Gilbert, 1982, pp. 104-107).

In short, the state faced what commentators have called a "legitimacy crisis" (Friedrichs, 1979) or a "confidence gap" (Lipset & Schneider, 1983): Citizens no longer trusted the motives or competence of government officials. Such feelings spread and intensified as the 1960s advanced and turned into the 1970s, and they created a context ripe for harvesting the ideas of labeling theorists who blamed the state for the crime problem. Due to their social experiences, it now made sense to many criminologists, policy makers, and members of the public that government officials would label the disadvantaged more than the advantaged and would operate prisons—such as Attica—that drove offenders deeper into crime. Accordingly, labeling theory won wide support and offered a stiff challenge to traditional theories of crime. The stage was set, moreover, for a reexamination of existing crime control policies.

The Consequences of Theory: Policy Implications

Labeling theory, LaMar Empey (1982) observed, "had a profound impact on social policy" (p. 409). As the ranks of the perspective's proponents swelled, an increasingly loud warning was sounded that pulling offenders into the criminal justice system only contributed to the crime problem. The prescription for policy change was eminently logical and straightforward: If state intervention causes crime, then take steps to limit it (Schur, 1973).

But how might this be accomplished? As Empey (1982) noted, labeling theorists embraced four policies—each coincidentally beginning with the letter *D*—which promised to reduce the intrusion of the state into offenders' lives: decriminalization, diversion, due process, and deinstitutionalization. These four reforms were implemented to different degrees and with uneven consequences. Even so, the agenda identified by labeling theory remains to this day an important vision of the direction criminal justice policy should take.

Decriminalization

Labeling theorists insisted that the "overreach of the criminal law" constituted a critical public policy problem (Morris & Hawkins, 1970, p. 2; Schur, 1965; Schur & Bedeau, 1974). Thus the criminal justice system has been used traditionally to control not only threats to life and property, but also a range of "victimless crimes" (e.g., public drunkenness, drug use, gambling, and pornography) as well as juvenile status offenses (e.g., truancy and promiscuity). The morality of these behaviors might be open to debate, theorists admitted, but using the criminal law as a means of control is an "unwarranted extension [that] is expensive, ineffective, and criminogenic" (Morris & Hawkins, 1970, p. 2).

Edwin Schur (1965; Schur & Bedeau, 1974), for example, argued that the criminalization of victimless deviance—such as drug use—creates crime in various ways. First, the mere existence of the laws turns those who participate in the behavior into candidates for arrest and criminal justice processing. Second, it often drives them to commit related offenses, such as when drug addicts rob to support their habits. Third, by prohibiting the legal acquisition of desired goods and services, criminalization creates a lucrative illicit market, whose operation fuels the coffers of organized crime. And fourth, the existence of such illicit exchanges fosters strong incentives for the corruption of law enforcement officials, who are enticed through payoffs to "look the other way."

Accordingly, labeling theorists argued for the prudent use of decriminalization: the removal of many forms of conduct from the scope of the criminal law. This policy might involve outright legalization or treating the act much like a traffic violation (such as speeding) for which penalties are limited to minor fines. In any case, the goal was to limit the law's reach and thus to reduce the extent to which people were labeled and treated as criminals.

The policy of decriminalization evoked much debate and encouraged some significant legal changes. Thus abortion was legalized by U.S. Supreme Court decision; possession of small amounts of marijuana frequently was reduced to a minor violation; the criminal status of pornographic material was left to communities to decide; forms of gambling—such as state-run lotteries and casinos—were legalized; status offenses were made the concern of social welfare agencies. These changes, however, did not occur across all states, and other forms of behavior remained illegal. Especially noteworthy, the most controversial of the labeling theorists' policy proposals—the call to decriminalize all forms of drug use—fell on deaf ears.

Indeed, as we have seen in recent years, an enormous campaign has been launched to stop the flow of drugs and to place those participating in this illicit market behind bars (Currie, 1993; Inciardi, 1986).

Diversion

Given that laws exist and offenders come to the attention of law enforcement officials, how should the criminal justice system respond? Labeling theorists had a ready answer: diversion. For juveniles, as Empey (1982) indicated, this policy might entail taking youths from the province of the juvenile court and placing them under the auspices of "youth service bureaus, welfare agencies, or special schools" (p. 410). For adults, it might involve release to a privately run mental health agency, community substance abuse program, or government-sponsored job training class. Diversion might involve also the substitution of a less severe intervention, such as when offenders are "diverted" from prison and are placed instead in the community under "intensive probation supervision" or under "home incarceration" (Ball, Huff, & Lilly, 1988; Binder & Geis, 1984; Latessa, 1987).

Diversion programs became widespread in the past two decades, a development that can be traced at least in part to the persuasive writings of labeling theorists (Klein, 1979). The current inmate crowding problem, moreover, is furnishing fresh incentives for jurisdictions to establish diversion programs that will help empty their prisons and jails. Diversion's popularity, however, has given labeling theorists little cause for celebration.

Originally conceived as an alternative to involvement in the criminal justice system or to incarceration, diversion programs have functioned most often as an add-on to the system. That is, participants in programs have not been those who would have stayed in the system or gone to jail, but rather those who previously would have been released, fined, or perhaps given a suspended sentence. Ironically, the very policy suggested by labeling theorists to lessen state intervention has had the effect of increasing that intervention: Diversion has "widened the net" of state control by creating a "system with an even greater reach" (Klein, 1979, p. 184; see also Binder & Geis, 1984; Frazier & Cochran, 1986).

Due Process

Labeling theorists were quick also to join the mounting due process movement, which sought to extend to offenders legal protections (e.g., right to an attorney, right not to be searched illegally). As Empey (1982) pointed out, although labeling theory did not prompt the concern for offender rights, the perspective and the concern for due process had a common source: "Both were part of the growing distrust of governmental and other institutions in the 1960s" (p. 410).

Labeling scholars' call for expanding due process was tied up with their critique of the "rehabilitative ideal." As noted in Chapters 2 and 3, reforms in the Progressive era had provided criminal justice officials with enormous discretion to effect the individualized treatment of offenders. Such discretionary powers were unbridled in the juvenile court, in which the state was trusted to "save children" by acting as a "kindly parent" (Platt, 1969; Rothman, 1978, 1980). Labeling theorists, however, accused state officials of abusing this trust. Individualized treatment, they claimed, was merely a euphemism for judicial decisions that discriminated against the powerless and for parole board decisions that denied release to inmates who dared to resist the coercive control of correctional officials.

The solution to this situation was clear. "Individualized justice," Edwin Schur (1973) urged, "must give way to a *return to the rule of law*" (p. 169; emphasis in original). The worst abuses must be curbed by an extension of constitutional protections, particularly to juveniles who had been left blindly in the hands of the state. Labeling theorists, moreover, embraced what amounted to the principles of the classical school: Punishments should be prescribed by law, and sentences should be determinate. Accordingly, discretionary abuse would be eliminated: Judges would be forced to sentence according to written codes, not to whim, and determinate sentences with set release dates would replace parole decision making.

Labeling theorists hoped that these policies would result in shorter and more equitable sentences and thus reduce the extent and worst effects of state intervention. This blind faith in the rule of law, however, has proven a mixed blessing. On the one hand, due process has provided offenders with needed protections against state abuse of discretion. On the other hand, it remains unclear whether the corresponding attack on rehabilitation has succeeded in creating a system that is less committed to interventionist policies and more committed to humanistic ideals (Cullen & Gilbert, 1982). As we will see in the final chapter, recent trends in criminal justice policy do not furnish reason for optimism on this point.

Deinstitutionalization

Finally, labeling theorists took special pains to detail the criminogenic effects of incarceration and to advocate vigorously the policy of lessening prison populations through deinstitutionalization. The time had come, they insisted, for a moratorium on prison construction and for the move to a system that corrected its wayward members in the community.

This proposal received a stunning test in 1972 when Jerome Miller, commissioner of Massachusetts's Department of Youth Services, took the bold action of closing the state's major juvenile facilities and of placing youths in community programs (Empey, 1982). Only a small number of youths remained in secure detention (Klein, 1979). Significantly, a subsequent evaluation revealed that recidivism rates were only slightly higher after the institutions were emptied. More instructive, the researchers found that in those sections of the state where the reform was pursued enthusiastically through the creation of "a large number of diverse program options, so that the special needs of each youth could be more nearly met," the recidivism rate was *lower* than before Miller's deinstitutionalization policy was implemented. The researchers termed these results "dramatic" (Miller & Ohlin, 1985, p. 70; see also *Corrections Magazine*, 1975).

One might have expected that these empirical results would have caused policy makers in other states to consider the wisdom of making a community rather than an institutional response to crime. But as we have noted, policy decisions are based less on research and more on what seems sensible and thus politically feasible. In the past decade, the tenor of American society changed, and new ways of thinking about crime emerged (see Wilson, 1975). Not surprisingly, policies have reflected this change in thinking, as we have abandoned the idea of deinstitutionalization and chosen instead to incarcerate offenders in unprecedented numbers.

Conclusion

Labeling theory's distinctive focus on societal reaction succeeded in sensitizing criminologists to the important insights that the criminal nature of behavior is socially constructed by the response to it and that a variety of factors can shape who comes to bear a criminal label. The perspective also forced consideration of the possibility that state intervention can have the ironic, unanticipated consequence of causing the very conduct—lawlessness—it is meant to suppress. Empirical research has yet to confirm convincingly this causal thesis, but neither has it shown that criminal labeling does not play a contributing role in stabilizing certain kinds of offenders in criminal careers. In any case, labeling theory provides an important reminder that the effects of criminal justice intervention are complex and may contradict what common sense would dictate. This warning assumes significance when we consider policy makers' current assurances that the panacea for the crime problem can be found in widening the reach of the criminal law and in the enormous expansion of prison populations.

6

SOCIAL POWER AND THE CONSTRUCTION OF CRIME

Conflict Theory

As shown in Chapter 5, theories purporting to explain crime by locating its sources in biological, psychological, or social factors associated with the offender have tended to ignore the way in which "crime" is produced and aggravated by the reaction to real or imagined attributes or behavior of those who are being labeled "offenders." Labeling theory tried to correct this oversight, going into great detail in an effort to explain the labeling process and its consequences. But as the previous chapter also indicates, some criminological theorists did not feel that labeling theory went far enough. The labeling theorists showed some appreciation for the way in which political interests and political power affected social reaction, but they did little to explore these deeper issues.

What determines whether a label will stick? What determines the extent to which those labeled are punished? The nature of the labeling may depend on differences between those labeled and those doing the labeling. Whether labels can be made to stick and the extent to which those labeled can be punished may depend essentially on who has power. Theories that focus attention on struggles between individuals and/or groups in terms of power differentials fall into the general category of *conflict theory*.

Some conflict theories try to search for the sources of the apparent conflicts. Some seek to elucidate the basic principles by which conflict evolves. Others try to develop a theoretical foundation for eliminating the conflict. Some try to do all this and more.

In this chapter we will examine some of the leading criminological conflict theories, beginning with conflict theory in general as found in the pioneering work of Marx and Engels and in the later work of Simmel. Next we will examine Bonger's attempt to develop a Marxist theory of crime, Sutherland's and Sellin's focus on the relationship between culture conflict and crime, and Vold's effort to build a criminological conflict theory on the tradition exemplified by Simmel. Because contemporary American criminological conflict theory, like other criminological control theories, drew much of its inspiration from the turmoil of the 1960s, it will be necessary to reexamine the 1960s from another point of view before proceeding to a consideration of such influential conflict theories as those of Turk, Chambliss, and Quinney. Finally, we will consider some of the consequences within criminology as well as the policy implications of conflict theory.

Forerunners of Conflict Theory

Marx and Engels: Capitalism and Crime

As indicated in Chapter 4, Karl Marx and Friedrich Engels already were expressing concern over the apparent decline in social solidarity by the middle of the 1800s, preceding Durkheim by several decades. For Marx and Engels as well as for Durkheim, crime was to some extent a symptom of this decline and would diminish (although Durkheim made it clear that it would never disappear) if social solidarity could be regained. They differed in their analysis of the source of the erosion of solidarity and their prescription for its restoration.

Durkheim saw the situation as a moral problem and argued that the social solidarity of the future would depend on an effective combination of controls through modes of social integration and social regulation that could operate in tune with the new division of labor that had been created by industrialization. Marx and Engels saw the problem in economic terms, denounced the new division of labor as the unjust exploitation of one social class by another, and insisted that social solidarity could be regained only with the overthrow of capitalism itself. They proposed revolution followed by a period of socialism. Because in their view the political state existed essentially as a mechanism for the perpetuation of capitalism, it was deemed historically inevitable that the state would then "wither away," leaving a society based on the true brotherhood and sisterhood of communism (Marx & Engels, 1848/1992).

Marx himself had very little to say about crime. Those criminological theorists who cite him as a major forerunner tend to extrapolate from his general approach, to cite his collaborator Engels's more directly relevant writings on the assumption that Marx agreed, or to do both by citing Marx in general with a specific quotation from Engels to nail down the point. Certainly Marx and Engels stressed differences in interests and in power much more than did Durkheim. For them, conflict was inherent in the nature of social arrangements under capitalism, for it was capitalism that generated the vast differences in interests and capitalism that gave the few at the top so much power over the many at the bottom. Above all, their theoretical approach was action oriented; they were less concerned with the pure understanding of social problems than with changing things for what they considered the better.

Although the work of Marx and Engels was extremely complex, certain basic propositions stand out (Turner, 1978). First there was the proposition that conflict of interests between different groups will be increased by inequality in the distribution of scarce resources (food, clothing, shelter, etc.). A second proposition was that those receiving less of the needed resources would question the legitimacy of the arrangement as they became aware of the nature of the "raw deal" they were getting. The third proposition was that these groups then would be more likely to organize and to bring the conflict out in the open, after which there would be polarization and violence leading to the redistribution of the scarce resources in such a way that they would be shared by everyone. Capitalism was considered to be at the root of the conflict because it was taken to be the source of the unjust inequality. In this view, greater integration and regulation simply would tend to perpetuate an unjust economic system. The way to solve the problem of collapsing social solidarity was not to find some new sources of faith in the social order or some more effective means of regulating its members but to destroy capitalism and build toward the one just form of social solidarity—communism.

Simmel: Forms of Conflict

Like Marx, George Simmel was a German intellectual with a deep interest in social theory. On the other hand, Simmel was a contemporary of Durkheim, doing his theoretical work a few decades later than Marx and concerning himself with a search for precise intellectual understanding of abstract laws governing human interaction rather than with changing the world. Simmel was an exponent of "sociological formalism" (Martindale, 1960, p. 233). He was concerned not so much with the changing *content* of social life as with its recurring *forms* or patterns. Speaking of Simmel, Wolff (1964) has remarked that his approach represented a "preponderance of the logical over the normative" (p. xviii). His interest was not in particular conflicts but in conflict in general, and he was less concerned with normative questions such as the justice of a particular outcome than with the abstract logic of conflict itself.

Although Simmel was interested deeply in conflict as a form common in social life, he was not as preoccupied with it as was Marx, seeing it as a normal part of life and as one form of interaction among others, some of which were operating in different and even opposite directions in an integrated social system (Turner, 1978). Conflict was regarded not as a problem necessarily calling for solutions or even leading to change but rather as a typical aspect of social order that often actually contributed to that order. Of equal importance is that although Marx focused on the *causes* of conflict and sought to find means for their elimination, Simmel focused on the *consequences* of conflict, with little interest in its sources and great interest in the complex, formal patterns through which it developed.

Bonger: Capitalism and Crime

Early in the 20th century, the conflict perspective of Marx and Engels was applied specifically to criminological theory by the Dutch criminologist Willem Bonger. As we will see later, the turbulence of the 1960s brought renewed interest in Marxist theory and in the work of Bonger (1916/1969). In the introduction to an abridged edition of Bonger's major work brought out near the end of the 1960s, the American criminologist and conflict theorist Austin T. Turk (1969b) spoke of him appreciatively as a man who "combined a passion to alleviate human misery with an equal passion for scientific research" (p. 3). Like Marx and Engels, and unlike Freud and Durkheim, Bonger felt that the human being was innately social. If so, crime would have to be traced to an unfavorable environment that distorted human nature. Bonger held that just such an unfavorable environment had been generated by the rise of capitalism.

Under capitalism, said Bonger, there had arisen a sharp division between the rulers and the ruled that did not originate in innate differences between them but in the economic system itself. In such an unfavorable environment, in which people were pitted against each other in the economic struggle, in which the individual was encouraged to seek pleasure by any means possible without regard for others, and in which the search required money, human nature was distorted into an intense "egoism" that made people more capable of committing crimes against one another. Thus, like the control theorists as far back as Durkheim, Bonger traced crime in part to individual egoism. Unlike them, however, he took the Marxist position that the decline of social integration and the rise of extremely disruptive individualism could be traced to capitalism. Such egoism could never be reduced by social controls that bound the individual more closely to society, for society under capitalism was itself the very *source* of the egoism.

Bonger traced much crime to the poverty generated by capitalism, both directly because crime among the subordinate class was sometimes necessary for survival and indirectly because the sense of injustice in a world in which many had almost nothing while a few had everything was held to demoralize the individual and stifle the social instincts. At the same time, however, he recognized that the more powerful bourgeoisie also committed crimes. He traced this to the opportunities that came with power and the decline of morality that came with capitalism. Crime was seen as a product of an economic system that fostered a greedy, egoistic, "look out for number one" mentality while at the same time making the rich richer and the poor poorer.

Long before the labeling theorists, Bonger stressed that although it was certainly true that crime fell into the category of immoral actions, definitions of morality varied. Indeed, he went further, insisting that the source of the prevailing definitions and of their variations could be found in the interests of the powerful. In Bonger's view, behaviors were defined as crimes when they significantly threatened the interests of the powerful and "hardly any act is punished if it does not injure the interests of the dominant class" (Turk, 1969b, p. 9). Thus he took note of the statistics showing a lower crime rate among the bourgeoisie and traced this to the fact that the legal system "tends to legalize the egoistic actions of the bourgeoisie and to penalize those of the proletariat" (p. 10). Given Bonger's theory of the causes of crime, his conclusion that the abolition of capitalism and the redistribution of wealth and power would restore a favorable environment and almost entirely eliminate crime followed as a matter of political logic.

Sutherland and Sellin:
Culture Conflict and Crime

In criminological theory, Edwin H. Sutherland is best known for his differential association theory discussed in Chapter 3. As indicated in that chapter, the concept of differential association was built on the concept of differential social organization, which was itself an attempt to move away from the value judgments entailed in describing situations organized differently as representing social disorganization. The concept of differential social organization represented one type of conflict perspective; inherent in the notion was the assumption that society did not rest on complete consensus but was made up of different segments with conflicting cultural patterns. Individual criminal activity could be explained by assuming that a person whose associations were dominated by relationships with those in a less law-abiding segment of society would tend to learn criminal techniques and develop criminal orientations.

Sutherland already had begun systematic research into the crimes of the wealthy and powerful by the middle 1920s. During the 1930s he pioneered the study of white-collar criminality, publishing a groundbreaking article at the beginning of the 1940s (Sutherland, 1940) and a widely cited book on the subject by the end of the decade (Sutherland, 1949). In these works he called attention to the fact that powerful economic interests such as the huge corporations that had arisen in the 20th century represented a segment of society whose organization and policy made them "habitual criminals," although their wealth and political power protected them from prosecution in the criminal courts. As was pointed out in Chapter 3, he explained the participation of *individuals* in the white-collar crimes of these corporations in terms of their *differential association* by way of immersion in the criminal patterns of the business.

During the Depression of the 1930s, another criminologist, Thorsten Sellin, best known today for his studies of capital punishment and his efforts at developing crime indices, argued, like Sutherland, for a broader definition of crime and a less conventional approach to criminological theory. Sellin (1938) stressed the problem of "culture conflict" as a source of crime, maintaining that different groups learned different "conduct norms" and that the conduct norms of one group might clash with those of another. As for which conduct norms would become a part of the criminal law, Sellin held that "the conduct which the state denotes as criminal is, of course, that deemed injurious to society, or in the last analysis, to those who wield the political power within that society and therefore control the legislative, judicial, and executive functions which are the external manifestations of authority" (p. 3).

Vold: Conflict and Crime

Near the close of the 1950s, George B. Vold (1958) set forth the most extensive and detailed treatment of criminological theory from a conflict perspective yet seen in criminology. Citing Simmel, he agreed that conflict should not be regarded as abnormal but rather as a fundamental social form characteristic of social life in general. He argued that "as social interaction processes grind their way through varying kinds of uneasy adjustment to a more or less stable equilibrium of *balanced forces in opposition,* the resulting condition of relative stability is what is usually called social order or social organization" (p. 204; emphasis added). In this perspective, social order was not presumed to rest entirely on consensus but in part on the stability resulting from a balance of power among the various conflicting forces that compose society. The conflict between groups was analyzed in Simmelian terms as potentially making a *positive contribution* to the strengthening of the different groups, because participation in the struggle resulted in group *esprit de corps* and in-group solidarity. According to this analysis, it was perfectly normal for groups in a complex society to come into conflict as their interests clashed and "politics, as it flourishes in a democracy, is primarily a matter of finding practical compromises between antagonistic groups in the community at large" (Vold, 1958, p. 208).

As to the nature of legal compromises, Vold (1958) cited Sutherland's work from the 1920s, noting that "those who produce legislative majorities win control over the police power and dominate the policies that decide who is likely to be involved in violation of the law" (p. 209). Vold considered politics the art of compromise and insisted that "the principle of compromise from positions of strength operates at every stage of this conflict process" (p. 209). His own theoretical interest in the *forms* rather than the *content* of such conflict may be seen in his comparison of the delinquent gangs' patterns to those formed by conscientious objectors in time of war. Both were analyzed as identical patterns or social forms in which group ideology existed in conflict with established authority. Like Simmel, Vold was concerned with the similarity of the forms of conflict rather than with normative distinctions such as the nature of the morality involved.

Vold (1958) pointed out that much crime was of an obviously political nature. He included crimes resulting from protest movements aimed at political reform, noting that "a successful revolution makes criminals out of the government officials previously in power, and an unsuccessful revolution makes its leaders into traitors subject to immediate execution" (p. 214). His formal analysis avoided the normative and stuck to the logical. Regardless of who was "right" and who was "wrong," those who lost were the "criminals." In this sense, their (formal) "crime" consisted of losing.

Vold (1958) also gave attention to crimes involving conflicts between union and management and between different unions themselves. In a statement portending what was to come in the civil rights movement in the United States of the 1960s and elsewhere in the world in the 1980s, he pointed out that "numerous kinds of crimes result from the clashes incidental to attempts to change, or to upset the caste system of racial segregation in various parts of the world, notably in the United States and in the Union of South Africa" (p. 217). He undertook an intensive analysis of organized crime and white-collar crime as examples of groups organizing themselves in the pursuit of their interests, examining the strategies and tactics employed in the conflict.

Theory in Context:
The Turmoil of the 1960s

Although the various forerunners of conflict theory discussed previously had anticipated much of what was to follow, it was not until the social upheavals of the 1960s that criminological conflict theory came into its own. The 1960s represented a major turning point for criminology. As we have seen already, it was within the context of those times that both control theory and labeling theory developed from theoretical seeds planted earlier. The same was true for conflict theory. Although control theory reacted by stressing the tenuous nature of complex society under conditions of rapid social change and insisted that crime and delinquency tended to spread with any significant weakening of forces containing the individual, conflict theory highlighted the newly revealed patterns of social division and questioned the legitimacy of the motives, strategies, and tactics of those in power. Although labeling theory exposed the way in which crime was a social construction of moral entrepreneurs and others in a position to influence the definitions developed by the political state and sometimes pointed to class bias in the labeling process, conflict theory was much more explicit about the connection between the criminal justice system and the underlying economic order, sometimes condemning the state itself.

Seeking to explain the rise of criminological conflict theory (there termed *critical theory*) during the 1960s, Sykes (1974) has pointed to three factors of special importance. First, there was the impact of the Vietnam War on American society. Second, there was the growth of the counterculture. Finally, there was the rising political protest over discrimination, particularly racial discrimination, and the use of the police power of the state to suppress political dissent, associated issues that had been smoldering and threatening to break into the open since World War II.

As the war in Vietnam escalated, doubts deepened not only about the wisdom of governmental policy but also about the fundamental motives and credibility of those in power. Reasons given for the escalating involvement seemed to many to be rather far-fetched, and doubts were increased by discoveries of *disinformation*—a bureaucratic term for governmental lies. Protest marches spread. Armed troops fired on and killed apparently peaceful protesters on college campuses. The conscientious objectors about whom Vold had written so coolly were everywhere, voluntarily choosing to become "criminals" by leaving for Canada or burning their draft cards in heated public protests.

As indicated in Chapter 4, the developing counterculture represented in large part a repudiation of middle-class standards. Countercultural behavior dramatized a fundamental conflict in values. Millions were engaging now in a variety of activities that they considered harmless but that the legal system regarded as criminal offenses—such so-called victimless crimes as fornication, vagrancy, and illegal drug use. The latter had in fact become not only a way to "get high" but a symbolic political protest.

As Chapter 4 has emphasized, along with the impact of the Vietnam War and the growth of the counterculture came the rise of social movements aimed at eliminating discrimination and demanding an end to the suppression of political dissent. The feminist movement spoke more and more militantly in terms of the political, economic, and sexual oppression of women. The homosexual community became more politicized, organizing to resist labeling and discrimination. Underlying social conflict came more and more into the open as the civil rights movement seemed to make it clear that Blacks were not going to gain social equality without civil disobedience, that the only way to deal with the unjust laws enforcing segregation was to violate them en masse, for the protesters to become "criminals" and spend some time in jail as the price for their beliefs.

At the same time, a society that had tolerated the McCarthyism of the 1950s was upset to learn that some of its most revered symbols of law and order, such as the FBI, had become involved in the dissemination of internal disinformation aimed at destroying political opposition and had fallen into the use of illegal tactics in dealing with citizens seeking to express legitimate grievances. It often appeared that the agents of the political state, whether southern sheriffs threatening Black schoolchildren with police dogs or members of Congress harassing as radicals or communists those who seriously questioned the political order, were really moral criminals disguised as legally constituted authority. The impression of society as composed of groups in conflict, with the legal system tending to brand as criminal significant threats to the interests of the powerful, became more and more prevalent, providing fertile ground for the development of conflict theory.

Varieties of Conflict Theory

The new criminological conflict theory went much further than criminologists had taken it before, appealing to Marx and Bonger as well as to Simmel. As Gibbons and Garabedian (1974) have pointed out in their own examination of the conflict theory movement (there termed *radical criminology*), "Sutherland certainly did not characterize the seventy corporations that he studied as 'exploiters of the people'; instead, he stopped far short of that sort of condemnation" (p. 51). Similarly, Sellin may have noted that the law is defined and applied in the interests of dominant groups, but he did not denounce them in the manner of Marx. As for Vold's analysis of the state of affairs, what had seemed like a bold outline of the conflict perspective in the late 1950s now struck some as in need of much more elaboration and others as far too abstract, academic, and aloof from the injustices that so angered them.

Sykes (1974) has listed four major factors behind the shift. First, there was now a profound skepticism toward any theory that traced crime to something about the individual, including not only the biological and psychological theories but sociological theories referring to inadequate socialization and the like. Second, there was a marked shift from the assumption that the inadequacies of the criminal justice system were to be traced to incompetent or corrupt individuals or minor organizational flaws to the conclusion that these problems were inherent in the system, either because it was fundamentally out of control or because it had been so designed by powerful interests. Third, the older assumptions that the criminal law represented the collective will of the people and that the job of the criminologist was to do theoretical analysis and empirical research and not to deal in normative issues of right and wrong increasingly were rejected as fallacies that made it impossible to ask the basic questions. Finally, as discussed in Chapter 5, it had become clear not only that official crime rate figures did not reflect the amount of criminal behavior actually present in society but also that what they did reflect was more often the labeling behavior of the authorities.

During the 1960s several criminologists, influenced by a blending of labeling theory with political theory, began to develop their own brand of criminological conflict theory. It is fair to characterize their work as part of a theoretical movement. Here we will concentrate on the efforts of three of the leading conflict theorists—Turk, Chambliss, and Quinney. As we will see, they were not working in isolation but rather in close contact within a particular sociohistorical context. Each of them presented the outlines of their own approach in articles written during the 1960s, and each published a book-length volume in 1969. Their differences were to depend to a considerable extent on influences from the various theoretical forerunners discussed previously.

Turk: The Criminalization Process

Completing his graduate work at the beginning of the 1960s, Austin T. Turk had come to be interested increasingly in the culture conflict perspective of criminologists such as Sellin and in the emerging labeling theory. As with any theorist, his perspective was influenced by his life experiences. Turk (1987) himself has put it this way:

Growing up as a working class boy in a small segregated Georgia town, I learned early that life is neither easy nor just for most folks; that irrationality and contradiction are very much part (maybe the biggest part) of social reality; that access to resources and opportunities have no necessary association with ability or character; that the meaning of justice in theory is debatable, and of justice in practice manipulable; and that whatever degree of freedom, equality, brotherhood, or security exist in a society are hard-won and tenuous. (p. 3)

By the end of the 1960s, Turk (1969a) had presented a complete statement of his own brand of conflict theory in *Criminality and the Legal Order*, quoting at length from Sutherland in the introduction and citing the more recent efforts of Vold and Dahrendorf. It was this effort to build on Dahrendorf's perspective, along with his Simmelian-Voldian approach that treated conflict not as some abnormality but as a fundamental social form, that distinguished Turk's theoretical contribution. For Turk, recognition of social conflict as a basic fact of life represented simple realism rather than any particular tendency toward cynicism.

Although also a conflict theorist, Dahrendorf (1958, 1968) disagreed with Marx on the question of inequality. Instead of tracing inequality back to an unjust economic system, Dahrendorf located the source in *power* differences, more specifically in differences in *authority* or power that had been accepted as legitimate. Unlike Marx, who had argued for the abolition of inequality, Dahrendorf took the position that because cultural norms always exist and have to depend on sanctions for their enforcement, some people *must* have more power than others to make the sanctions stick. In Dahrendorf's view, it was not the economic inequality resulting from capitalism that produced social inequality; rather inequality was an inescapable fact because the basic units of society *necessarily* involved dominance-subjection relationships. Thus the idea of eliminating inequality was treated as a utopian dream.

Turk (1969a) seems to have been persuaded of the essential relativity of crime in much the same way as the labeling theorists. For him the theoretical problem of explaining crime lay not in explaining varieties of behavior, for these may or may not be crimes depending on time and place. Instead, the problem lay in explaining "criminalization," the process of "assignment of criminal status to individuals" (p. xi), which results in the production of "criminality" (p. 1). Dahrendorf's influence was clear in Turk's definition of the study of "criminality" as "the study of relations between the statuses and roles of legal *authorities . . .* and those *subjects*—

acceptors or resisters but not makers of such law creating, interpreting and enforcing decisions" (p. 1; emphasis in the original).

Such an approach was deemed necessary if the criminologist was to explain such "facts" as variations in crime rates or to develop better methods of dealing with "criminals." Turk (1969a) stressed that assignment of criminal status to an individual may have less connection with the behavior of that person than with his or her relationship to the authorities. "Indeed, criminal status may be ascribed to persons because of real or fancied *attributes*, because of what they *are* rather than what they *do*, and justified by reference to real or imagined or fabricated behavior" (pp. 9-10; emphasis in the original). From this point of view, even if the criminologist could succeed eventually in explaining the *behavior* of criminals, such an achievement would not help in accounting for their *criminality*, which had more to do with the behavior of the authorities in control of the criminalization process.

Central to the concept of *authority* is its accepted legitimacy; authority differs from raw power because it is regarded as legitimate power, the use of which is accepted by those subject to it. Any theorist concerned with the relationship between subjects and authorities must investigate the basis for such acceptance. Like some of the control theorists, Turk (1969a) rejected the argument that acceptance of authority must be the result of internalization. He maintained that acceptance could be explained as a consequence of people learning the *roles* assigned to the *statuses* they occupied and simply acquiescing and going along as a matter of routine. Some have the status of authorities; others play the part of subjects. "The legality of norms is defined solely by the words and behavior of authorities," to which subjects will tend to defer (p. 51).

Like Simmel and Vold, Turk (1969a) was concerned with the logical *consequences* of the fact that some people had authority over others, not with the sources of this authority or whether it was just or unjust according to some normative conception of justice. In fact, logical consistency might be expected to force anyone who was convinced that concepts such as crime were a matter of labeling relative to time and place to a similar position with respect to concepts such as justice. In any case, Turk focused on the logical consequences of authority relationships, holding that "how authorities come to be authorities is irrelevant" to such an analysis (p. 51).

Because of his (1969a) argument that the assignment of the criminal status would have to be justified by the authorities "by reference to real or imagined or fabricated behavior" (pp. 9-10) that was held to represent a violation of legal norms, Turk found it important to make a formal distinction between two types of legal norms—cultural norms and social norms. The first he defined as those set forth in symbolic terms such as words, as norms dealing with *what is expected*. The second he identified as those found in patterns of actual behavior, in terms of *what is being done* rather than what is being said. Turk pointed out that the cultural norms and the social norms in a given situation might or might not correspond.

According to Turk (1969a), a satisfactory theory accounting for the assignment of criminal status would include "a statement of the conditions under which cultural and social differences between authorities and subjects will probably result in conflict, the conditions under which criminalization will probably occur in the course of conflict, and the conditions under which the degree of deprivation associated with becoming a criminal will probably be greater or lesser" (p. 53). Like Simmel, he proceeded to examine the nature of these conditions through a series of formal, logical propositions.

Thus Turk argued that given that cultural and social norms may not agree, the existence of a difference between authorities and subjects in their evaluation of a particular attribute, such as past membership in a radical political organization, or a particular act such as marijuana use, logically implies four situational possibilities. Each logical possibility carries a different conflict potential. The conflict probability would be highest, for example, in the "high-high" situation in which there was (a) high congruence between the cultural norms preached by the authorities and their actual behavior patterns and (b) similarly high congruence between the cultural evaluation of a particular attribute or act and the actual possession of that attribute or commission of that act on the part of the subjects. If both sides not only *hold* different standards but also act *in accordance* with them, there is no room for compromise. In a situation in which the authorities not only say "smoking marijuana is wrong" but also act to stop it, for example, *and* marijuana users not only say "pot is okay" but also insist on using it in spite of the normative clash, the conflict potential would be logically greatest.

On the other hand, Turk's logic suggested that the conflict potential would be lowest in situations where there was neither agreement between authorities' stated cultural norms and their actual behavioral norms nor between the cultural norms and the social norms of subjects. In such situations, the preachments would clash, but because neither side practices what it preaches in any case, the probability of conflict would be low. Why should they fight over words when neither side lives by them anyhow?

A third logical possibility was described as one in which authorities' talk and behavior were highly congruent, although there was little if any agreement between the words and actions of subjects. Such a situation would fall somewhere in the middle in terms of Turk's formal logic of conflict potential, but with a somewhat higher conflict potential than that logically inherent in the fourth and final possibility. The latter situation was described as one in which the attribute or act as described in the announced cultural norm happened to be in close agreement among subjects while the cultural norm preached by the authorities actually had little relationship to their behavior. According to Turk, the third possibility would entail somewhat more conflict potential than would the fourth because the authorities would be less likely to tolerate norms different from their own when their cultural norms were reinforced by their social norms.

According to Turk's analysis, the logic of the relationships between cultural and social norms is complicated by additional formal propositions. Under the assumption that an individual who has group support is going to be more resistant to efforts to change him or her, he concluded that the probability of conflict with authorities grows with the extent to which those having the illegal attributes or engaging in the illegal activities are *organized*. Under the assumption that the more sophisticated norm resisters would be better at avoiding open conflict through clever tactical maneuvers (e.g., pretending to submit while secretly continuing as before), he concluded that the probability of conflict increases as the authorities confront norm resisters who are less *sophisticated*. The logical possibilities resulting from combination of the two variables of organization and sophistication were set forth as follows: (a) organized and unsophisticated, (b) unorganized and unsophisticated, (c) organized and sophisticated, and (d) unorganized and sophisticated. Conflict odds were attached to each combination.

Proceeding through formal analysis of the four formally distinct possibilities, Turk reached certain conclusions. First, he concluded that conflict between authorities and subjects is most probable where the latter are *highly organized and relatively unsophisticated* (e.g., delinquent gangs). He then concluded that the odds of such conflict declined to the extent that the subjects involved are *unorganized and unsophisticated* (e.g., skid row transients) and still further to the extent that they are *organized and sophisticated* (e.g., syndicate criminals). It followed logically that the lowest probability of conflict would be associated with a situation in which the norm-resisting subjects are *unorganized and sophisticated* (e.g., professional con artists). These formal deductions may or may not match empirical reality, but they have a certain logical consistency, and Turk encouraged research designed to assess their actual empirical validity.

As for the authorities themselves, Turk pointed out that they must be *organized* or by definition they would not be the authorities but some sort of illegitimate mob. He concluded that the probability of conflict between these authorities and subjects resisting their norms would be greatest where the authorities were *least sophisticated* in the use of power. Interestingly enough, his logic carried him to the same conclusion as that reached by the control theorist Hirschi at the same time—that the probability of conflict was affected by the "nature of the bonds between authorities and subjects" (Turk, 1969a, p. 61). He concluded that "where subjects are strongly identified with the authorities and generally agree in moral evaluations, an announced norm may be accepted in a 'Father knows best' spirit" (p. 61). But where Hirschi stressed these bonds as central, Turk devoted much less attention to them, considering society to be less a matter of Durkheimian bonds and more a matter of constant Simmelian conflict working itself out over time. We must remember, of course, that Hirschi was focusing theoretical attention on juvenile delinquency, while Turk was devoting considerable attention to organized crime, political crime, and white-collar crime in general. Accordingly, the relative stress on bonds as compared with conflict potentials is hardly surprising.

For Turk (1969a), an analysis of conflict probabilities was only a first step. The key question was: "Once conflict has begun, what are the conditions affecting the probability that members of the opposition will become criminals . . . that they will be subjected to less or more severe deprivation?" (p. 64). Part of the answer was traced to the same factors outlined above, which would continue to affect probabilities throughout the criminalization process. Turk concluded, however, that additional variables tended to come into play with actual criminalization.

First, he admitted that although the crucial norms defining the conflict were those of the higher authorities, the major factor in the probability of criminalization was likely to be the extent to which the official, legal norms agreed with both the cultural norms and the social norms *of those specifically charged with enforcing the legal norms,* especially the police, but also prosecutors, judges, and the like. Because of the importance of police discretion and decisions on the spot, he concluded that the extent to which the police agreed with the legal norms they were expected to enforce would have a major effect on the odds of arrest and criminalization. Prosecutors, judges, juries, and others were expected to affect the probabilities somewhat, but ultimately it would be the police as the front line enforcers who would determine the extent to which norm resisters actually would be defined as criminal.

In Turk's analysis, the *relative power of enforcers and resisters* became still another variable affecting the odds of criminalization. He proposed that the greater the power difference in favor of norm enforcers over resisters, the greater would be the probability of criminalization. He asserted that the reluctance of the enforcers to move against very powerful resisters would keep the criminality of the very powerful low regardless of their behavior. He added the qualification, however, that some of the disapproved behavior of the least powerful might be ignored also if they seemed to pose no threat and "weren't worth the bother."

The final set of variables to which Turk assigned special significance in determining the odds of criminalization had to do with the *realism of conflict moves*. Although in part a matter of the sophistication mentioned above, success in avoiding criminalization or producing criminalization was regarded also as dependent on factors beyond the use of knowledge of others' behavior patterns in manipulating them. Any move by *resisters* was considered to be unrealistic if it (a) increased the *visibility* of the offensive attribute or behavior, thus increasing the risk that the authorities would be forced to act; (b) increased the *offensiveness* of the attribute or behavior (e.g., by emphasizing it, calling attention to additional offensive attributes, or violating an even more significant norm of the authorities); (c) increased *consensus* among the various levels of enforcers (e.g., by moving from simple opposition to a particular norm or set of norms to a wholesale attack on the system with emphasis on stereotyping of enforcers as brutal, ignorant, and corrupt); or (d) increased the *power difference* in favor of the enforcers (e.g., by upsetting the public in such a way that enforcers would be able to get significantly increased resources such as budget increases).

In Turk's analysis, any move by the *authorities* was likely to be unrealistic if it (a) *shifted the basis of their legitimacy away from consensus* toward the "norm of deference" or obligation to obey despite disagreement, which would be likely in the case of power plays; (b) represented a *departure from standard legal procedures*, especially if the shifts were unofficial, sudden, or sharp; (c) *generalized from a particular offensive attribute* so that additional attributes of the opposition also became grounds for criminalization (e.g., if roundups of similar types were used in lieu of a systematic search for a particular offender); (d) *increased the size and power of the opposition* (e.g., by creating martyrs among them so that they gained sympathy and other resources from other segments of society); or (e) *decreased consensus* among the various levels of enforcers.

Turk went much further than this in pointing out additional factors that may be expected to alter the nature and outcome of social conflict. He attempted to provide a logical integration of his propositions to demonstrate how various combinations affect conflict probabilities differently and went into great detail in describing possible indicators that might be used to operationalize his propositions to facilitate research. Thus he dealt with the means by which legal norms could be classified in practice; with the question of the best measures of key concepts such as normative-legal conflict, the significance of legal norms, relative power, and realism in conflict moves; and with other issues that would have to be solved if his theory were to be tested by data.

Chambliss: Crime, Power, and Legal Process

Finishing his own graduate work in the same year (1962) as had Turk, William J. Chambliss (1964) had become interested in the development of criminal law, specifically in "sociologically relevant analyses of the relationship between particular laws and the social setting in which these laws emerge, are interpreted, and take form" (p. 67). Chambliss (1987) too has been candid about the relationship between his theoretical perspective and his life experiences.

> After I graduated from UCLA I hitchhiked across the country again to see my father. It was 1955 and in short order I was drafted into the army and sent to Korea with the Counter Intelligence Corps (CIC). I learned a lot about crime during that period. American and Korean soldiers raped, stole, assaulted, intimidated and generally terrorized the Koreans. Because they had the power, nothing was done about it. . . . How could crime be understood from the paradigms I learned in psychology and sociology? (pp. 5-6)

Chambliss completed his graduate work at Indiana University before going on to teach at the University of Washington and then to postdoctoral studies at the University of Wisconsin. It is worth noting (a) that both Turk and Richard Quinney, the third of the contemporary criminological conflict theorists to be examined in this chapter, completed their graduate work at the University of Wisconsin in the same year that Chambliss was completing his at Indiana and (b) that Turk himself joined the faculty at Indiana after completion of his graduate work at Wisconsin. The ties between these institutions were very close, and there was considerable mutual influence.

> Our lives are far more dependent on chance occurrences than we ever want to acknowledge. A year after I arrived at Washington the University hired Pierre van den Berghe, who was extremely knowledgeable about Marxism. I organized a faculty seminar on the sociology of law with Pierre, a philosopher, and two anthropologists. . . . About this time the Russell Sage Foundation decided to support the resurrection of the sociology of law. I was awarded a fellowship to study law at the University of Wisconsin. (Chambliss, 1987, pp. 3, 7)

Like Turk, Chambliss was impressed by the relativity of crime and the way in which the criminal label seemed to be the product of social conflict. But although Turk's work was influenced by a formal, Simmelian approach, Chambliss was at first inspired less by the older, European tradition of conflict theory than by the American tradition of *legal realism*, the pioneering work of the American legal scholar Jerome Hall, and by the results of his own empirical research. Chambliss (1964) had undertaken a study of the development of vagrancy law in England, concluding that these laws could be traced to vested interests. "There is little question that these statutes were designed for one express purpose: to force laborers . . . to accept employment at a low wage in order to insure the landowner an adequate supply of labor at a price he could afford to pay" (p. 69).

In the same year that Turk published *Criminality and the Legal Order,* Chambliss (1969) published *Crime and the Legal Process,* an edited volume consisting of actual empirical research studies of the legal system, tying them together with his own theoretical framework. This was soon followed by a more elaborate presentation, *Law, Order, and Power,* in collaboration with Robert T. Seidman, a professor of law at the University of Wisconsin (Chambliss & Seidman, 1971). In the earlier statement, Chambliss (1969) simply identified his position as representing an "interest-group" perspective rather than a "value-expression" perspective, a distinction that he compared to that seen in "the debate in social science theory between the 'conflict' and 'functional' theorists" (p. 8). His approach was very much influenced by the American school of legal realism, which concerned itself with the distinction between the "law in the books" and the "law in action." It insisted that the study of abstract legal theory must be complemented by the study of the law as it works itself out in actual practice. It is interesting to note that although the first of these had been the focus of the classical school discussed in Chapter 2, the new attention to the law in action represented the influence of positivism in legal studies. Chambliss hoped to develop a theory of the law in action, a theory based on empirical research.

Early in the second volume, Chambliss and Seidman (1971) sounded an almost Durkheimian theme, asserting that the "first variable in our theoretical model is the relative complexity of the society" (p. 31). They went on, however, to insist that (a) the complexity, which comes with technological development and necessitates more complicated, differentiated, and sophisticated social roles, actually operates to (b) put people *at odds with one another,* thus (c) requiring *formal institutions* designed to sanction what some consider norm violations. This argument was reminiscent of Dahrendorf's, with the major difference being that formal, sanctioning institutions were not regarded as inherently necessary to society but as a contemporary necessity resulting from increasing social complexity. Their conflict perspective led them to a theory of legal development almost exactly opposite to that expounded in Durkheim's (1964) control theory approach, which maintained that increased societal complexity tended to lead society from an emphasis on "repressive" law to a stress on "restitutive" law. Instead, Chambliss and Seidman (1971) argued that "we may formulate, therefore, the following proposition: The lower the level of complexity of a society, the more emphasis will be placed in the dispute-settling process upon reconciliation; the more complex the society, the more emphasis will be placed on rule-enforcement" (p. 32).

Chambliss and Seidman (1971) had begun by arguing that increasing *social complexity* itself tended to call for sanctioning institutions designed to keep order among the conflicting interests. Going further, they maintained that this sanctioning process would become even more pronounced to the degree that the social complexity became a matter of *social stratification* with some groups having more wealth and power than others: "The more economically stratified a society becomes, the more it becomes necessary for the dominant groups in the society to enforce through coercion the norms of conduct which guarantee their supremacy" (p. 33). Here was something of a Marxian theme, although Chambliss and Seidman stopped short of a clear-cut Marxian position that traced the most serious problems of social stratification to polarization produced by capitalism.

Chambliss and Seidman (1971) stressed also the significance of the fact that the developing sanctions tended to be enforced through *bureaucratic organizations.* In their view, the basis of the sanctioning would be organized in the interests of the dominant groups, but the actual application of the sanctions tended to come through bureaucracies *that had their own interests.* In this sense, the law in action might be expected to reflect a combination of the interests of the powerful and the interests of the bureaucratic organizations created to enforce the rules.

Because the essence of Chambliss's theory was aimed at explaining the law in action in contemporary, complex, industrial societies, we can concentrate on the second and third variables in the theory of the law in action—*social stratification* and *bureaucracy.* In *Crime and the Legal Process* Chambliss (1969) stressed that "the single most important characteristic of contemporary Anglo-American society influential in shaping the legal order has been the emerging domination of the middle classes," along with "the attempt by the middle class to impose their own standards and their own view of proper behavior on people whose values differ" (pp. 10-11). In this view, the middle class was coming to represent the conventional morality, but Chambliss emphasized that behind the values lay self-interest.

In *Law, Order, and Power,* Chambliss and Seidman (1971) set forth five fundamental propositions with respect to the relationship between social stratification and the law, beginning with the proposition that (a) *the conditions of one's life affected one's values and norms.* They then asserted that (b) *complex societies were composed of groups with widely different life conditions,* and that (c) *complex societies therefore were composed of highly disparate and conflicting sets of norms.* As for the relationship between these conflicting norms and the law itself, they maintained that (d) *the probability of a given group's having its particular normative system embodied in law was not distributed equally but was closely related to the political and economic position of that group.* These propositions taken together led them to the final proposition that (e) *the higher a group's political or economic position, the greater was the probability that its views would be reflected in the laws* (pp. 473-474).

Most of Chambliss and Seidman's theoretical explanation for the law in action was focused on the argument that although the law represents the values and interests of the more powerful elements in the stratification system of complex societies, it is specifically created and enforced by bureaucratic organizations with their own agendas. In *Crime and the Legal Process* Chambliss (1969) insisted that "the most salient characteristic of organizational behavior is that the ongoing policies and activities are those designed to maximize rewards and minimize strains for the organization"

(p. 84). Furthermore, "this general principle is reflected in the fact that in the administration of the criminal law *those persons are arrested, tried, and sentenced who can offer the fewest rewards for nonenforcement of the laws and who can be processed without creating any undue strain* for the organizations which comprise the legal system" (pp. 84-85; emphasis in the original). In Chambliss's view, the criminal justice bureaucracies tended to treat those of lower social-class position more harshly for the same offenses committed by middle-class and upper-class people because they had little to offer in return for lenience and they were in no position to fight the system. Meanwhile, he insisted, these bureaucracies tended to ignore or deal leniently with the same offenses when committed by those higher in the stratification hierarchy.

The process by which the goals of bureaucratic efficiency and avoidance of trouble displace the official goal of impartial law enforcement has been termed *goal displacement* or goal substitution. According to Chambliss, a bureaucratic organization might be expected to take the easy way out, the path of least resistance, especially in contexts in which (a) the members have little motivation to resist the easy way out, (b) they have a great deal of discretion in how they will actually behave, and (c) adherence to the official goals is not enforced. "It will maximize rewards and minimize strains for the organization to process those who are politically weak and powerless, and to refrain from processing those who are politically powerful" (Chambliss & Seidman, 1971, p. 269). Thus "the failure of the legal system to exploit the potential source of offenses that is offered by middle- and upper-class violators . . . derives instead from the very rational choice on the part of the legal system to pursue those violators that the community will reward them for pursuing and to ignore those violators who have the capability of causing trouble for the agencies" (Chambliss, 1969, p. 88).

Speaking of the police, Chambliss and Seidman (1971) presented evidence leading to the conclusion that as a bureaucracy, "they act illegally, breaching the norms of due process at every point: in committing brutality, in their searches and seizures, in arrests and interrogation" (p. 391). This illegality takes place not because the police are evil, but because they are not committed to due process in the first place, they have enormous discretion, and there is little enforcement of due process norms by the public or other agencies of the criminal justice system. As for prosecution following an arrest, Chambliss and Seidman concluded that "how favorable a 'bargain' one can strike with the prosecutor in the pretrial confrontations is a direct function of how politically and economically powerful the defendant is" (p. 412). The alleged safeguards provided by the right to trial by jury were taken to be largely a matter of myth because of the "built-in hazards of the jury trial . . . which exert the greatest pressure on accused persons to plead guilty," leading the powerless to surrender the so-called right in 9 cases out of 10 (p. 444). Finally, Chambliss and Seidman attempted to establish the validity of the proposition that "the tendency and necessity to bureaucratize is far and away the single most important variable in determining the actual day-to-day functioning of the legal system" by demonstrating how even in sentencing "institutionalized patterns of discrimination against the poor are inevitable" (pp. 468-469).

For several years prior to Chambliss's original presentation of his theoretical framework, he had been involved in a study of the relationship between professional crime and the legal system in a large American city. His experiences while conducting this study clearly influenced his thinking, especially with respect to the impact of bureaucracy on the legal system. Pointing out that although at first glance "it would appear that the professional criminal (be he a thief, gambler, prostitute, or hustler) would have little to offer the law enforcement agencies," he noted that there appeared in practice to be a situation of "symbiosis" or mutual dependence there (Chambliss, 1969, p. 89). He argued that because law enforcement agencies in fact depend on the professional criminal for inside information that makes their job easier, they tend to cooperate with these offenders rather than enforcing the law against them. In the later elaboration Chambliss and Seidman (1971) went into much more detail with respect to the symbiosis involving organized crime, presenting evidence in support of the proposition that "from the standpoint of the sociology of legal systems, the most important aspect of the widespread presence of organized crime . . . is that such organizations are impossible without the cooperation of the legal system" (p. 489).

Chambliss (1969) used this argument to explain some characteristics of the Anglo American legal system that seem somewhat illogical. As he pointed out, "Ironically, most of the criminal-legal effort is devoted to processing and sanctioning those persons *least* likely to be deterred by legal sanctions" (p. 370; emphasis in the original). He cited the use of harsh punishments against drug addicts and capital punishment against murderers as examples of severe sanctioning in exactly those cases where it has little deterrent effect. In contrast, he cited the reluctance to impose stiff sanctions against white-collar criminals and professional criminals as examples of allowing precisely those criminals who do tend to be deterred by sanctions to escape them. According to his argument, such a policy went directly against the formal logic of deterrence, but fit perfectly the bureaucratic logic of demonstrating "effectiveness" by harsh treatment of the powerless while avoiding the organizational strains that would follow from taking on the powerful.

As for Durkheim's control theory argument that law contributed to social solidarity, Chambliss (1969) concluded that "the imposition of legal sanctions is likely to increase community solidarity only when the emergent morality also serves other interests of persons in positions of power in the community" (p. 373). Although admitting that law might *occasionally* contribute to social solidarity, he stressed instead the manner in which the law in action *splintered the community* by labeling and excluding certain of its (powerless) members and the way in which policies such as the death penalty "may play an extremely important role in the general attitude toward the legitimacy of the use of extreme violence to settle disputes" (p. 376). In Chambliss's view, the creation and enforcement of law grew out of social conflict and then tended to *add to and reinforce that conflict.*

By the middle 1970s, however, political events in general and developments in social theory in particular seem to have combined to produce a significant shift in Chambliss's perspective. The social changes of the 1960s, which had influenced both Turk and Chambliss, had at the same time led a number of important social theorists to return to the Marxist tradition that had lain dormant during the war years of the 1940s and the McCarthyism of the 1950s. These Marxist theorists traced the problem of racial discrimination and the involvement in Vietnam directly to the economic interests of capitalists, and they argued that the countercultural response to the American dream was politically naive and would be crushed unless its adherents developed a revolutionary, socialist mentality. As we will see in greater detail later, the end of the 1960s saw the emergence of a political backlash that threatened not only to block the prospects for reform that were implicit in Chambliss's critique of the law in action but also to "turn the clock back" to restore the social and political climate of the 1950s. Chambliss apparently concluded that the problems lay deeper than he had suspected, that the Marxists had come closer to the truth, and that his own analysis must be turned in a Marxist direction.

Chambliss's (1975) shift was reflected in nine specific propositions. With respect to the *content and operation of criminal law,* he now asserted (a) that "acts are defined as criminal because it is in the interests of the ruling class to so define them," (b) that "members of the ruling class will be able to violate the laws with impunity while members of the subject class will be punished," and (c) that "as capitalist societies industrialize and the gap between the bourgeoisie and the proletariat widens, penal law will expand in an effort to coerce the proletariat into submission" (p. 152). As for the *consequences of crime for society,* he maintained (a) that "crime reduces surplus labor by creating employment not only for the criminals but for law enforcers, welfare workers, professors of criminology, and a horde of people who live off the fact that crime exists," (b) that "crime diverts the lower classes' attention from the exploitation they experience and directs it toward other members of their own class rather than toward the capitalist class or the economic system," and (c) that "crime is a reality which exists only as it is created by those in the society whose interests are served by its presence" (pp. 152-153).

Summarizing his position and its implications, Chambliss (1975) argued (a) that "criminal and noncriminal behavior stem from people acting rationally in ways that are compatible with their class position . . . a reaction to the life conditions of a person's social class," (b) that "crime varies from society to society depending on the political and economic structures of society," and (c) that "socialist countries should have much lower rates of crime because the less intense class struggle should reduce the forces leading to and the functions of crime" (p. 153). The similarity to Bonger's position was clear, and the use of terms such as *bourgeoisie, proletariat, exploitation,* and *class struggle* stressed the shift to a more Marxist formulation focusing on capitalism as the problem and socialism as a way of dealing with it.

Quinney: Social Reality, Capitalism, and Crime

As pointed out previously, the third of the criminological conflict theorists to be examined in this chapter, Richard Quinney, also completed graduate work in 1962, entering criminology along with Turk and Chambliss at a time when the ferment of the 1960s already was producing a markedly different social atmosphere. Quinney was to become not only the most prolific of the criminological conflict theorists but also the most controversial, revising his theoretical perspective time after time. Beginning with a position similar in many ways to that of Turk and Chambliss, he was to alter it almost immediately, only to develop a Marxist perspective at about the same time as did Chambliss and then to move in still another direction. Quinney has explained these theoretical turns as follows:

I have moved through the various epistemologies and ontologies in the social sciences. After applying one, I have found that another is necessary for incorporating what was excluded from the former, and so on. Also, I have tried to keep my work informed by the latest developments in the philosophy of science. In addition, I have always been a part of the progressive movements of the time. My work is thus an integral part of the social and intellectual changes that are taking place in the larger society, outside of criminology and sociology. One other fact has affected my work in recent years: the search for meaning in my life and in the world. (Bartollas, 1985, p. 230)

In the same year that saw publication of Turk's (1969a) *Criminality and Legal Order* and Chambliss's (1969) *Crime and the Legal Process,* Quinney (1969) set forth his own position in the introduction to an edited volume on the sociology of law called *Crime and Justice in Society.* At this point, Quinney's perspective was similar to that of Turk in some ways and to that of Chambliss in others. Like Chambliss, he focused on the sociology of conflicting interests. He preferred, however, to begin with the *sociological jurisprudence* of Roscoe Pound (1942) rather than with the "so-called legal realists," arguing that it was Pound who had first made the "call for the study of 'law in action' as distinguished from the study of 'law in the books' " (Quinney, 1969, pp. 22-23). But unlike Pound, who had seen law as operating for the good of society as a whole, Quinney, like Turk, and also citing Dahrendorf, took a position "based on the coercion model of society as opposed to the integrative" (p. 29).

Quinney (1969) defined law as "the creation and interpretation of specialized rules in a politically organized society" (p. 26). He then asserted that "politically organized society is based on an interest structure," that this structure "is characterized by unequal distribution of power and by conflict," and that "law is formulated and administered within the interest structure" (pp. 27-29). Referring to the "politicality of law," Quinney argued that "whenever a law is created or interpreted, the values of some are necessarily assured and the values of others are either ignored or negated" (p. 27). In this view, law was seen as part of the interest structure of society, with changes in the law reflecting changes in the interest structure, and as changing with changes in that structure.

One year later, Quinney (1970a, 1970b) published *The Problem of Crime* and *The Social Reality of Crime,* two volumes in which he presented somewhat different versions of criminological conflict theory. Like both Turk and Chambliss, Quinney was impressed by the relativity of crime. In *The Problem of Crime* (1970a) he began by taking the position, like Turk's, that crime must be considered in relative terms as a "legal status that is assigned to behaviors and persons by authorized others in society" with the criminal defined as "a person who is assigned the status of criminal on the basis of the official judgment that his conduct constitutes a crime" (pp. 6-7). Like both Turk and Chambliss, he also argued that social differentiation and social change tended to produce complex societies with different and often conflicting conduct norms prevailing in different segments. His critique of criminal justice statistics was quite similar to those of Turk and Chambliss. He asserted that "the crucial question is why societies and their agencies report, manufacture, or produce the volume of crime they do" (Quinney, 1970a, p. 16), and his analysis of American society as a criminogenic social system drew from the traditions described in earlier chapters— except for the accent on the "politicality of crime" (p. 180). By the "politicality of crime" Quinney meant that "the actions of the criminally defined are not so much the result of inadequate socialization and personality problems as they are conscientious actions taken against something . . . the only appropriate means for expressing certain thoughts and feelings—and the only possibilities for bringing about social changes" (p. 180).

In his discussion of philosophical principles underlying his approach, however, Quinney diverged considerably from Turk and Chambliss. This distinct difference was to set him apart. Quinney (1970a) pointed out that a number of criminologists had expressed concern over the positivistic conception of "cause," outlined deeper issues beneath this philosophical debate, and concluded that "under the impact of the philosophical implications of modern physics, most physical scientists have abandoned the idea that science is a *copy of reality*" (p. 134; emphasis in the original). This amounted to a total rejection of positivism. Drawing on the European tradition of *philosophical idealism,* he took the position that "accordingly, to state the extreme, there is no reality beyond man's conception of it: *reality is a state of mind*" and argued that "there is no reason to believe in the objective existence of anything" (pp. 136-138; emphasis in the original). As Quinney saw it, the problem was not to understand some reality that stood apart from the observer but rather to formulate ideas that were helpful in terms of one's purposes.

To criminologists untrained in philosophy, this may sound highly implausible or even ridiculous. Nevertheless, philosophical idealism (the theory that the world is a product of mind) has a long and distinguished history going back to Plato and beyond. It holds that what we take to be the objective world outside us is an image produced by our senses and the thoughts that interpret what they seem to reflect. Thus, for example, the world would be different for another creature with different senses and a different mind, and no creature's world is any more real than that of another. Labeling theory itself had represented a modest move in this direction, throwing light on crime as a matter of perception and definition. Quinney was going a step further, following the lead of the social constructionists in pointing out that social reality in general, as well as deviance or crime in particular, is a matter of changing perceptions and interpretations.

Many variations on some form of philosophical idealism were "blowing in the wind" in the 1960s, from the political commitment to achieving major social change through moral persuasion and nonviolence that Martin Luther King had learned from Gandhi to the "far-out" activities of the so-called countercultural yippies, who may be taken as an example of the extremes to which this approach can be taken. In some ways the 1960s seemed to be a time when it appeared possible to *change things* by *redefining them* through the development of a new consciousness. The more extreme version of such "consciousness politics" aimed at "blowing people's minds" is captured in the following summary:

> To blow people's minds was to confront them with a situation that could shatter their cultural assumptions and, perhaps, liberate them from ruling-class images. . . . Without question, the master mindblowers in the New Left were a scruffy band of self-described "anti-intellectual action freaks" who called themselves the Youth International Party (YIP).
>
> Lacking any theory or organization and with a narrow social base, the Yippies concentrated on tactics. They used dramatic irony to reveal absurd contradictions in a social order whose legitimacy depended on the appearance of rationality.
>
> The Yippies' first major prank was to shower dollar bills from the visitors gallery onto the floor of the New York Stock Exchange.
>
> The Yippies appeared naked in church; invaded university classrooms, where they stripped to the waist and French kissed; dressed as Keystone Kops and staged a mock raid on the State University of New York Stony Brook campus to arrest all the whiskey drinkers; planted trees in the center of city streets; dumped soot and smokebombs in Con Edison's lobby; and called a press conference to demonstrate a drug called "lace," which when squirted at the police, made them take their clothes off and make love. (Starr, 1985, pp. 267-270)

Quinney was no yippie, but he clearly was influenced by the pervasive sense of the way in which the taken-for-granted aspects of social life were really a matter of collective definitions with which people went along largely without thinking. His position was laid out in greater detail in *The Social Reality of Crime* (Quinney, 1970b). There Quinney developed an analysis of the social reality of crime, drawing from Schutz (1962), Berger and Luckmann (1966), and others. Whatever physical reality may be, these theorists had argued that *social reality* consisted of the "meaningful world of everyday life" that was tied together by the fact that "human behavior is *intentional,* has *meaning* for the actors, is *goal-oriented,* and takes place with an *awareness* of the consequences" in such a way that the individuals share a collective reality made up of shared meanings and understandings (Quinney, 1970b, p. 14; emphasis in the original). For Quinney the theoretical problem lay in the exploration and explanation of the *phenomenological processes* by which this collective meaning is developed and sustained.

The theory set forth in *The Social Reality of Crime* consisted of six propositions, beginning with a general definition of crime in which it is to be regarded as "a definition of human conduct that is created by authorized agents in a politically organized society," followed by the proposition that "criminal definitions describe behaviors that conflict with the interests of segments of society that have the power to shape public policy" (Quinney, 1970b, pp. 15-16). Here Quinney indicated his indebtedness to both Vold and Turk; thus he observed that the probability of powerful segments of society formulating criminal definitions becomes greater with an increase in the conflict of interests between the segments of a society, and he insisted that the history of law reflected changes in the interest structure of society.

Quinney's (1970b) third proposition focused on the "law in action," asserting that "criminal definitions are *applied* by the segments of society that have the power to shape the enforcement and administration of criminal law" (p. 18; emphasis added). He argued that "the probability that criminal definitions will be applied is influenced by such community and organizational factors as (1) community expectations of law enforcement and administration, (2) the visibility and public reporting of offenses, and (3) the occupational organization, ideology, and actions of the legal agents to whom authority to enforce criminal law is delegated" (pp. 19-20). In a fourth proposition dealing with the sources of the behavior resulting in the criminal label, he asserted that "behavior patterns are structured in segmentally organized society in relation to criminal definitions, and within this context persons engage in actions that have relative probabilities of being defined as criminal" (p. 20). Taking the position that it is not the quality of the behavior but the action taken against it that makes it criminal, Quinney went on to say that "persons in the segments of society whose behavior patterns are not represented in formulating and applying criminal definitions are more likely to act in ways that will be defined as criminal than those in the segments that formulate and apply criminal definitions" (p. 21).

Quinney (1970b) argued further that the definitions of crime developed by certain social segments had to be successfully diffused within the overall society before the generally accepted social reality could be altered: "Conceptions of crime are constructed and diffused in the segments of society by various means of communication" (p. 22). His final proposition summarized the entire theoretical framework: "The social reality of crime is constructed by the formulation and application of criminal definitions, the development of behavior patterns related to criminal definitions, and the construction of criminal conceptions" (p. 23).

Four years later, however, Quinney (1974a, 1974b) published *Criminal Justice in America: A Critical Understanding* and *Critique of the Legal Order: Crime Control in Capitalist Society,* two volumes that reflected a significant shift to a Marxist approach. He now criticized not only positivism but also the sort of social constructionism and phenomenology that he had used so effectively 4 years earlier, charging that "positivists have regarded law as a natural phenomenon; social constructionists have regarded it relativistically, as one of man's conveniences; and even the phenomenologists, though examining underlying assumptions, have done little to provide or promote an alternative existence" (1974b, p. 15). Like Marx, he seems to have concluded that the point was not simply to understand social life as a collective construction but to change it, going on to say that "with a sense of the more authentic life than may be possible for us, I am suggesting that a critical philosophy for understanding the social order should be based on a development of Marxist thought for our age" (p. 15).

This shift in thinking was influenced by his reading of the work of the Frankfurt school of German social theorists, including Marcuse (1960, 1964, 1972) and Habermas (1970, 1971), recent American work in the revived Marxist tradition mentioned previously (Baran & Sweezy, 1966; Edwards, Reich, & Weisskopf, 1972; Milibrand, 1969), and by his own interpretation of the backlash, particularly the "War on Crime" as it had developed in the Johnson and Nixon administrations. Just when Chambliss and Quinney were calling for further change, the backlash appeared, exemplified initially by the crackdown on crime in the Johnson administration and then by the election of Richard Nixon, a political figure who had been rejected twice by the voters in the early 1960s only to be elected president by the end of the decade. Although criminologists such as Chambliss and Quinney were crying for *more* reform, the voters were electing a president who promised just the opposite.

It is also apparent that Quinney himself felt, much like many people around him, that the foundations of American life had to be changed if people were to regain a more "authentic existence." Quinney's (1974b) six Marxist propositions read as follows:

> (1) American society is based on an *advanced capitalist economy;* (2) The state is organized to serve the interests *of the dominant economic class,* the capitalist ruling class; (3) Criminal law is an instrument of the state and ruling class to *maintain and perpetuate the existing social and economic order;* (4) Crime control in capitalist society is accomplished through a variety of institutions and agencies *established and administered by a governmental elite,* representing ruling class interests, for the purpose of establishing domestic order; (5) The contradictions of advanced capitalism—the disjunction between existence and essence—require *that the subordinate classes remain oppressed by whatever means necessary,* especially through the coercion and violence of the legal system; and (6) Only with the collapse of capitalist society and the creation of a new society, *based on socialist principles,* will there be a solution to the crime problem. (p. 16; emphasis added)

This line of argument followed Engels in asserting that the institution of the political state arises only at a point in the development of society when private property appears and then becomes concentrated in the hands of a few and that the law is "the ultimate means by which the state secures the interests of the ruling class" (Quinney, 1974b, p. 98). Developing the argument contained in *The Social Reality of Crime* in a Marxist direction, Quinney (1974b) maintained that the clever manipulations of the ruling class were obscured by an ideology serving to justify the system and that "manipulating the minds of the people is capitalism's most subtle means of control" (p. 137). He stressed that the sort of socialism advocated was not that of a centralized state bureaucracy such as existed in the (then) Soviet Union and some East European societies but rather a "democratic socialism" based on equality and giving everyone a chance to participate in control over his or her own life (p. 188).

Quinney's thought continued to evolve in reaction to criticisms leveled at Marxist criminology and newer contributions to Marxist theory. Three years later he published *Class, State, and Crime* (1977), a volume in which he criticized recent theories of justice, arguing that they all were rooted in an implicit acceptance of the current economic order. He now laid great stress on the Marxist argument that capitalism generates a *surplus population* made up of unemployed laborers. The general problem of the capitalist state was seen as providing support for the growth of capitalism while trying to manage the resulting problems by such mechanisms as the welfare state and the criminal justice system. According to Quinney (1977), some members of the surplus population are not co-opted by such mechanisms as the welfare system, especially in view of the fact that capitalism finds it difficult to fund this mechanism adequately. They may adapt to their plight by turning to crime. "Nearly all crimes among the working class in capitalist society," he held, "are actually a means of survival, an attempt to exist in a society where survival is not assured by other, collective means" (p. 58).

At the same time, he moved from a position that seemed to suggest that the state was in the hands of a powerful and all-seeing elite to one emphasizing a dialectical concept of social class. Thus Quinney (1977) asserted that "a theory which posits an opposition between an elite (or a 'ruling class') and the 'masses' (or the 'people') fails to provide an adequate understanding of the forces of capitalist society" (p. 64). His new emphasis was closer to a structural Marxism that saw political outcomes as natural results of the dynamics of the economic system than to an instrumental Marxism that saw political strings being pulled by a small elite looking out for itself. Crime was considered in Engels's terms as a "primitive form of insurrection, a response to deprivation and oppression," but one that "in itself is not a satisfactory form of politics" (pp. 98-99). Although there were still signs of the older conception of the politicality of crime, crime was now considered clearly an unsatisfactory form of politics: It was not a sufficiently rational response to oppression unless it succeeded in developing a revolutionary consciousness so that it represented an *informed rebellion* against capitalist conditions.

Class, State, and Crime also presented a typology of crime, including *crimes of domination* and *crimes of accommodation and resistance.* Crimes of domination were said to include *crimes of control* (e.g., police brutality), *crimes of the government* (e.g., Watergate-style offenses), and *crimes of economic domination* (e.g., white-collar crime and organized crime). Crimes of accommodation and resistance were said to include *predatory crimes* (e.g., theft) and *personal crimes* (e.g., homicide), which were provoked by the conditions of capitalism, and *crimes of resistance* (e.g., terrorism), which involved the political struggle against the state.

Throughout Quinney's theoretical turns there was a constant tension between the realms of the subjective and the objective. Although *The Social Reality of Crime* had taken a subjectively oriented, phenomenological, or constructionist view of the world, *Critique of Legal Order* had thrown him into a Marxist tradition of strict *materialism*, a tradition that not only explicitly rejected philosophical idealism but that regarded it as the enemy. This tension broke through in the second edition of *Class, State, and Crime* (Quinney, 1980), which is heavily theological in content. Indeed, it is interesting that current textbooks tend to remain content with an examination of Quinney's social reality period and his later Marxism without mention of this later development, almost as if it is either embarrassing or irrelevant. It was certainly not irrelevant to Quinney, whose thought tended thereafter to deal less with criminology per se and more with existential philosophy and theology.

In the preface to the second edition of *Class, State, and Crime* Quinney (1980) argued that "ultimately, the answer to the human predicament is a salvation achieved through the overcoming and healing of the disparity between existence and essence" (p. ix). Although continuing to advocate a socialist solution to the crime problem, he increasingly emphasized the *religious* nature of the goal, going so far as to reject Marxist materialism in favor of the theology of Tillich: "The contemporary capitalist world is caught in what Tillich, going beyond Marx's materialistic analysis of capitalism, calls a *sacred void*, the human predicament on both a spiritual and a sociopolitical level" (Quinney, 1980, p. 3; emphasis in original). The deeper problem was described as follows: "Among the vacuous characteristics of present civilization are a mode of production that enslaves workers, an analytic rationalism that saps the vital forces of life and transforms all things (including human beings) into objects of calculation and control, a loss of feeling for the translucence of nature and the sense of history, a demotion of our world to a mere environment, a secularized humanism that cuts us off from our creative sources, a demonic quality to our political state, and a hopelessness about the future" (p. 3). Returning to the theme of justice and citing the biblical prophets, he asserted that "justice is more than a normative idea; it is charged with the transcendent power of the infinite and the eternal, with the essence of divine revelation" (pp. 30-31). What was necessary, he now argued, was a "prophetic understanding" of reality (p. 40).

Much of the second edition of *Class, State, and Crime* was devoted to discussions of the religious implications of socialism. "The rise of political consciousness in the late stage of capitalism," Quinney (1980) asserted, "is increasingly accompanied by a consciousness about matters of ultimate concern" (p. 112). He held that Marx had erred in considering religion merely the "opium of the people" and that "a social criticism that does not consider the sacred meaning of our existence systematically excludes the full potential and essence of our being" (p. 199). "Prophetic criticism," he held, "takes place with an awareness of divine involvement in history." Quinney drew heavily from theological writings such as Tillich's work on religious socialism, seeing the effort in this direction as one in which "we hope to recover our wholeness, to heal our estrangement from the source of our being." "The socialist struggle in our age," he concluded, "is a search for God at the same time that it is a struggle for justice in human society" (p. 204).

Conflict Theory and the Causes of Crime

During the 1960s many criminologists had turned away from the search for the causes of crime. As we have seen, control theory focused on the sources of *conformity*, under the assumption that crime and delinquency should be expected when there was a decline in the holding power of the conformity influences. Labeling theory treated crime as a matter of definition, with the source of the definition being the labelers. The early work of the conflict theorists Turk, Chambliss, and Quinney explored the criminalization process with a focus on factors that might explain *the behavior of the authorities* rather than that of the offenders.

Still, criminological conflict theory did have something to say about the causes of offenders' behavior. We already have seen some examples. Turk had referred to cultural and social norms; Chambliss had considered crime as a rational reaction to exploitation; Quinney had discussed the politicality of crime as involving the use of the only available and appropriate means to express certain thoughts and bring about certain changes. The question of causality, however, became more important in the criminological conflict theory that began to appear with the shift in the social climate at the end of the 1960s and the beginning of the 1970s. Although mentioning possible sources of offenders' behavior from time to time, the earlier conflict theorists had concentrated on the way in which the traditional search for causes of criminal and delinquent behavior had deflected attention away from the fact that crime was the result of the criminalization of certain behavior by the powerful. Having made the point so powerfully, criminological conflict theory then turned more attention to the sources of the *behavior* that was being criminalized.

Early in the 1970s, for example, Gordon (1971) offered a Marxist economic analysis that traced a great deal of crime to the underlying economic structure of American society. He attempted to show how many crimes represented a rational response to the fact that the economic position of many people was kept in constant danger by the very nature of capitalism. By the middle of the decade, Spitzer (1976) had set forth the argument that capitalism generated both a *surplus population* that consisted essentially of economic outcasts and a series of *internal contradictions* in the institutions developed to maintain capitalist domination. He maintained that members of the surplus population were chronically unemployed outsiders who sometimes turned to deviant behavior including crime and that additional deviance resulted from the tensions in such institutions as schools, which are said to serve youth but really serve the ruling class.

Focusing on the sources of delinquency, Greenberg (1977), for example, argued that theft was one response to a situation in which adolescents in capitalistic society were put under heavy pressure to spend considerable money in a consumption-oriented youth culture even as the economic system was eliminating their employment opportunities. This lack of employment opportunities was said to produce considerable anxiety about prospects for achieving secure adult status, just at a time when institutions such as the school were taking away any sense of independence and subjecting the young people warehoused there to a variety of humiliating experiences. Greenberg maintained that such circumstances tended to produce a deep resentment and fear of failure that precipitated violent behavior, itself a reflection of a demand for respect.

Early in the 1980s Colvin and Pauly (1983) attempted to combine control theory with a Marxist approach to social class issues. In their view, capitalist society tended to exert a pattern of "coercive control" over the lower classes, threatening those at or near the bottom with loss of jobs or of any economic assistance unless they conformed completely to the expectations of the powerful. Colvin and Pauly maintained that this pressure produced an "alienative involvement" on the part of those under such oppression, breaking what Hirschi might term their "bonds to society" and increasing the likelihood of criminal activity.

A number of other conflict theorists have also attempted to say something about the causes of criminal and delinquent behavior, but the focus has remained on the notion of crime as an outcome of definitions imposed as part of the consequences of conflict among various segments of society. Seen this way, the central theoretical problem still is to understand the nature of social conflict. Some of the more recent developments in criminological conflict theory will be examined in Chapter 7.

Consequences of Conflict Theory

Criminological conflict theory has had notable consequences in terms of subsequent theorizing and rethinking within mainstream criminology but has had relatively little direct impact on social policy. As indicated earlier, and as we will see in greater detail in Chapter 8, the period of social turmoil that gave rise to contemporary criminological conflict theory was followed by a period of exhaustion and a social backlash of conservatism—as if people were trying to pretend that the 1960s had not happened and were determined to recapture the sense of tranquillity of the complacent 1950s. Some of the conflict perspective could be integrated into contemporary criminological theory and applied to social policy, but much was rejected. What was accepted and what was rejected depended primarily on whether the formulations called for further social reform in the tradition of some of the earlier theories or demanded social revolution.

Turk's conflict approach had been formalized highly and had treated conflict patterns as essentially inevitable, so it was not to be expected that his theoretical perspective would lead to specific alterations in social policy. It did, however, have considerable impact not only within criminology but also within the more general field of "deviant behavior" studies. The concept of "criminal" as a *status* assigned by the authorities as a result of a process working itself out through conflict probabilities was especially appealing to those with a formal, sociological orientation who were interested in the conflict perspective but were put off by the ideological fervor of many Marxists.

As for the conflict perspective presented by Chambliss in *Crime and the Legal Process* and elaborated in the later work with Seidman, it is worth noting that a number of the policy implications inherent in that approach already had been addressed by the U.S. Supreme Court under Chief Justice

Earl Warren. Indeed, the Warren Court was in its own way as much a part of the turbulent 1960s as was the civil rights movement, the counterculture, and the Vietnam protests. Years before Chambliss began his work, the Warren Court had shown considerable appreciation for the legal realists' distinction between the law in the books and the law in action. It had extended the legal rights of convicted offenders as well as suspects and private citizens to provide them with additional protections in their struggles with the bureaucratic agendas of the police, courts, and corrections. Chambliss himself was well aware of this, and he actually dedicated his first book to Chief Justice Warren. It is ironic that it appeared at the time of President Nixon's appointment of the conservative Warren Burger to replace the retiring Earl Warren, which took the Court back into a posture that gave much *less* attention to the way in which the law in action might differ from the law in the books.

Chambliss's use of the tradition of legal realism has been of considerable influence within criminology and, like Turk's work, has been influential also within the field of deviant behavior studies. Quinney's early work had essentially the same theoretical implications as Turk's, but any interpretation of its policy implications depends on one's interpretation of philosophical idealism. As noted earlier, Quinney later decided that his earlier phenomenological, constructionist approach tended to impede efforts to change things. Nevertheless, the earlier position seems to have had more impact on both criminological thought and deviant behavior studies than his later Marxist or theological approaches. The concept of crime as a result of the "social construction of reality" is broader still than labeling theory, and the general perspective has become extremely influential in the larger field of "social problems" theory (Ball & Lilly, 1982).

As long as the conflict theories went only one step further than the theories tracing crime to criminogenic elements in society as discussed in Chapter 3 or the labeling theories pointing to the relativity of crime as discussed in Chapter 5, they tended to strengthen the case for policies of social reform suggested by those perspectives. In fact, they gave the appearance of greater political realism. They recognized that the inequalities stressed by the opportunity theories and the stigmatizing processes emphasized by the labeling theories had a great deal to do with the perceived interests of the powerful, and they suggested how the powerful and the bureaucracies representing them might be held more accountable. Thus, for example, some of the radicals took an active part in community campaigns to curb police brutality, raise bail for poor defendants, abolish the death penalty, stop the repression of political dissidents, and provide support for prisoners (Greenberg, 1981). Some pushed for policies allowing for greater social diversity without criminalization of those who were different and for more informal, community-based policies of conflict accommodation such as arbitration, informal dispute settlement, and conflict resolution through negotiation outside the mechanisms of the political state (Mathiesen, 1974; Pepinsky, 1976; Quinney, 1974b).

But when they called for the abolition of capitalism, the radical criminologists produced mostly charges of either misunderstanding Marxism (which indicated that they were not to be taken seriously) or of understanding it too well (which indicated that they were dangerous revolutionaries of the sort Senator McCarthy had warned America against in the 1950s). This was in general the fate of the later work of both Chambliss and Quinney.

Even if society had been ready for further dramatic social change in the late 1970s, the problem of policy impact probably would have remained simply because of the inability or unwillingness of Marxist conflict theorists to provide blueprints for policy. The tendency of Marxists was to condemn capitalism and insist that individuals equipped with a revolutionary consciousness would be able to work their way through policy changes as they came. They generally held, for example, that it was too early to try to spell out exactly what law and criminal justice (if such continued to exist) would look like under democratic socialism. Although some were willing to predict, for example, that prisons probably still would be needed, although for many fewer prisoners in a very different setting, others were less inclined to offer blueprints for the future. Although this stance can be understood in terms of the Marxist focus on principles of dialectical logic, it made no sense to contemporary policy makers (and many criminological theorists) who knew and trusted only the instrumental logic of ends-means calculation that insists that the policy makers spell out precisely what they expect to find at the end of the political journey before undertaking it in the first place (Ball, 1978, 1979).

Although conflict theory had little direct impact on social policy, it has had a great deal of impact within criminology itself. It led to considerable rethinking as to the nature of law, with most textbooks taking a more critical stand than was the case at the beginning of the 1960s. More recent criminological conflict theorists working in the Marxist tradition have moved toward structural Marxism and away from the instrumental Marxism that seemed so close to the notion of a conspiracy of dominance by a tiny elite at the top. This instrumental Marxism had tended to portray the capitalist elite as an omniscient few who knew everything and always pulled the strings at exactly the right moment to see that their interests were served. Structuralism locates the basis of social control factors such as law in class *relations* generally rather than asserting that it was entirely within the total, conscious control of the capitalists at all times. Structural Marxism bears a resemblance to the formalism of Simmel, Vold, and Turk because it maintains that social conflict is a matter of the inherent social dynamics of a particular system. It differs by taking a more historically relative position, maintaining that the key to understanding these dynamics lies not in formal logic that deals with social systems *in the abstract* but in a dialectical logic that is rooted in an understanding of the structural features of capitalism *in particular.*

At the same time that the Marxist conflict theories were attacking capitalism, they had criticized conventional criminology. This criticism had consequences, even if only in making it more difficult to be complacent about the field. These criticisms included charges that conventional criminology was itself a part of the capitalist system and tended to support it, thereby contributing to the crime problem rather than to its understanding or its solution. The more radical conflict theorists insisted that conventional criminology had tended to accept the law as given, concentrating on the behavior of the offender and searching for some pathological source of this behavior in biological, psychological, or social factors. They maintained that this very search tended to exaggerate the notion that the criminal was in some important way "different from the rest of us" when in fact the problem lay in the creation and enforcement of the laws that produced the criminals. Some demanded that crimes also be considered from the perspective of the criminal, using the writings of prisoners as part of an attempt to escape a narrow, class-biased point of view.

Some of the radical criminologists leveled heavy criticisms at the efforts of conventional criminology to maintain a value-free, "scientific" posture that refused to get involved in political debate or political action, insisting that scientific criminology confine itself to the "facts." This position went back to the development of the positivistic approach discussed in Chapter 2. By refusing to take a moral stand, the critics of positivism charged, conventional criminology was accepting implicitly the moral ideology provided by the powerful and forced on the powerless. When mainstream criminologists responded that they not simply were accepting the ideology of the powerful at all but in fact were operating on the basis of broad social consensus, the radicals argued that this public consensus was a misleading mirage based on the power of the elite to shape public opinion (Michalowski & Bolander, 1976; Quinney, 1970b; Reiman, 1979). As such, it seemed to them to represent a "manufactured consensus" (Greenberg, 1981, p. 9). Indeed, conventional criminologists seemed to some of them to "reproduce the hegemony of the existing relations of property, race, and sexual privilege," either "to regain prestige, to build research empires, or because they truly believe in the ideas of those in positions of power" (Krisberg & Austin, 1978, p. 119).

Even the reforms urged by conventional criminology, the radical theorists had insisted, were simply minor tinkering that tended to support the further survival of a corrupt social system by making it appear that the powerful do care and that progress is being made toward economic and political justice. Meanwhile, they added, conventional criminology was providing the knowledge necessary to detect and control those seen as threats to the powerful. Thus, for example, Platt (1969) had argued that the original establishment of the juvenile court was not a means of helping youth but rather a technique by which upper-class, Republican, Protestant women extended control over the children of the Catholic and Jewish immigrants. In a similar vein, the concept of rehabilitation was criticized as a tool of political oppression that justified prolonged and invasive tinkering with the minds and bodies of prisoners under the guise of assisting them (Smith & Fried, 1974; Wright, 1973).

One does not have to accept radical conflict theory to realize that it is easy to be taken in by the assumptions of the times. Indeed, this volume itself represents an effort to show how thinking about crime is shaped intimately by the nature of social context. Complacency has no place in criminology, and conflict theory, especially of the radical variety, is anything but complacent. Whatever its defects, criminological conflict theory certainly has succeeded in providing for a broadened reorientation and an increased sensitivity to issues previously overlooked or treated only in passing (Thomas & Hepburn, 1983).

7

NEW DIRECTIONS
IN CRITICAL THEORY

Criminological theory, as this book demonstrates, has a long and productive history. In this chapter we introduce two additional perspectives that have been developed in response to theoretical arguments and empirical results, as well as to societal changes: feminist perspectives on crime and recent developments in what once was called the "new criminology."

Feminist Perspectives

Background

Before examining contemporary feminist perspectives in criminological theory, we first must recognize that feminism's roots rest in antiquity. Among other origins, it has been traced to the Roman Empire, where several women championed emancipatory issues. Cornelia, the "Romans' own 'favorite woman,' " led a reform movement of the plebeians against the patricians (Boulding, 1992, p. 8). Even after social unrest that saw the death of her two sons, she remained a voice for equality and became an international figure visited by men of affairs seeking her advice. A monument erected to her by the Romans indicates the reverence in which she was held. Two other Roman women, Seneca and her mother Helvia, both taught the equality of the sexes to their offspring and were promoters of women's emancipation (Boulding, 1992). Although their actions did not constitute a sea change ending the subordination of women and others, neither did emancipatory issues disappear throughout the ages.

The beginning of the first wave of the feminist perspective in the United States is located conventionally in the mid-19th century when the first women's rights convention was held at Seneca Falls, New York, in 1848 (Daly & Chesney-Lind, 1988, p. 497). From this meeting's "Declarations of Sentiments and Resolutions" it was resolved that "the history of mankind is the history of repeated injuries and usurpations on the part of man toward woman, having in direct object the establishment of an absolute tyranny over her" (Miles, 1989, p. 221).

This resolution and the first wave of the feminist perspective was itself part of another emancipatory movement, the abolition of slavery. In fact, Miles (1989) argued that of "all the causes that fuelled the fight for the rights of women, most important was the parallel struggle against the slavery of the southern states in America" (p. 242). This and the feminist struggle, however, reached beyond the United States to include some European countries. But it was from England during the 1840 World Anti-Slavery Congress that abolitionists "imparted their feminist vision to their American sisters" (p. 237). This was a major impetus for the 1848 Seneca Falls convention. But as important as the antislavery and women's movements were as mid-19th-century emancipatory developments, they were not the only two social struggles.

It is well to remember that the early to mid-19th century witnessed what some have termed the apex of one of the most profound and dramatic transformations in history—the industrial revolution. Begun in the mid-18th century in England, by the mid-19th century it, coupled with the rise of capitalism, largely had changed traditional family and village economies into factory production. One result was the near destruction of what had been previously a valued and necessary "household" partnership between spouses, their offspring, and extended households. Writing from Paris in 1848, the utopians Marx and Engels (1848/1992) argued in their *Communist Manifesto* that the bourgeoisie had:

> pitilessly torn asunder the motely feudal ties that bound man to his "natural superiors," and . . . left remaining no other nexus between man and man than naked self-interest, than callous "cash payment." It . . . drowned the

most heavenly ecstasies of religious fervor, of chivalrous enthusiasms, of phil-
istine sentimentalism, in the icy water of egotistical calculation. It has resolved personal worth into exchange value, and in place of the numberless
indefeasible chartered freedoms, has set up that single, unconscionable freedom—Free Trade. In one word, for exploitation, veiled by religious and
political illusions, it has substituted naked, shameless, direct, brutal exploitation . . . [it] has reduced the family relation to a mere money relation. (pp.
20-21)

It is against this broader background of human struggle and exploitation that we now examine the feminist perspectives on criminology.

Early Pioneers and Themes

Until recent years the criminality of women had a long history of neglect; however, in both the late 19th and early to mid-20th centuries there
was a small group of writings specifically concerned with women and
crime. Throughout this early literature there were different analytical
approaches, yet there were many shared assumptions about the nature of
women and the crimes they committed (Klein, 1973). These assumptions
focused on crime as the result of *individual physiological* or *psychological*
characteristics of women. It was thought also that these characteristics were
universal to women and that they transcended any historical time frame.
Central, too, was the assumption that there is an *inherent nature of women*
(Klein, 1973).

The focus on crime as a result of *individual* characteristics rather than
on conditions in the existing social structure generated theoretical and
research attention directed toward determining the differences between
criminal and noncriminal women. One result was the creation of two
distinct classes of women: good women who are not criminal and bad
women who are criminal (Klein, 1973). Built into this distinction was
another important assumption: Crime resulted from individual choices.
Women, therefore, were conceptualized as freely choosing to act criminal
or noncriminal, void of any influences from the social, economic, and
political world.

Cesare Lombroso. Often called the father of modern criminology (see
Chapter 2), Lombroso had a great interest in tracing an overall pattern of
evolution in the human species. According to his arguments, evolution
accounts for the uneven development of groups. For instance, Whites were

more advanced than non-Whites, men more than women, and adults more than children. In 1903 he published *The Female Offender* (1903/1920) in which he described female criminality as an inherent tendency of women who, in effect, had not developed properly into feminine women with moral refinements. He buttressed his argument with physiological evidence that he thought explained why female criminals were biological atavists. Included here were cranial and facial features, moles, height, dark hair, and skin color. Short, dark-haired women with moles and masculine cranial and facial features were good candidates for crime.

He went further than this, however, and argued that women were characterized also by physiological immobility, psychological passivity, and amorality featuring a cold and calculating predisposition. Criminal women, then, were in fact more *masculine* than feminine; they could "think like a man" whereas "good women" could not. Criminal women were thought also to be "stronger" in some ways than men. Lombroso concluded that criminal women could, for instance, adjust more easily than men to mental and physical pain. As an example he argued that criminal women often adjusted so well to prison life that it hardly affected them at all. For Lombroso, criminal women were abnormal.

W. I. Thomas. A modified emphasis on the physiological explanations of female crime offered by Lombroso appeared in the work of W. I. Thomas (1863-1947). Born in an isolated region of Virginia and a graduate of the University of Tennessee, Thomas wrote his doctoral dissertation in sociology, "On a Difference in the Metabolism of the Sexes," at the University of Chicago (where he taught his first sociology course in 1886). He wrote two influential books on sexual behavior and society, *Sex in Society* (1907) and *The Unadjusted Girl* (1923). Separated by 16 years between publication, the shift in emphasis in these books moved the discussions of women's behavior to more sophisticated theories that "embrace physiological, psychological and social-structural factors" (Klein, 1973, p. 11).

In *Sex and Society* (1907) Thomas began by offering the age-old dichotomy that men and women are fundamentally different. For Thomas, men are destructive of energy and what can flow from it, although women store energy much like plants; they are more motionless and conservative than men. This difference has contributed, according to Thomas, to a relative decline in the stature of women, especially in "civilized" societies. Thomas was ambivalent as to why the stature of women had declined, however. At one point he attributed it to a lack of superior motor fitness on the part of women. At another point he argued that women's decline can be explained by their loss of sexual freedom. Women, he claimed, under the development of monogamy, had to confine their sexual behavior to being wives and mothers and adjust to the fact they were treated as property controlled by men.

Underlying these arguments of the inferior status of women is a focus primarily on *physiological* issues. Men, for instance, have more sexual energy than women. This allows men to pursue women for sexual reasons, who in turn exchange sex for domesticity (Klein, 1973). In essence, monogamy and chastity become a form of accommodation to men's basic urges.

In *The Unadjusted Girl* (1923) Thomas shifted his position on female criminality in two directions. First, he argued that female delinquency is normal under certain circumstances given certain assumptions about the nature of women. Unfortunately, Thomas does not specify the nature of his "assumptions about the nature of women" (Klein, 1973, p. 14).

Second and more important, however, is his shift in focus from punishing criminals to *rehabilitation* and *prevention*. This point represented a radical departure from the Lombrosian biological position, which claimed that crime-prone individuals must be locked away or sterilized as a preventive strategy (Klein, 1973). One important implication that followed was Thomas's contention that there is no individual who cannot be made socially useful (Thomas, 1923). For him, individuals could be socialized to prevent antisocial attitudes, even if they had been poorly socialized in a slum family or neighborhood. The key to this strategy lay in how individuals were taught to define the situation. Thomas claimed that the way to prevent women dissatisfied with their conventional sexual roles from committing crime, for instance, was to socialize them to change their attitudes. In other words, they needed to adjust to the situation by first redefining it as acceptable. This, he explained, was one of the important reasons why middle-class women commit so little crime; they had been socialized to accept their position and to treasure their chastity as an investment (Klein, 1973). Lower-class women, on the other hand, had not been socialized to suppress their need for security and instead committed crimes rather inadvertently out of a desire for excitement and new experiences (Klein, 1973). Sexual behavior in delinquent girls, Thomas maintained, was used as a means for realizing other wishes.

Despite Thomas's shift in focusing attention away from biological determinism and toward rehabilitation, he nevertheless relied on the ever-present dichotomy of the good and bad woman to explain female crime. Bad women exploited men for fulfillment of their desires; good women used sex as a protective measure against the future and uncertainty. Not unlike other men who had attempted to explain female crime, Thomas also underemphasized the importance of economic factors in favor of psychological characteristics.

Sigmund Freud. A similar emphasis is found in the work by Freud. For him, the position of women was based on explicit biological assumptions about their nature. In essence, for Freud, "anatomy is destiny," and because women's anatomy is inferior to men's, it is appropriate that compared to men, women are destined to occupy an inferior social status, including being mothers and wives (Klein, 1973, p. 16). The specific anatomical characteristics that Freud considered were men's and women's sex organs. According to Freud, the inferiority of women's sex organs is recognized universally. Beginning in childhood, for example, male and female children are aware of this distinction, and a girl grows up assuming she has lost her penis as a form of punishment. One central consequence, according to Freud, is that girls develop penis envy and become revengeful, whereas boys come to dread their envy and vengeance.

An additional difference between men and women based on women's anatomical inferiority, according to Freud, is the fact that women also develop an inferiority complex and try to compensate for it by being exhibitionistic, narcissistic, and well dressed (Klein, 1973). This concern with personal matters helps to explain why women have, again according to Freud, little sense of justice, scant broad social concerns, and few significant contributions to building civilization. Because they cannot sublimate their individual needs, they are concerned with marginal matters. Men, on the other hand, as builders of civilization, recognize that individual urges, especially the sex drive, must be repressed in order to get on with worldly affairs. Otherwise little of lasting value would be accomplished or produced. Men, therefore, are rational, and women are irrational.

In this framework, "the deviant woman is one who is attempting to be a *man*" (Klein, 1973, p. 17, emphasis in the original). Female aggression and rebellion, for instance, are expressions of longing for a penis, and if not "treated" women will only end up "neurotic." Freudian-based treatment for women, therefore, is intended to have them adjust to appropriate sex roles. Again, as we have seen, the emphasis is placed on changing women to fit into society as defined by men, rather than changing society. To be normal, women must adjust and accommodate to the glorified duties of wives and mothers at the expense of gender equality. As Klein (1973) observed, one clear implication of Freud's logic is a class bias: "Only upper and middle class women could possibly enjoy lives as sheltered darlings" (p. 18). The lives of poor and Third World women are not so fortunate.

Another important implication is that Freudianism has had a powerful influence in transforming a gender and sexual ideology of proper female behavior and sexuality into a *scientific* framework. As such, Freudianism has been used for decades to maintain female sexual repression, sexual passivity, and the "woman's place" in the nuclear family. This legacy influenced the writing of many scholars, including Otto Pollak.

Otto Pollak. For Pollak, one of the most influential post-World War II scholars in the field of female crime, female involvement in crime compared to male involvement was largely "hidden" from public view (Klein, 1973, p. 21; Pollak, 1950). Pollak advanced this theory based on the idea that women are inherently deceitful because of physiological reasons. Because men, unlike women, must achieve an erection to perform the sex act, he reasoned that they cannot hide their emotion nor deny their failure to perform sexually. Women's *physiological* nature, however, permits them to a degree to hide their emotional involvement in sex. Women, Pollak suggested, are therefore innately deceitful. When combined with the domestic opportunities they have as maids, nurses, teachers, and homemakers, this deceitful nature permits them to commit undetectable crime (Klein, 1973).

Women are also vengeful, according to Pollak, especially during their menstrual period. During this time, women once again recognize that their "anatomy is destiny" and that any desire to be men is doomed. False accusations, for example, are typical female crimes because they are an outgrowth of their nature and treachery. Shoplifting, too, is a special type of female crime, reflecting the mental disease kleptomania.

A final factor that Pollak advanced for explaining female hidden crime is chivalry in the criminal justice system. His argument is that although there is no actual discrepancy between crime rates for men and women, women are treated differentially by the law, which keeps the rates of their crimes hidden (Pollak, 1950; Klein, 1973). He failed to consider that female criminals are often poor or women who have stepped outside of chauvinistic, classist, and racist definitions of women's proper roles.

Unfortunately, Pollak, like many other early theorists, failed to see that in some instances female crime can be explained by economic necessity. Instead, psychologically based and physiologically based sexual motives or mental illness often were invoked to explain female economic crimes. Only within the last few decades has this logic been challenged.

Recent Theorists

In 1961 criminologist Walter C. Reckless (1961) questioned whether any theory of delinquency would be accepted if a criminologist paused to consider if it applied to women. It was nearly a decade later, however, before Bernard (1969) and Heidensohn (1968) drew attention to the "omission of women from general theories of crime" and "signaled an awakening of criminology from its androcentric slumber" (Daly & Chesney-Lind, 1988, p. 507). Indeed, in hindsight the discovery of *women* as a conceptual term that could be incorporated into criminological theory has been called "quite literally, pioneering" (Young, 1992, p. 289).

Two issues were critical at this stage of the development of the feminist perspectives in criminology. The first issue was the uncertainty identified by Reckless of whether general theories of crime generated by men to explain crime by men and boys could be applied or generalized to women and girls. The second issue involved social structure and categories of risk. The question here was whether class, race, and age structures found to be the core of criminological theory for males also held for gender. This issued addressed the gender-based ratio question of why women commit less crime than men (Daly & Chesney-Lind, 1988).

Early feminist writing in criminology did not always focus on these problems, however, and centered instead on what British criminologist Gelsthorpe (1988) called criminologists' "amnesia" of women (p. 98). What followed was a number of critiques on the intellectual and institutional sexism found in explanations of female crime and criminal justice systems (Daly & Chesney-Lind, 1988). Some feminist writings focused on how women were represented or misrepresented in conventional criminological literature. This work, essentially a critique of "accumulated wisdom" about female offenders (cf. in Britain, Campbell, 1981; Smart, 1976), was of immense importance for demonstrating that theories of criminality developed by and "validated on men had limited relevance for explaining women's crime" (Gelsthorpe, 1988, p. 98). Examples of such work abound and are found easily in leading criminology texts.

For many generations of American criminologists, no better example exists than the rabbit hole through which so many of them "fell" into the study of crime and justice, Sutherland and Cressey's *Criminology* (1970). Of the many introductory textbooks on criminology published in the United States so far, not one has been "born again" in as many editions as this book (Lilly & Jeffrey, 1979). Even its 11th edition published in 1992 contained no discussion of a feminist perspective per se on crime. Although recognizing that recent research indicates a narrowing of the sex ratio between men and women for some reported crimes, this relationship was explained partially as a result of modifications in law enforcement practices that witnessed changes in the "somewhat chivalrous treatment they [women] traditionally received" (Sutherland, Cressey, & Luckenbill, 1992, p. 162).

This type of explanation of female crime, although perhaps having some empirical basis, points to a wider and more serious shortcoming: Sutherland and other early criminologists had little or no understanding of the social worlds of women and girls. It is therefore not surprising that historical explanations of female crime and deviance often focused more on biological than social or economic forces (see Daly & Chesney-Lind, 1988; Heidensohn, 1985; Morris, 1987). Nor is it surprising that examinations of juvenile and criminal justice system responses to girls' misbehavior found that they were more concerned with girls' proper sexual behavior than for the sexual behavior of boys (Chesney-Lind, 1973). In fact there is very little juvenile justice system concern about boys' sexual behavior. This suggests a sexist ideology reflecting "a set of ideas about the place of women in the social order that emerged in the . . . nineteenth century . . . [I]t . . . placed men in the public sphere . . . and women in the private sphere" (Daly & Chesney-Lind, 1988, p. 509). Here men were found in the paid workforce, politics, and law while women were located as the moral guardians of the household and family life.

The first wave of feminism ended in the United States in 1920 with ratification of the 19th amendment to the U.S. Constitution, which gave nationwide suffrage to women. Second-wave feminism denounced the domestic or private "sphere as oppressive to women and sought to achieve equality with men in the public sphere" (Daly & Chesney-Lind, 1988, p. 509). This ideological shift contributed to the development of a number of feminist critiques of criminology and to additional questions about equality being raised by feminists.

Women's Emancipation and Crime

The late 1960s and early 1970s saw the beginning of renewed emphasis on women's issues, a development that came to be known as the women's movement. Born in part because of questions about social, political, and economic equality with men, it was to have a profound impact on the nation's social agenda, especially on how women and crime were examined. Prior to this development, criminologists often reported that women simply committed less and different crimes than men. Subsequent to an increased participation of women in the workforce, new explanations of female crime were developed.

In 1975 two controversial books—Adler's *Sisters in Crime* (1975) and Simon's *Women and Crime* (1975)—proposed ideas about women's criminality based on analyses of female arrest trends in the 1960s and early 1970s. Both books reached somewhat different conclusions but were largely "an outgrowth of the unexamined assumption that the emancipation of women resided solely in achieving legal and social equality with men in the public sphere" (Daly & Chesney-Lind, 1988, p. 510). Adler argued that a lifting of restrictions on women's opportunities in the marketplace gave them the chance to be as greedy, violent, and crime-prone as men. Simon read the evidence to conclude that women's increasing share of arrests for property crime (she found no increases for violent crime) might be explained by their increased opportunities in the workplace to commit crime. Simon also wondered if the emancipation of women might encourage law enforcement and courts to be more interested in treating men and women the same.

Both books attracted critical attention, and several scholars called into question many of the issues raised by Adler and Simon. Steffensmeier (1978, 1980) and his colleagues, for instance, found that research contradicted the view that women were committing more masculine, violent crimes. He did report that arrest rates for women had been increasing but that the gap between male and female crime rates was not closing. Rather, because female arrest rates have been so much lower than those of males historically, any small increase in the *absolute* number of female arrests show up as a *relatively* large percentage increase. However, Steffensmeier (1980) did find that there were rate increases for women in the larceny-theft category, a type of crime in which women always have been found in great numbers.

Steffensmeier (1981) also disputed the claim that changes in the occupational structure generated increases in women's white-collar crime. Here he argued that Simon was wrong to classify larceny, fraud, forgery, and embezzlement by women as traditional white-collar or occupational crime. Women, Steffensmeier argued, were not committing stock fraud or embezzling large sums of money. Instead, they were being arrested for shoplifting and for writing bad checks. For Steffensmeier, these crimes do not fit the white-collar criminal image presented by Simon. Overall, Steffensmeier and Cobb (1981) concluded that any increase in female arrest rates matches the daily activities of women, such as shopping and paying family bills, not those associated with occupational positions.

This raises an important question: If increased occupational opportunities do not explain increased female crime, what does? Two suggestions were offered by Steffensmeier. First, today there is greater opportunity than in the past for women to commit petty theft and fraud because of a self-service marketplace. With this type of market comes a greater availability of credit for women, which in turn provides new opportunities for old crimes: shoplifting, bad checks, and credit card fraud. These new opportunities also are associated with increased security and detection procedures, which improve the arrest rates for female offenders. Second, Steffensmeier and Cobb (1981) provided data indicating that law enforcement and court attitudes toward female offenders are changing and that now there is a greater willingness to arrest and prosecute them.

Steffensmeier and his colleagues, however, are not without their critics. Giordano, Kerbel, and Dudley (1981) argued that women's roles may be changing more gradually than can be measured in the relatively short time periods Steffensmeier examined. Giordano et al. analyzed police records from 1890-1976 and found that present-day female crime patterns differ greatly from those at the turn of the century. In the early years of the century high percentages of female arrests were for prostitution, a marked contrast with the reasons women were arrested in the late 20th century.

Herein lies, as critics have noted, a serious problem: the failure to examine whether the trends early research on female crime associated with the women's movement were actually occurring (Daly & Chesney-Lind, 1988). Were low-income women, as Adler argued, actually seeking equality with their male counterparts in the public sphere? Or as Simon claimed, were female arrests for property crime the result of opportunities? Or was their reading of the arrest data hampered by a liberal feminist perspective on gender that "ignores class and race differences among women, and defines gender either as the possession of masculine or feminine attitudes or as role differences between men and women" (p. 511)? Both books ignored the impact of power relations in a patriarchy where the social structure allows men control over women's labor and sexuality. By focusing on the public sphere's aspects of equality and opportunity of women compared to men, these scholars failed to consider one of the more important features of the dominant social structure—patriarchy.

Patriarchy and Crime

The "emancipation thesis" had great value in focusing attention on female crime, but it carried insights on female criminality only so far. Following Adler's and Simon's pioneering work, the next generation of feminist criminologists went from focusing on emancipation to patriarchy. As Akers (1994) noted, the theme today in current feminist theories of crime "are the pervasiveness of male dominance in patriarchal society and its impact on crimes committed both by and against women" (p. 175). This shift in attention seems to distinguish feminist theory of criminal behavior from the earlier focus on women's liberation. But it is not a total departure from criminological theories that focus on power such as conflict and Marxist theories. The difference, however, is on what "*type* of power is placed at the center" (p. 175; emphasis in original). Marxist theories of crime focus, for instance, on the power of the ruling class, and most conflict theories focus on the conflict between various powerful and powerless groups. For feminist theory, men's power over women is the dominant theme.

This emphasis fits nicely with feminists' contributions to our understanding of the nature of the crimes women commit as well as some of the crimes women experience at the hands of men. Thus power differences lead women into types of crime that are "powerless," such as prostitution and small-scale fraud (Messerschmidt, 1986). These crimes bring little reward because women are marginalized by economic destitution. As such, some female crime is a manifestation of and helps to reproduce sexual stratification in society (see also Cloward & Piven, 1979).

Rape, other forms of sexual abuse including date and marital rape, and domestic violence each has been explained by patriarchal dominance. Again, these crimes by men—and thus the victimization of women—reflect the ability of men to use their power against women. Unfortunately, thus far there has been relatively little research testing the notion that patriarchy explains female crime. The problem here is that as an independent variable, patriarchy is difficult to measure so that its explanatory value can be determined in different settings. Until this occurs, progress in assessing patriarchy theory will be slow.

Consequences of the Feminist Perspectives

Although the debate over women's emancipation and crime has not been very fruitful empirically, greater attention has been given to women as victims and survivors of sexual and physical violence (Daly & Chesney-Lind, 1988). Aided by the women's movement, popular and important works including Susan Brownmiller's famous *Against Our Will* (1975), and numerous media reports of women as victims and survivors (such as the 1993-1994 case of Lorena Bobbitt severing her husband's penis after years of alleged physical and psychological brutalization and the 1994 double murder of O. J. Simpson's former wife Nicole and her companion Ronald Goldman), this topic—especially rape and intimate violence—has become central to the feminist perspective in conventional criminology and to left realism, as well as in public consciousness (*New York Times,* 1994b, *Newsweek,* 1994).

According to some observers, there are several reasons why the victimization of women as a topic has had such relative success compared with explaining female crime by the emancipation movement. First, victimization of women and girls can be tied to a number of feminist perspectives including Marxist, social, and radical feminisms. This expansion of the explanation of female victimization has permitted men's violence against women to be more easily linked to some of the more salient features of patriarchy, especially power. Victimization of women is one way in which patriarchal power can be defined and perpetuated. Second, this linkage between patriarchy and power moved "large numbers of grass-roots feminists and some academic feminists to document the then-hidden forms of violence suffered almost exclusively by women" (Daly & Chesney-Lind, 1988, p. 513). Third, the whole milieu of the women's movement affected criminology, including nonfeminist criminologists who had to "digest and deal with feminist scholarship" (p. 513). The increasingly documented record of men's violence against women itself had to be integrated into criminology; it could not be ignored. Last, while these developments were taking place, more women and feminists were moving into criminology and other academic disciplines. Although this aspect of the feminist perspective in criminology has not been well charted, the presence and impact of women on criminology have been debated.

One indication of this impact is found in the presidency of the American Society of Criminology (ASC). Founded in 1941, ASC has had 39 different presidents, only three of whom have been women, and each of these have held office since 1989. The most recent female president of this organization, Professor Freda Adler, Rutgers University, was elected in 1993. The Academy of Criminal Justice Sciences (ACJS), by comparison, has had 28 presidents since its first one was elected in 1963, two of whom have been women. One female scholar held office in 1984-1985; another was elected to office in 1994. By 1994 a majority of ACJS's executive board members were women. These developments, especially the increased female membership in previously male-dominated professional organizations, were no doubt of great importance in developing a sense of urgency and affinity toward female victims (Daly & Chesney-Lind, 1988, p. 513).

Writing in 1977, British criminologist Paul Rock observed in a review of Smart's (1976) *Women, Crime and Criminology* that he doubted that "analytic losses" had been inflicted on criminological theory by not considering women. Today it is doubtful whether this conclusion would be accepted as much more than sexist rhetoric. More recently, in a brief review of the impact of feminist work on criminology, British criminologist Allison Young (1992) argued that by revealing the partiality and inaccuracy of conventional criminology regarding female crime, feminists sent a jolt "through the entire criminological enterprise" (p. 292). Slowly, she claimed, course syllabuses were altered to include women and crime, new courses were designed, and conferences began to include sessions on women and criminal justice. Texts, too, on deviance and criminology were revised to reflect feminists' arguments including, in Britain, Downes and Rock's classic *Understanding Deviance* (1988). In the United States, Sykes's *Criminology* (1978) contained only one feminist's interpretation of female property crime. Its second edition, however, contained an entire section titled "Feminist Criminology" (Sykes & Cullen, 1992). These changes and modifications were interpreted by one female observer as so influential as to have "revivified a discipline that had come to seem bogged down in its own internal arguments" (Young, 1992, p. 290). The question remains, nonetheless, whether today there is a "feminist criminology." The record appears to be mixed.

Addressing this question in 1988, Gelsthorpe concluded that the term *feminist criminology* as used then created confusion. There are two problems involved: One concerns just who the feminist criminologists are; the other more difficult issue questions the existence of core elements that would identify feminist criminology. Certainly, according to Gelsthorpe, *a* feminist criminology cannot exist, just as there cannot be *a* feminist sociology, history, philosophy, or any other single feminist discipline. There are multiple feminist perspectives in criminology. Some feminists argue that men and women should be dealt with equally by criminal justice systems; others claim they should be treated differently. Some argue that men and women differ in their capacity to commit crime; others disagree. Still others claim that feminist criminology should develop alternative interpretations of social reality; others argue that feminist criminology should focus on explaining the gross differences between men's and women's crime rates.

Although not dismissing the importance of these different emphases, Renzetti (1993) asked whether feminism has had enough of an impact to transform criminology/criminal justice education so that gender is a central organizing theme. Organizing her evaluation around curriculum, pedagogy, and campus climate for students and faculty, Renzetti concluded that feminist criminology/criminal justice education seems to remain at the margins of the "male-stream" (p. 219). In support of her conclusion, she pointed out that although women currently constitute more than 52% of the general undergraduate population, 40.4% of bachelor's degree recipients in criminology, and 68.4% of bachelor's degree recipients in sociology, they are still "largely invisible in our courses and textbooks" (p. 226). At best, she explained, women are marginalized in special courses as special topics or in separate token chapters. They are not integrated fully into the criminology/criminal justice curriculum.

Campus culture also has contributed to the marginalization of gender issues in criminology/criminal justice. Drawing on the work of McDermott (1992), Goodstein (1992), and Hall and Sandler (1985), Renzetti (1993) reported that classroom interaction patterns among faculty and students, including sexist humor and language, "breeds other, less subtle forms of discrimination including sexual harassment" (p. 228). According to Stanko (1992), this contributes to women's marginalization because these experiences are reminders that they are "only women."

Feminist critiques of traditional pedagogy and research methodologies denounce the rigid separation of the "knower" from the "known." Greater emphasis is placed on qualitative methodologies employing interactive or participatory research strategies. As Daly and Chesney-Lind (1988) stated, "They are more interested in providing texture, social context, and case histories . . . presenting accurate portraits of how . . . women become involved in crime" (p. 518). They object to insensitive quantification (Renzetti, 1993). More central to developing feminist criminologies is the emphasis on gender. This is not to deemphasize the feminist perspectives' concern about stereotypical images of women and methodologies sympathetic to these concerns (Gelsthorpe, 1988). Gender, however, is not only about women. As Renzetti (1993) explained, "the goal of feminism is not to push men out so as to bring women in, but rather to gender the study of crime" (p. 232). Theories that do not consider it not only are incomplete but also are misleading because gender carries great social, economic, and political significance (Gelsthorpe, 1988).

Additional consequences of the feminist perspectives on crime are found in a number of public social policies. Mandatory arrest for domestic violence, for example, is now widespread throughout the United States, although its long-term impact on domestic violence is questioned (Sherman, 1992). Changes in rape laws represent another example of the impact of the feminist perspectives on social policies. Traditionally, explanations of rape have focused on the sexual component of the offense with emphasis given to offenders' excessive sexual tensions or maladjustment and the manner in which the victims "asked for it." In recent years the focus has changed from defining and prosecuting rape as a sexual act to its treatment as an act of violence. Key to this shift in emphasis is recognizing that rape is an act of subjugation/domination reflecting cultural definitions of male roles. This interpretation emerged with the development of the women's movement and the feminist perspectives on crime and has been elaborated on by several observers. Susan Griffin (1971), for example, claimed that rape is ingrained deeply in patriarchal societies and is used as a form of mass terrorism to deny women self-determination.

Others have given attention to what now is called "date rape," a topic unthinkable a generation ago. The heart of the issue here is when is sex considered sex and when is sex considered rape. It developed in large measure as college women began to report that they were raped not by strangers, but by men they knew well or casually. As colleges and universities learned of this phenomenon, new reporting policies were created, and now the federal government and several states have laws requiring educational institutions to report crime statistics. Other responses include new college and university educational programs on acquaintance rape and consensual sexual relations (Celis, 1991).

Rape shield laws are another example of the impact of the feminist perspectives on criminal justice policy. These laws grew out of the need to protect rape victims from being raped twice, once by the accused and again by the accused's defense attorney probing the victim's past sexual behavior. Every state has adopted some type of rape shield law, but these laws vary considerably, especially regarding whether the victim previously had consensual sexual relationships with the defendant.

No one knows exactly how many women are raped annually, but it is clear that redefining rape as an act of violence, recognizing the existence of date and acquaintance rape, and the development of rape shield laws represent dramatic changes in how rape is defined and prosecuted. These are not, however, the only evidence of the influence of the feminist perspectives on rape. Now more and more rape victims are finding justice through civil courts; experts on rape say that the number of civil suits has grown from a few 15 years "ago to a steady stream, as women have become less ashamed by rape and more aware of the legal options for fighting back" (*New York Times*, 1991, p. A-1; copyright © 1991 by the New York Times Company. Reprinted by permission.).

The British Influence

Background

For a perspective with specific concern for the causes and for the social, economic, and political significance of crime, we turn to what in the late 1960s and early 1980s was called the "new" criminology. Known during this period by other terms—including Marxist criminology; materialist criminology; dialectical criminology; and radical, social, and critical criminology—today its heir apparent is left realism/realist criminology. Although this tradition experienced strong popularity and support on both sides of the Atlantic, of particular concern here is the British version of the new criminology because of the "exceptional success of radical criminology in this country" (Young, 1988, p. 159). (See Chapter 6 for a discussion that focuses primarily on U.S. theorists' work on social power and the construction of crime.) And of special importance beyond its appeal in Britain is the fact that it not only had a significant impact on academic criminology more than two decades ago, but also remains an important influence, albeit somewhat outside conventional criminology. Unlike so many criminological theories that have enjoyed relatively brief moments of popularity and then faded away, the new criminology had a brief period of decline and is now experiencing a resurgence of interest and influence.

Early on, it was much influenced by what Young (1988) identified as the "impact of the West Coast labelling theory centering around Howard Becker which set the creaking chariot of radical criminology off [in Britain] on its course" (p. 163). According to Young, this involved a transformation of U.S. ideas that, rather like popular music, play back to the United States the culture of Europe. But this development did not involve the simple translation of U.S. ideas to Britain. It was a transposition of ideas that had to travel "a considerable distance politically, culturally and, indeed, in terms of the contours of crime itself" (p. 163).

More than this specific influence was at work. In the late 1960s British criminology was at a crossroads because traditional positivism, with its emphasis on crude and simple biological, psychological, and sociological determinism, was in a crisis. The central problem was that unlike what traditional criminological explanations of crime would have predicted, a "wholesale improvement in social conditions resulted, not in a drop in crime, but the reverse" (Young, 1988, p. 159). Confounding as this problem was for conventional deterministic explanations of crime, it was not the only social abnormality that needed to be explained and corrected. It was part and parcel of a number of social problems challenging the British post-World War II welfare state, including urban housing problems and the destruction of communities, public health, and education issues. "Thus the crisis in criminology did not . . . come out of the blue, it was part . . . of the particular crisis in politics and culture . . . which was refracted in the internal problems of criminology" (p. 160). It is against this background that the new criminology in Britain emerged.

Theoretical Arguments

Published in 1973 (and still in print 20 years later) with a highly complimentary foreword by American sociologist Alvin Gouldner, this perspective's major tome, *The New Criminology* (Taylor et al., 1973), was described as so powerful in its critique of traditional criminology that "it redirects the total structure of technical discourse concerning 'crime' and 'deviance' " (Gouldner, 1973, p. ix). One year later Elliott Currie (1974) praised it as an important document in the "effort to build a more humane criminology" and "probably the most comprehensive critical review of 'the field' that has been produced so far" (p. 133). This radical criminology perspective was different in important ways from its counterpart in the United States. It was, for instance, often more intellectually sophisticated and well-grounded in criminology literature and continental philosophy than found in the United States. And unlike the minority position of radical criminology in the United States (Inciardi, 1980), it grew to share equal partnership with conventional criminology.

Central to its early development was its objections to (a) structural functionalism's assumption that the social order was based on a public consensus and (b) traditional criminology's overly deterministic treatment of crime. Writing of its early focus, Cohen (1988) stated: "The initial intellectual shape taken by the break . . . was a systematic attempt to overturn the taken-for-granted assumptions of the positivist criminological tradition" (p. 9). To overturn these assumptions the first job was to demonstrate that conventional studies of crime were too narrowly entrenched in more general theories and paradigms, which assumed they had a monopoly on the "correct," "scientific," and "deterministic" understanding of human nature and social order. To explain crime as the result of broken homes, for example, was too simple. The task facing the new criminology in part was to challenge successfully this narrow position and to demonstrate that conventional criminology was grounded in ideological constructs central to the policies of the state. The challenge required establishing that "there *was* a debate going on in criminology" over these issues (Young, 1988, p. 161; emphasis in original).

Next the task was to make crime the central focus of concern for social scientists, rather than a peripheral topic—for crime had been placed in an intellectual ghetto by traditional positivism. In other words, new criminology claimed that studying crime illuminates both social order and disorder. Crime is indeed not a marginalized topic, but a central plank of social scientists' explanations of stability and change. In order for this argument to take hold and change the direction of traditional criminology, the new criminology had to "undo the notion of . . . objectivity which [deterministic] positivism had created in its pursuit of a mistaken scientificity" and to focus on the political nature of crime (Young, 1988, p. 161). This was accomplished by focusing on the political and economic structures and the institutions of capitalism and on how these form the social conditions that generate crime.

For the new criminology, capitalism is an exploitative and alienating social order in which inequality is institutionalized by an elite ruling class. Under these conditions, crime is therefore a rational response to forced social arrangements; it is a by-product of the political economy. According to Young (1976), one of the major contributors to the new criminology, "central to our concerns is the explanation of law and criminality in terms of the dominant mode of production and the class nature of society" (p. 14).

Under capitalism, criminal law all too often is manipulated to benefit particular interest groups to the detriment of all others; more particular, criminal law is used by the state and the ruling class to secure the survival of the capitalist system (Bohm, 1982). For the new criminology, then, crime would be defined as capitalist policies and interests that contribute to human misery and deprive people of their human potential. Here the violation of human rights is of central concern for the definition of crime and includes imperialism, capitalism, racism, and sexism. This focus, although assaulted by more than a decade of nonintervention and privatization of social services ideology under then-Prime Minister Margaret Thatcher, remains an important part of the British criminological enterprise.

Critique of "New" Criminology

This perspective was as soundly and thoughtfully criticized early on as it was praised, sometimes by the same people. Currie, for example, was quick to notice that *The New Criminology* (Taylor et al., 1973) was in many ways far too "close to the tradition it supposedly sets out to criticize and replace" (Currie, 1974, p. 133). Three specific problems were identified that for Currie made the new criminology resemble the old: (a) the way it criticized the old theories; (b) its style, language, and expected audience; and (c) its own theoretical perspective.

First, Currie (1974) stated that although Taylor and colleagues provided a solid and illuminating critique of the shortcomings of conventional criminology, especially ethnomethodology and conflict theory, they were often sketchy and "sometimes just plain wrong" (p. 134). Further, their discussion of the classical school was incomplete and the critique of positivism was about biological determinism, avoiding other varieties of determinism; accordingly, they gave the misleading impression that criticism of biologicalism applied equally to psychological and sociological determinism. Nor did their critique of biological determinism go beyond previous criticisms of the same topic. Taylor et al.'s (1973) work also did not live up to their assertion that they would "explain why certain theories . . . survive" (p. 31). Instead, they treated criminological theories as if they existed in a scholarly limbo, rather than in wider ideological currents "rooted in material conditions ... in advanced capitalist societies" (Currie, 1974, pp. 134-135). This oversight not only obscured the connections conventional criminology has with state intervention into crime and other social problems but also gave credence to the claim that Taylor et al. (1973) were themselves "conventional" because they did not go into a "deeper level of critical analysis" (Currie, 1974, p. 136).

Second, the writing style of Taylor et al. (1973) was closely akin to people with finely tuned interests in the field of criminology (Currie, 1974). To some, this might sound like an unfair criticism, but for Currie it was an indication that Taylor et al. were actually writing for traditional criminology rather than for radicalized people working to create meaningful social change for the exploited.

The third and most damaging criticism is that in its rush to offer a more heuristic social explanation of crime than offered by traditional criminology, the new criminology failed first to present a cogent discussion of human nature and of the social order. Without this information, it is unclear just what it was offering as an alternative to traditional criminology. Part of the explanation for this weakness is that new criminology's concentrated critique of biological theories threw out the baby with the bathwater. As Currie (1974) stated, "A more useful approach is not to reject biological and psychological conceptions altogether, but to integrate them with an overall vision of human nature" (p. 138). For these and other reasons, Currie concluded that *The New Criminology*'s main theoretical assumptions were a bit confused and fundamentally misleading.

Left Realism

Other factors contributed eventually to diminishing the initial praise and impact of the new criminology, not the least of which was the changing political context of Britain with the rise of the "new" right under Prime Minister Margaret Thatcher. In 1979, the new right succeeded in a Conservative/Tory party victory in Britain's General Election and brought into office a government determined to effect change (Jenkins, 1987). The Conservative party was committed specifically to ending Britain's domestic and international economic and political decline. To do this, the first target of the victorious Conservatives was to make an ideological and political break with the assumptions and rules restraining government under the ideology of social democracy circa 1940 and post-World War II.

This represented a major change in British politics. At the heart of social democracy was a four-decade expansion of the functions and responsibilities of the state. The public enterprise sector, for example, was substantially "increased through the nationalization of major public utilities such as gas, electricity, coal and railroads" (Gamble, 1989, p. 2). In the social arena, this expansion meant that welfare provisions were extended as were national health care, housing, and education. But by the 1970s, social democracy and its welfare policies came under attack in Britain and in many other countries. The 1979 Conservative victory ushered in a new governmental ideology, which used as its major agenda the privatization of government industries and the placing of restrictions on welfare, national health care, and educational support. At the time of this writing, 15 years after the 1979 General Election victory, the Tories continue dismantling the welfare state, although markedly weakened in popularity by failed social policies and high-level governmental scandals (*New York Times*, 1994a; *Observer*, 1993).

As the new right's governmental policies were being formulated and implemented, radical criminology recognized that its tide had turned. Writing about the impact of radical criminology, Stanley Cohen (1981) stated:

> There are more corners and cavities than ten years ago, but for the most part the institutional foundations of British criminology remain intact and unaltered, for the Establishment saw the new theories as simply fashion which would eventually pass over or as a few interesting ideas which could be swallowed up without changing the existing paradigm at all. (p. 236)

In a reflective comment about radical criminology's two-decade history, Matthews and Young (1986) stated that it had "concentrated on the impact of the state—through the process of labelling—on the criminal at the expense of neglecting the effect of crime upon the victim" (p. 1). In their words this neglect was improper because radical criminology should have concentrated on "the basic triangle of relations which is the proper subject matter of criminology—the offender, the state and the victim" (p. 1).

In part as a remedy to this oversight and the claim in some circles that radical criminology was in a state of crisis of its own, radical criminology developed a different approach to studying crime called *left realism*, a name used because of its emphasis on the *real* aspects of crime. Central to left realism was a strong concern that the new criminology not only had placed perhaps too much emphasis on the state, but also had neglected the etiology of crime (Young, 1986). This point cannot be overly emphasized because it marked a significant shift in Britain's radical criminology, one not so much *from* theoretical issues as *toward* research and statistical analyses of crime causation and its consequences.

More specifically, left realism was explicitly, though not exclusively, concerned with the origins, nature, and impact of crime in the working class. This emphasis was conducive to creating a research agenda that included "an accurate [study of] victimology" (Young, 1986, p. 23). But this was not just an emphasis on "victims"; it was a broader approach that not only stressed the geography and social dimensions of vulnerable sections of a community but also included studying the "risk rate of vulnerability" in the community. One way of conceptualizing this point is to think of the working class as a victim of crime from all directions. The more vulnerable a person is economically and socially, for example, the more likely it is that *both* working-class and white-collar crime will occur against them (Young, 1986, p. 23).

One example of left realism's concern for victims is the emphasis it places on feminist perspectives in criminology. With the growing awareness in the 1970s of the problem of rape and other feminist issues, feminists forced a rethinking of criminological theory itself, as has been discussed here. This development has not been lost on left realism, as it stresses that crime should be studied as "problems as people experience them" (Young, 1986, p. 24). As Young stated, "It takes seriously the complaints of women" (p. 24). This should not be interpreted to mean that left realism is concerned only about women as crime victims. Its agenda is concerned equally with racism, police brutality, and a number of other "everyday crimes" (see Young & Matthews, 1992; Matthews & Young, 1992). The uniqueness of its perspective is that it is interested decidedly in the class and power dimensions of crime causation and what can be done about it. Finally, today left realism is at least a decade old and its appeal and contributors are found in a number of countries, including Canada, the United States, Australia, and Britain.

Consequences of New Criminology/Left Realism

The early contributions by the new criminology and realist criminology were not created in a social and political vacuum. Initially they were part of the emergence of the New Left in North America and Britain during the late 1960s and early 1970s. It held in its scope of criticism not only the issues discussed here within traditional criminology, but also what has become known as the antipsychiatry movement, prison support groups, campus sit-ins, and community action efforts (Young, 1988). Moreover, during the late 1960s and 1970s, higher education social science in Britain was expanded at an unprecedented level, and sociology/criminology/deviance offerings were developed not only in the well-established universities but also in lesser universities and the expanding polytechnics. The new courses were often "taught . . . by individuals in or around the new radical criminology . . . to sociology students heavily imbued with the New Left ideas and practice" (p. 168). Many of these scholars and their students remain in academia and are active critical criminologists.

In addition to leading the attack on traditional positivism, which held sway between post-World War II and the late 1960s, radical and realist criminologies have contributed to a long list of concepts that "are now staples of criminological culture, whatever its political persuasion" (Young, 1988, p. 164). These include a powerful critique of the mechanical determinism associated with biological explanations of crime, the social construction of statistics, emphasis on the endemic rather than a solely class-based nature of crime, and the largely invisible victimization of racist crime, domestic violence against women, and the abuse of children.

Unlike conventional or "establishment criminology," which claims generally to be apolitical, value-free, and objective and which receives research funding from central government, radical criminology/left realism has "its powerbase in those areas of what one might call unsubsidised criminology" (Young, 1988, p. 164). Not unlike early feminist work in conventional criminology, left realism research funding is usually outside of the support provided in Britain by the Home Office and in the United States by the National Institute of Justice. Not infrequently, in recent years its funding has come from radical, left-leaning local government services. The political and economic support from the left combined with its continuing criticism of establishment criminology's focus on the effectiveness of the state's effort to construct and operate efficient social control apparatuses has permitted left realism to be a rich theoretical and research alternative outside conventional criminology. Furthermore, local funding of left realism research is indeed one consequence of this perspective's theoretical insightfulness and research findings. Primarily for these reasons, left realism is the new criminology's heir apparent and a major alternative to establishment criminology.

8

CONSERVATIVE CRIMINOLOGY

Revitalizing Individualistic Theory

As we have seen in the earlier chapters, during the 1980s and early 1990s some of the theoretical paths that had emerged in previous periods continued to develop, but with a shift in emphasis in accordance with the context of the times. This chapter will center on the way in which the conservatism of the 1980s formed a context contributing to the revitalization of those perspectives that locate the sources of crime in the individual. In many ways it was as if criminological theory had come full circle in the 1980s, with a return to the classical school depiction of crime as the result of individual actors exercising rational choice or the positivistic portrayal of crime as the result of organic anomalies or psychological defects.

We have focused deliberately much of the contextual material on the United States of the 1980s and early 1990s because of sources readily available in the mass media. Because it is difficult to analyze this period from a point too close to the time to allow for historical perspective, a more balanced analysis must await the work of future scholars. Our hope here is both to capture something of the flavor of the times and to encourage the reader to ponder the images portrayed in the mass media of the period as something more that "just news," something amounting to the construction of a collective sense of social reality, which in turn had its effect on criminological theorists.

Context: The United States of the 1980s and Early 1990s

To make our analysis more manageable, we will concentrate on developments in the United States. As indicated in Chapter 6, the turmoil of the 1960s was succeeded by a political backlash leading to the election of Richard Nixon to the presidency. Nixon was elected in part because of promises to get tough on crime and because he indicated that he would extricate the United States from the quagmire of Vietnam by way of a "secret plan." He made "perfectly clear" his extreme distaste for the dress and drugs of the counterculture, and his election signaled the return to power of those who had little enthusiasm and limited tolerance for the civil rights, countercultural, and feminist movements of the time.

By the early 1970s, however, certain economic and political shifts that had been building for decades began to be felt. These underlying shifts had been very important to the sense of peace and prosperity of the 1950s and the radical developments of the 1960s, and they were to have major effects in the decades to come. The structural shifts were both economic and political. The economic dominance of the United States came into question in the 1970s, leading to a sense of something "gone wrong" by the end of the decade. Politically, the United States adapted with a shift to even more conservative political rhetoric in the 1980s, with a sort of cultural nostalgia for the "good old days" of the 1950s along with spending generating an enormous national debt.

The Economic Decline of the United States

By the close of World War II in 1945, the United States' share of world manufacturing was nearly 50%, a proportion so great that never before or since has it been attained by a single nation. The United States came out of the war so strong economically that Henry Luce, one of the nation's leading publishers, proclaimed that it was the beginning of the "American century." Indeed, such a prediction was reasonable at the time; in 1945, for example, the United States owned two thirds of the world's gold reserves and all of its atomic bombs. It was truly the initial stages of the Americanization of the Old World. In view of the United States' vast economic power, it did little good for countries such as France to try to outlaw the importation and sale of items such as Coca-Cola (Kennedy, 1987, p. 29).

With such immense resources, it is not surprising that in the late 1940s the United States continued to extend its military protection (some would say "capitalistic-militaristic imperialism") throughout the world. By 1970 the United States had more than 1 million soldiers in 30 countries and was a major supplier of military aid to nearly 100 nations around the world (Kennedy, 1987, p. 29). As the United States' military commitments began to increase after 1945, however, its positions in world manufacturing and world gross national production already were beginning to decline, slowly at first and then with increasing speed. Military expenditures under Presidents Eisenhower and Kennedy (prior to the military buildup in Vietnam) were already approximately 10% of the gross national product (GNP), but the economic burden was obscured by the fact that the United States' share of global production and wealth was about twice what it is now.

Something of the precarious nature of underlying economic conditions in the United States of the 1980s can be seen by recognizing that during these years under President Reagan defense spending increased at least 50% more than what was spent in the late 1970s under President Carter, Reagan's predecessor. Meanwhile, the national debt was growing at remarkable speed. In 1980 the federal deficit was $59.6 billion; in 1985 it was already $202.8 billion and growing rapidly. Interest alone on the debt was already $52.5 billion by 1980, but by 1985 it had reached $129 billion (Kennedy, 1988, p. 33). By 1988 the United States had a $500 billion federal deficit, a far cry from when it owned two thirds of the world's gold reserves in 1945. Some observers termed this situation the "Argenting of America" (*Newsweek*, 1988a, p. 22). Many predicted that the United States' world economic position would continue to decline and that the next century would belong not to the United States but to countries in Asia, especially Japan. By the late 1980s it was forecast that by 1995 private Japanese investors would own $1 trillion, or 10%, of all assets in the United States (*Newsweek*, 1988a, p. 45).

Changes in other parts of the world also contributed to the United States' predicament. Over the last two decades, for instance, some foreign countries increased their world production in areas in which the United States once ranked supreme, such as in the production of textiles, iron and steel, shipbuilding, and basic chemicals. In addition, the United States faced stiff international competition in the production and distribution of robotics, aerospace technology, automobiles, machine tools, and computers (Kennedy, 1987, p. 29). And in food production, another area in which the United States ranked supreme even into the 1970s, Third World countries and the European Economic Community began to export food, thus competing with U.S. farm production and sales.

The Persistence of Inequality in the United States

During the 1980s it became increasingly clear that the roots of inequality discussed by the strain theorists and conflict theorists ran even deeper in the United States than many had suspected. College attendance became more and more difficult for young people, some feminists began to rethink their position in the light of such slow progress toward gender equality, and racism reappeared in some especially ugly forms. Because of the underlying economic shifts outlined above, the economic pie was no longer as large to the relative number of those hungry for a slice as it had seemed in the 1960s and early 1970s. Because the power of youths declined as the huge number of baby boomers who had fueled the protests of the 1960s moved toward middle age, and perhaps because many of the more energetic, educated, and articulate women and Blacks had been successful in obtaining their own slices of the pie, thus becoming a part of the "system," pressure for basic social change ebbed. By the end of the 1970s, Lasch (1978) already had cited the rise of a "culture of narcissism," and some were proclaiming the coming of the "Me Decade." More and more people seemed to focus on their own problems, although basic social problems that had seemed on their way to at least partial solution began to worsen.

The race issue may be taken as an example. During the late 1960s, President Lyndon B. Johnson had appointed the Kerner Commission, charging it to investigate the causes of the racial riots of the time. The commission had concluded that the riots were the result of White racism and cautioned that unless White attitudes and behavior changed, the United States would continue to move toward a system made up of two societies, one Black, one White—separate and unequal. Twenty years later it was evident that although some progress had been made, the impact had affected three different segments of the Black community quite differently (*New York Times,* 1988a). The Black middle class, a group that had relative economic success during the two decades prior to the 1980s, had achieved even more economic success, along with success in the political arena, but late 1980s members of the Black working class in the late 1980s often experienced great difficulty sustaining their economic position, being very vulnerable to the loss of jobs coming with downsizing and deindustrialization. Things were much worse, however, for a third group of Blacks, who now seemed permanently "stuck" at the bottom.

This third group, the emerging "Black underclass," is composed of people who had succumbed to the economic and social strains inherent in slum living (Wilson, 1987). The mass media have described them as the "miserable human residue, mired in hard-core unemployment, violent crime, drug-use, teen-age pregnancy and one of the world's worst human environments, [which] seems to be a partial, perverse result of the very success of other blacks" (*New York Times,* 1988a, p. 13).[1] In the early 1970s the Black median income was 57% that of Whites, but it has since declined as the Black-White income gap has widened during the past 25 years.

Unfortunately, until the 1990s no reliable data exist on racial, religious, or ethnic violence for the entire United States (*New York Times,* 1987c, 1994d). Only a few cities in the 1980s created special units for crimes motivated by hatred, but reports of racial strife and violence are on the increase. In mid-1987 the U.S. Justice Department's Community Relations Service released information indicating that racial incidents reported to the government rose from 99 in 1980 to 276 in 1986 (*New York Times,* 1987c, p. 13). In 1993 more than 7,000 hate crimes were reported to the FBI (*New York Times,* 1994d). Corroborative information is present in investigations of arson and cross burning that have followed the move of minorities into mostly White neighborhoods. The Klanwatch Project of the Southern Poverty Law Project (Montgomery, Alabama) found that between 1985 and 1986 there were hundreds of acts of vandalism and other incidents directed at members of minority groups who had moved into mostly White areas (*New York Times,* 1987d, p. 22).

Reports such as these were not restricted to the Deep South. In New York City alone the number of reports of incidents of racial assaults in which Blacks and Whites were injured in the first 8 months of 1987 were the highest in the 7-year investigating unit. There were 235 incidents in all of 1986, and 301 incidents were reported in the first 8 months of 1987. A similar trend was reported by the Mayor's Management Report; it stated that the number of bias incidents doubled between fiscal year 1986 and 1987 (*New York Times,* 1987e, p. 19). Further, the Anti-Defamation League of B'nai B'rith reported that anti-Semitic acts rose 12% in 1987. New York, the state with the largest Jewish population, led the nation with vandalism incidents, followed by California, New Jersey, and Florida (*New York Times,* 1987f, p. 13).

Part of the mood that arose in the 1980s was symbolized by the Bernard Goetz case. Just 3 days before Christmas 1984, Goetz, a middle-class White, shot four Black youths on a New York subway, after one of them had asked for five dollars. In June 1987 a jury acquitted Goetz on the shooting charge. Throughout the proceedings, a debate raged over issues of racial tension, self-defense, and the perception that Goetz's acquittal would be interpreted as widening the circumstances justifying deadly force, at least of Whites against Blacks (*Newsweek,* 1987b, pp. 20-21; *New York Times,* 1987g, p. 11).

The Rhetoric of Stability

Those who do not wish to consider fundamental changes in the social order tend to locate the sources of social problems such as crime either in defective individuals or in failures of the institutions of socialization (Rubington & Weinberg, 1971). The increase in racial discrimination and violence outlined above represented but one example, albeit a very important one, of tendencies to see certain *types of people* as the problem. As for the focus on the alleged *failures of our institutions of socialization,* it amounts to a belief that the "American way of life" is either exemplary or at least fundamentally sound, but that the institutions of work, family, education, and religion are somehow failing to integrate potential troublemakers into the mainstream and are in need of reaffirmation and strengthening. If the first of these perspectives may be said to characterize President Nixon, the second was well represented by the Democratic successor to the Nixon-Ford years, James Earl ("Jimmy") Carter.

Carter's rise to the U.S. presidency is in itself an instructive example of the way in which economic and political changes affect public policy, including which criminological theories are implemented. Long before the underlying problems of the United States' economic decline were apparent to the mass media or the general public, important American financial interests were well aware of the situation and had responded with the creation in 1973 of the Trilateral Commission, a combined effort of powerful interests in America, Europe, and Japan. The one-time director of the commission, Zbigniew Brzezinski, summarized public disenchantment over Watergate, Ford's subsequent pardon of Nixon, and a host of related signs of loss of faith in the system by writing that "the democratic candidate in 1976 will have to emphasize work, the family, religion, and increasing patriotism to be elected" (Allen, 1977, pp. 2-7). Partly as one aspect of the "southern strategy" to win back the electoral votes of the South, Carter was selected as a southern governor exemplifying these attributes. Upon Carter's election, Brzezinski became Carter's national security adviser.

President Carter was elected not only because of powerful supports from influential political kingmakers, however, but also because he symbolized the mood of the times better than any other candidate. Indeed, it is important to remember that political figures in America are successful in large part because of their ability to mold themselves to the public mood to "become what they want." Carter succeeded in reaffirming the work ethic to the extent that he often was called a workaholic, and he was well known for his familial affection for wife, daughter, and even his "bad-boy" brother, Billy. As a self-proclaimed born-again Christian with evangelicals in his immediate family, he represented some of the longing for a return to more traditional religious values and for moral leadership in the aftermath of the Watergate scandal. His presidency floundered, however, on his inability to reaffirm the power of patriotism with a victory over the hostage holders in Iran, and he in turn was succeeded by Ronald Reagan, who became even more a symbol of America in the 1980s than Carter had been in his time.

During the late 1970s President Carter spoke publicly of surveys showing a pervasive malaise in the United States. The public had lost much of its traditional faith in education as a force for socialization. Many seemed to feel that the changes of the 1960s had destroyed the cohesion of the family and undermined its capacity to socialize and control American citizens. Religion seemed to offer personal solace to an increasing number of citizens, but perhaps it became less of a vehicle for community building and reform as more and more people turned to charismatic televangelists for spiritual direction.

By the end of the 1970s, the mood of the American public seemed to fit nicely with candidate Reagan's position that too many naysayers were spending too much time criticizing America and focusing on the dark side when what was needed was a patriotic public to "stand up for America." As indicated earlier, society as a whole seemed to be tired of social concerns and eager to turn its back on internal problems of economic decline, racism, poverty, environmental pollution, and all the rest, almost as if they did not exist. Although labeling theory received some lip service, it was not a time in which strain theories—much less conflict theories—were likely to gain much of a hearing.

The inauguration of President Reagan suggested to some that the U.S. public was about to embrace the 1950s spirit once again. The theme of the "Me Decade" that had been proclaimed in the late 1970s began to take on a somewhat different tinge. Although the focus was much on the individual "looking out for number one," there was at the same time more and more condemnation of the permissive society. Thus, for example, the society as a whole seemed to view much more positively the somewhat cynical pursuit of individual material success in the rat race, although growing much less tolerant of individualistic pursuits of pleasure in the form of sex and drugs. In fact, it became fashionable to call for surveillance over sexuality and for compulsory drug testing on the principle of restriction of individual rights for the protection of society.

The embrace of materialism. The America of the 1980s often seemed like a case of "life imitating art," if the mass media portrayals can be called "art." The top-ranked television series in 1981 was the prime-time soap opera *Dallas,* featuring scenes of Texas high rollers led by the conniving Ewing oil baron "J. R." Later in the decade, the real-life Wall Street wheeler-dealer Ivan Boesky, who had summarized the thinking of many in his assertion that "greed is not a bad thing" (*Newsweek,* 1988b, p. 42), was named by *Fortune* magazine as "Crook of the Year" (*Newsweek,* 1988b, p. 44) after agreeing to relinquish illegal profits of $50 million and indemnify another $50 million and was later honored with a 3-year prison sentence. In 1984, *Lifestyles of the Rich and Famous* became a hit television show (*Newsweek,* 1988b, p. 42), and in that same year *Newsweek* declared the real-life "Year of the Yuppie." In direct contrast to the yippies of the 1960s, the yuppies (young upwardly mobile urban professionals) represented a symbol of the times as a demographic cohort of self-centered materialists bent entirely on "making it" with no social conscience getting in the way.

The reaffirmation of traditional sexual preachments. By the early 1980s the open, hedonistic sexuality that many associated with the rise of the 1960s counterculture was declared a thing of the past in articles with titles such as "Sex in the 80s: The Revolution Is Over" (*Time,* 1984, pp. 74-78). A *Newsweek* cover story announced that the "Playboy Party Is Over," and *Time* referred to an era of "Sex Busters." Examples of the new mood abounded:

congressional opposition to the Braille editions of *Playboy* magazine that
had been published monthly since 1970 under the National Library Service for the Blind and Physically Handicapped; a highly criticized government-sponsored study of how children are portrayed in *Playboy, Penthouse,*
and *Hustler;* increased violence against homosexuals; and a hotly disputed
Justice Department report on pornography.

The debate over sexual values also reached into the nation's courts. For
example, in *Bowers v. Hardwick* (1986), decided in the middle of the decade, the Supreme Court upheld (by the narrowest of margins in a 5-4 split)
a Georgia law that made it a felony punishable by 20 years in prison for
consenting adults to engage in oral or anal sexual relations. The case
developed innocently enough when a police officer went to Hardwick's
apartment to serve a warrant for carrying an open container of alcohol in
a public place (part of a crackdown on drinking). The officer was ushered
into the apartment by a guest and told that he could find Hardwick in his
bedroom. There the officer discovered Hardwick engaged in oral sex with
another man and made an arrest. In effect, the court ruled that individuals
under Georgia law had no right to engage in such acts even as consenting
adults in a private bedroom, taking the position that the state had a legitimate right to restrict and control such behavior as part of its responsibility
for enforcing public morality even in private places.

In a matter also related to balancing privacy versus state interests, the
1980s witnessed the increasingly heated debate on the right of women to
terminate pregnancy through abortion. The courts were asked repeatedly
to reconsider *Roe v. Wade,* the 1973 Supreme Court case that had declared
as unconstitutional laws prohibiting abortion, largely on the judgment
that state interests were not compelling enough to justify interference in
the personal privacy of women. As a difficult moral dilemma, the stance
taken on abortion often cut across usual ideological lines (e.g., liberal
Catholics opposing pro-choice). Even so, the growing pro-life movement
was nourished by America's turn to the right, as conservative politicians,
religious leaders, and right-to-life groups played prominent roles in the
crusade to overturn *Roe v. Wade.* They argued that the interest of the state
in maintaining public morality—represented most fully in the moral
choice to protect the lives of the unborn—was more than sufficient to
allow state legislatures once again to restrict, if not criminalize, the practice
of abortion.

Finally, the 1980s saw the emergence of AIDS as a growing threat. AIDS's
mounting toll initiated much discourse in the media and in political fo-

rums over existing sexual practices. For liberals, AIDS precipitated a call for more pragmatism in sexual relationships: the prudent selection of partners, the practice of "safe sex," and broader efforts to educate about the transmission of sexual diseases. For conservatives, the AIDS menace provided incontrovertible evidence of the dire consequences of the breakdown of sexual morality. Ultimately, conservatives warned, the problem of AIDS reflected a moral failing—the result of sex outside the boundaries of marriage—and it could be eliminated only by a reaffirmation of traditional sexual values.

The "War on Drugs." Early in the Reagan administration there had been antidrug campaigns, and in 1986 the federal government declared a new $250 million "War on Drugs," a so-called war that was to extend the compulsory drug testing of employees in the world of business and athletics to federal employees (*Newsweek,* 1986a; *Time,* 1986a, pp. 12, 13). The announcement of the new testing policy came after a 5-month congressional study that had concluded that "urinalysis procedures were expensive, 'useless in most cases' and often inaccurate" (*Washington Post,* 1986, p. 15), but the policy was to be implemented despite the lack of any evidence that those to be tested had used illegal drugs or had committed any crime at all. The federal government was described as in a "frenzy" over drugs (*New York Times,* 1986a, p. 25). Despite arguments that what employees do on their private time was their own business unless it affects job performance and that such testing replaces the due process assumption of innocence with an assumption of guilt until proven otherwise, a White House poll reported that the public was less concerned about the federal budget deficit and arms control than about drugs (see *Time,* 1986a).

The Department of Justice and the Supreme Court. Although it may not be true that the positions taken by units of federal government reflect the times exactly, they do provide clues. Thus it is instructive to consider trends in both the U.S. Department of Justice and the Supreme Court during the 1980s. In both cases there was increasing reluctance to focus on possible social conditions underlying crime and a tendency to demand harsher treatment of ordinary street criminals.

At the beginning of President Reagan's second term, his close friend Edwin Meese was appointed attorney general. Meese declared in 1986 that Supreme Court decisions should not be regarded necessarily as the supreme law of the land (*Newsweek,* 1986b, p. 9). He argued that Supreme

Court decisions were binding *only* for those involved in a specific case (*New York Times*, 1986b). A similar position was advocated by the chief of the Justice Department's civil rights division, William Bradford Reynolds, who not only questioned the competence of a Supreme Court judge but also argued that efforts to achieve a radically egalitarian society would pose perhaps a major threat to individual liberty (*Newsweek*, 1986c, p. 27). Reynolds was the leader of assaults on federal civil rights and school desegregation programs, efforts to enhance equality in women's college athletics, and efforts to halt discrimination in housing. According to Griffin Bell, attorney general under President Carter, "That's what he was hired to do" (*Newsweek*, 1986c, p. 27).

In matters closely related to criminal justice, the leadership of the Justice Department was equally conservative. Attorney General Meese, for example, advocated overturning the 1966 *Miranda* decision, which required the police to inform criminal suspects of their legal rights, referring to the decision as "infamous" (*New York Times*, 1987h, p. 13). Chief Justice William H. Rehnquist sounded a similar refrain by calling for a limit on last-minute appeals filed by death row inmates. He argued that such appeals create "chaotic conditions . . . within a day or two before an execution" (*New York Times*, 1988b, p. 7). Unfortunately the "chaotic conditions" that concerned Rehnquist resulted in part from the fact that the Supreme Court "made it clear that the constitutional right to assign counsel [did] not apply to litigation beyond the first appeal" (*New York Times*, 1988c, p. 27). Meanwhile, Attorney General Meese advocated execution for teenage killers (*Cincinnati Enquirer*, 1985a).

In addition to military spending and criticism of those at the bottom of the economic ladder, part of the politics of the 1980s in the United States revolved around a perceived need to reaffirm faith in the American way of life in the face of problems that seemed difficult to handle. On the 100th birthday of the Statue of Liberty in 1986, after 2 years of refurbishing at a cost of $39 million, the statue and all that it symbolizes was celebrated with the most expensive and extravagant party ever held in the world. It was attended by more than 5 million people. As testimony to the themes of liberty, freedom, and a new life, each central to the core of American values and symbolized by the Statue of Liberty, more than 25,000 immigrants took the citizenship oath on July 4, 1986, in 44 different locations across the nation. The reaffirmation celebration was attended also by foreign dignitaries, and no fewer than 35 foreign warships stood by in New York Harbor as a symbolic gesture supporting the American way of life. In keeping with the times, an expensive dance was held on Governors Island at a cost of $10,000 per couple (*Time,* 1986b; *Newsweek,* 1986d).

Content: Individualistic Theories Revitalized

Rather than being a period of new theories cut from whole cloth, the 1980s and early 1990s were primarily a time that witnessed the revitalization of old theories. Many of the revitalized theories stressed explanations of crime that focused on the question, "What's wrong with individual criminals?"—a question that directs attention to looking *within* individuals for explanations of their behavior.

The 1980s, as we have seen, ushered in a period of rising conservatism— so much so that politicians scurried to avoid the label of liberal. Such conservatism represented a principled defense of individual responsibility, respect for tradition, and need for social order but often tended to turn a blind eye to the difficult social circumstances endured by many citizens. Sociological explanations of crime still accrued substantial support, but now they lost ground to explanations seeking to revitalize the thinking of the early classical and positivist schools of criminology and thus to locate crime's causes within an individual's will, mind, and body (Flanagan, 1987).

In this context, certain research findings began to attract more attention. First, there were all the data showing that many if not most people in high crime environments did not commit serious crimes themselves. Then there was the increasing evidence tracing a large proportion of crimes to a small percentage of individual offenders (Wolfgang, Figlio, & Sellin, 1972), suggesting that there must be something about these particular individuals themselves that led them to commit many more offenses than committed even by other criminals in the same social environment. Fear of violence had increased, and data showing that violent criminals tended to begin their aggression and crime at an especially early age (e.g., Loeber & Dishion, 1983) suggested that the environment might not be the problem.

Prevalence of Biological Theorizing

As suggested in Chapter 2, the earlier biological theories of Lombroso and others had achieved their prominence in part because of the fact that biology, especially in the form of Darwinism, had become perhaps the most fashionable science of the late 19th century. By the middle of the 20th century, biology had lost some of its prominence to physics and the rapidly growing social and behavioral sciences, but by the 1980s biology had been revitalized by new discoveries in the laboratory, especially in the subfield of genetics as exemplified by the explosion of work on DNA. Now major breakthroughs were being hailed, including such remarkable feats as the expected cloning of humans themselves. In 1985 a major newspaper reported that the brains of executed prisoners were being studied at the University of Florida (*Cincinnati Enquirer*, 1985b). A study at the New York University Medical School soon reported that convicted murderers had once suffered head injuries (*New York Times*, 1986c). Two medical doctors reported at the 1985 Fourth World Congress of Biological Psychiatry that 90% of all excessively violent people had brain defects (*New York Times*, 1985, pp. 17, 19).

Although the claims of most of this type of research were presented in rather general terms such as "brain damage" or "neurological defects," reports identifying a *specific* defect began to appear in 1987. One report that made the front page of the *New York Times*, for instance, linked manic depression to a "specific genetic defect" (*New York Times*, 1987i, p. 1). As some noted at the time, the medical claim that a specific genetic structure can explain a specific form of behavior is only a short step from the creation of policies that would require "special treatment" for people with such an identifiable genetic structure. In 1988 the National Research Council, the operating arm of the National Academy of Sciences that Congress chartered to advise the federal government, called for a 15-year study effort "to diagram the possible 100,000 human genes" (*New York Times*, 1988d, p. 1, 13). At an estimated cost of $3 billion, it would "set the stage for constructing the ultimate physical map—the complete DNA sequence of the human genome" (*New York Times*, 1988d, p. 13). By the late 1980s DNA "fingerprinting" had been used already to obtain convictions for rape and murder in both the United States and England, and there was increasing talk of identifying the DNA structure of convicted criminals as a basis for screening the public for potential offenders with similar DNA structures.

Of course, few of the new theoretical approaches are as purely biological as the media make it appear. They are by and large biosocial rather than biological, although they tend to emphasize nature much more than nurture in their arguments. The more sophisticated approaches rarely make the simple argument that some individuals are inherently criminal. Instead, they trace antisocial behavior to many precursors, which if ignored or inappropriately treated are said to combine with any negative environmental conditions to produce serious crime by adolescence and adulthood (Fishbein, 1990). One example of this process is cited in an alleged link between low IQ or learning disabilities and criminal behavior. Although neither low IQ nor learning disability is considered inherently criminogenic, in the absence of appropriate intervention the model suggests that a child will become frustrated with mainstream activities such as school, suffer a drastically lowered self-esteem in general, and begin to interact with others experiencing similar frustrations as they move in the direction of delinquency and crime (Fishbein, 1990). Such a model suggests that the earlier the detection and intervention, the more likely they will succeed in preventing criminal outcomes, which may be beyond prevention by adolescence.

The newer biosocial approaches tend to acknowledge the importance of learning, but they emphasize the extent to which the learning and conditioning of behavior occur differently for different individuals because of neurological variations (Fishbein, 1990; Moffitt, 1983; Zuckerman, 1983). Thus psychopaths are said to be impulsive and unemotional because their nervous systems are more difficult to condition, and schizophrenics are said to suffer from brain anomalies, disturbances of the limbic system, or damage to neural structures. What an individual inherits, however, is not a specific behavior but a tendency to respond to environmental factors through general predispositions (Fishbein, 1990).

Like the earlier biological theories, the newer biosocial theories have focused considerable attention on family studies aimed at locating genetic factors by examining behavioral similarities among members of the same family, although today they stress behavioral characteristics such as hyperactivity or attention deficit disorder. Twin studies have been very popular also, despite their methodological deficiencies. In an excellent review of the literature, Fishbein (1990) has noted a number of biochemical differences between controls and individuals with psychopathy, antisocial personality, violent behavior, and conduct disorder, including levels of certain hormones, neurotransmitters, peptides, toxins, and metabolic processes, as well as psychophysiological correlates of psychopathy such as electroencephalogram (EEG) differences, cardiovascular differences, and electrodermal variations.

The 1980s saw publication of a series of works in criminal biology, with the biosocial theory of Mednick and his associates attaining special prominence (Mednick, Gabrielli, & Hutchings, 1984; Mednick, Moffitt, & Stack, 1987; Mednick, Pollack, Volavka, & Gabrielli, 1982; Mednick, Volavka, Gabrielli, & Itil, 1981), which had begun to appear in the late 1970s (Mednick, 1977; Mednick & Christiansen, 1977; Mednick & Shoham, 1979). Eysenck's (1964) work, which associated low cortical arousal with extroverted personality, lower "conditionability," and a consequently weaker moral conscience, had received some attention in the mid-1960s, but the social context was more accepting of biosocial approaches by the time Mednick's (1977) similar theory appeared in the late 1970s. Mednick proposed that certain high-risk individuals have inherited an autonomic nervous system (ANS) that is less sensitive to environmental stimuli and that such slow arousal makes it less likely that they will develop the responses necessary to inhibit antisocial behavior. Mednick had focused on the ANS in an effort to discover why the approximately 1% of the population that seems to be responsible for more than half of the crimes reported appear either unable or unwilling to learn from their continued mistakes. He stressed that conformity is learned and that the key involves learning of the fear response that becomes associated with consideration of antisocial behavior. The theory stresses that an individual with a normal ANS will experience a reduction of fear immediately on inhibiting antisocial activity and that because this fear reduction is a powerful reinforcement, such a person will learn to inhibit such activity. If, on the other hand, an individual's ANS reduces the fear too slowly or ineffectively to produce the necessary reinforcement, the theory suggests that normal inhibition may not be developed.

Theories suggesting faulty chromosomes (e.g., the XYY syndrome) that had produced little research support and much confusion in the 1960s and 1970s were supplanted in the 1980s by more careful research leading to theories arguing for disorders of the central nervous system (CNS), such as the cortical immaturity hypothesis (Mednick, Volavka, Gabrielli, & Itil, 1981). By the late 1980s this work had crystallized with the publication of an influential volume (Mednick, Moffitt, & Stack, 1987) including an elaborate study of 14,427 Danish adoptees (Mednick, Gabrielli, & Hutchings, 1987). Newer theory centered on the CNS by suggesting variations of a hypoarousal hypothesis (Volavka, 1987).

Recent biochemical theories have focused on sex hormones and neurotransmitters. For males, sex hormone theory has been concentrated on possible connections between testosterone and aggression. For females, various theories have suggested hormonal shifts occurring several days before menstruation and leading to a premenstrual syndrome (PMS) characterized by seriously distorted judgment and tendencies toward violence, along with postpartum depression syndrome occurring as a result of hormonal imbalances following pregnancy and childbirth, which has been used as a defense in infanticide cases.

Neurotransmitters are chemicals mediating signals between brain neurons. Of these, serotonin, dopamine, and norepinephrine have received the most attention. Animal studies have shown that serotonin may operate to inhibit aggression, and there is evidence associating low levels of serotonin with both habitual violence and suicide. Animal studies have also shown some association between both dopamine and norepinephrine and aggressive behavior under certain circumstances. The problems here are, however, extremely complex. Just as high levels of testosterone, for example, may be as much the product of aggression as the cause, so low levels of serotonin may be as much the product of environmental stress leading to chronic depression as the cause of such phenomena as suicidal behavior. The association between biochemical factors and antisocial behavior is perhaps the clearest example of the "chicken or egg" problem facing criminological theory. Which causes which? Or are both interrelated in some complex feedback process? If the associations eventually are established, should policy focus on changing the biochemistry of high-risk individuals (e.g., with pills or injections designed to produce the "proper" level of serotonin or dopamine) or on changing the environment that produced these unusual physiological consequences in certain individuals? Such decisions are, of course, political decisions, but they depend in part on whether criminological theory tends to focus on "chicken" or "egg." It is not surprising that the biologist wishes to focus on one and the sociologist wishes to focus on the other.

Of the various environmental factors influencing physiology, biological theorists have focused on diet, with special attention to protein intake, refined carbohydrates, food allergies, vitamin deficiencies, exposure to lead or cadmium, and certain substances such as monosodium glutamate (MSG), caffeine, and chemicals found in chocolate (Curran & Renzetti, 1994). Serotonin, for example, is produced by an amino acid found in high-protein foods. Thus it has been suggested that aggression due to low serotonin levels may be corrected through a high-protein diet. Diets high in refined carbohydrates such as are found in sugar and most junk foods produce large amounts of glucose in the bloodstream, which may trigger excessive insulin release and a dopamine increase leading to impaired behavioral control. As early as the end of the 1970s this carbohydrate theory was used to establish diminished capacity in the famous "Twinkie defense" involving former San Francisco Supervisor Dan White, who confessed killing Mayor George Moscone and Supervisor Harvey Milk (Curran & Renzetti, 1994). White was convicted, but of manslaughter rather than of the more serious charges of murder.

Crime and Human Nature:
Wilson and Herrnstein

The new biosocial theories concentrate attention on the body, which is presumed to play the major role in affecting the mind. The best publicized example of the return of individualistic explanations of crime appeared in James Q. Wilson and Richard J. Herrnstein's *Crime and Human Nature* (1985). It was greeted by numerous reviews in such well-known publications as *Time, Newsweek, U.S. News & World Report, Vogue, New York Times,* and the *Chronicle of Higher Education.* It also was treated as a news item by the Associated Press (see *Cincinnati Enquirer,* 1985c). The basic argument offered by Wilson, then a Harvard University political scientist, and Herrnstein, a psychologist also from Harvard, was based on a biosocial explanation of behavior that focused attention primarily on "constitutional factors" (Wilson & Herrnstein, 1985, chap. 3). Such factors, some of which are genetic, were treated by Wilson and Herrnstein as predisposing individuals to engage in criminal behavior. In their words, they wanted to explain "why some individuals are more likely than others to commit crime," and "why some persons commit serious crimes at a higher rate and others do not" (pp. 20-21). Their effort was directed toward explaining *criminality* rather than *crime.*

Although Wilson and Herrnstein (1985) did not give their theory a specific label or name, its biosocial focus was clear:

> The existence of biological predispositions means that circumstances that activate behavior in one person will not do so in another, that social forces cannot deter criminal behavior in 100 percent of the population, and that the distribution of crime within and across societies may, to some extent, reflect underlying distributions of constitutional factors. Crime cannot be understood without taking into account predispositions and their biological roots. (p. 103)

In certain respects, Wilson and Herrnstein's (1985) perspective harkens back to the theories of Lombroso, Hooton, Sheldon, and the Gluecks (see Chapter 2) and to the positivist school of criminology. Although largely ignored by today's criminologists because of theoretical and methodological problems, Wilson and Herrnstein claimed that a distinctive body type exists that distinguishes criminals from noncriminals: "Wherever it has been examined, criminals on the average differ in physique from the population at large. They tend to be more mesomorphic (muscular) and less ectomorphic (linear). . . . A corresponding argument is that the more muscular criminals are more likely to have biological parents who are themselves criminals." On the importance of family and its contribution to crime Wilson and Herrnstein stated that "bad families produce bad children" (p. 215). These authors buttressed this position by an extensive review of the work published on twins and adopted children (pp. 69-103).

The major argument here is that if there is a genetic connection to crime, it should show up when identical twins raised in the same environment are compared with fraternal twins also raised in the same environment. The findings suggest that if one identical twin has committed crimes, the other twin is likely also to have committed crimes. Research does not support this finding for fraternal twins.

Research on adopted children has focused on the criminality of the children compared to the criminality of their biological and adoptive parents. It is argued that children whose biological parents are criminals would engage in crime more than the adoptive parents. If genetics are connected to crime, it would have an influence despite the environment. Some research findings suggest that the criminality of biological parents is more significant in explaining the criminality of children than the criminality of adoptive parents.

Just how constitutional factors influence criminality is a point on which Wilson and Herrnstein expressed caution. They based their answer on what people consider rewarding and their ability to postpone gratification until some time in the future. According to Wilson and Herrnstein, constitutional factors have an impact on the ability to consider future and immediate rewards and punishments. For example, aggressive and impulsive males with low intelligence are at a greater risk of committing crimes than young males who have developed "the bite of conscience," which reflects a higher cognitive and intellectual development.

Gibbs (1985) interpreted an emphasis on rewards and punishments to mean that Wilson and Herrnstein attempted to develop an "operant-utilitarian" theory of criminality, although they did not give it a label at all. Again it is necessary to mention that an emphasis on rewards and punishments was pursued by the scholars in the classical school of criminology. They attempted to deter individual acts of crime by imposing punishments sufficiently severe to outweigh the benefits of illegal conduct.

The evaluations of *Crime and Human Nature* did not heap praise on Wilson and Herrnstein. The reasons were many but they can be divided into two categories: conceptual/empirical and ideological. The conceptual/empirical criticisms focused on the authors' lack of "concern about the empirical applicability of their terms" (Gibbs, 1985, p. 383). They used such concepts as "ratio of rewards," "material and nonmaterial crime," "approval of peers," "sense of inequity," and many other concepts (see Wilson & Herrnstein, 1985, chap. 2—"A Theory of Criminal Behavior"). However, they failed to offer any numerical or operational expressions for the concepts. Consequently there was a lack of clarity about what they were trying to communicate, thus creating difficult obstacles to conducting research that would test their theory.

Another troublesome dimension of their work was their claim that they were confining their attention to serious street crimes and predatory crimes such as murder, robbery, and burglary. But their failure to include such offenses as white-collar crimes under the label of predatory crimes and their failure to explain why burglary should be considered a street crime raised serious doubt about the generality and conceptual clarity of their theoretical arguments. As Gibbs (1985) stated, the relatively loose manner in which Wilson and Herrnstein used labels for crimes is "better suited for journalism than criminology" (p. 382).

An equally troublesome aspect of *Crime and Human Nature* was that although the authors gave the impression that they were objective in the selection and presentation of relevant literature, they may have in fact been highly selective in what they reviewed (Kamin, 1985). The problem here is that although the reader was given the impression that their arguments were based on solid *science* and therefore should be *believed*, in more than one instance their arguments were based on shaky evidence. The reader, however, was not given this information. For example, Wilson and Herrnstein's (1985, p. 418) observation that young people growing up in the 1960s were less willing to delay gratification than young people growing up 15 years earlier was based on a "single experimental study, [taken] at face value" (Kamin, 1985, p. 22). In addition, the authors failed to cite published research that indicated that noncriminals were found to be *more* mesomorphic in body type than delinquents (Kamin, 1985, p. 24). Apparently Wilson and Herrnstein elected to emphasize resources that supported their arguments for constitutional factors related to crime rather than address the literature that questioned or confounded this argument.

These criticisms, however serious, did not overshadow the ideological implications of some of Wilson and Herrnstein's arguments and the reasons their arguments were given wide attention. On this point, Kamin (1985) stated:

> The Wilson and Herrnstein work ought not to be judged in isolation. Their selective use of poor data to support a muddled ideology of biological determinism is not unrepresentative of American social science in the sixth year of the Reagan presidency. The political climate of the times makes it easy to understand why social scientists now rush to locate the causes of social tensions in genes and in deep-rooted biological substrata. (p. 25)

Wilson and Herrnstein's work implied that certain biological predispositions, found frequently in the poor, may be responsible for excessive criminal behavior. This message, particularly when read by those lacking criminological expertise and who do not pause to read the authors' caveats about their argument, suggests to some disquieting policy implications. We have seen in Chapter 2 that early biological theories were used to justify repressive and physically intrusive policies. The historical record teaches that attempts to root crime in human nature exempt the social fabric from blame and lend credence to the idea that offenders are largely beyond reform and in need of punitive control.

Varieties of Conservative Theory

The emphasis on crime's biological roots represents only one theme found in conservative writings about crime. At the risk of simplifying complex arguments, three additional types of conservative theorizing can be delineated (Currie, 1985). By revitalizing classical school principles, some have developed *rational choice/routine activities/econometric* models that conceive of individuals as logical actors choosing crime when the benefit exceeds the cost. Others have attempted to revitalize the psychological approach by suggesting that offenders persist in crime because they think not logically but differently. Still others of a conservative bent have gone beyond an individualistic approach, but only to the point of linking crime to a distinctive type of social influence: the allegedly permissive culture that they trace to developments in the American society of the 1960s, such as those discussed in earlier chapters.

Rational choice and routine activities. Rational choice theory represents an approach favored by many economists. Based on the concept of expected utility, it proceeds on assumptions similar to Bentham's utilitarian assertion that individuals operate by rational decisions expected to maximize profits and minimize losses. Gibbs (1975) has argued that as sociologists became more interested in the deterrence issue, economists became interested in rational choice models of crime. There is little doubt that both shifts were products of the times.

According to Cornish and Clarke (1986), rational choice theory can account not only for the decision to engage in crime but also for the selection of specific crimes at specific times and places. Unlike the more rationalistic exponents of the classical school, however, contemporary rational choice theorists do not insist on the pure rationality of decision making but make allowances for factors such as morality, inaccurate information, and fear that might distort the hedonistic calculus. Rational choice theorists tend to exaggerate the "irrationality" of other psychologically oriented theories; however, by making so many exceptions to the pure rationality they purport to stress in their own theories, some critics have insisted that there is little to set them apart from other theoretical models (Akers, 1994).

The more ecologically oriented routine activities theory looks beyond the individual to the larger context, particularly the combination of motivated offender, potential victim, and absence of capable guardians in conjunction at a particular time and place (Cohen & Felson, 1979). Such an approach is, of course, much less individualistic and less conservative in that it stresses the logic of social systems in addition to that of actors (Williams & McShane, 1994). The probability of a conjunction of the three key crime factors is held to be a product of the usual, recurrent, routine daily activities of human beings in particular times and places. According to routine activities theory, changes in these patterns of daily living simply alter the odds of crime as they bring the various crime-generating factors into conjunction. This theory does not purport to explain the nature of the criminal motivation on the part of the potential offender or probe very much into reasons why potential guardians are unavailable, incapable, or unwilling to help. Like control theory, it assumes that crime will tend to occur. Like ecological theory, it traces this to "natural" features of certain social systems.

In terms of policy consequences, the rational choice theories are largely deterrence theories. The political implications drawn from the theories are especially revealing. Although the logic they adopt suggests that crime might be reduced by either increasing the risks of punishment (e.g., through tighter citizen surveillance and harsher penalties) or increasing the rewards for conformity (e.g., through increased employment at higher wages), or both, these theorists tend to concentrate on the first policy approach.

The psychological approach. Although by the middle 1970s psychoanalytic theory had lost considerable standing and was to come under considerable attack by the early 1990s, partly because of new evidence suggesting that Freud had either misjudged or actually suppressed much of his critical case material and partly because of sharp feminist critique, Samuel Yochelson and Stanton Samenow (1976) published a popular book, *The Criminal Personality,* arguing that crime was the result of pathological thought patterns constituting a "criminal mind." Offenders were described in the traditional language of psychopathy as manipulative, calculating, and largely immune to efforts to treat them. By the 1980s the notion that the criminal must be characterized by some pathological mentality, if only it could be identified, had gained more favor, with many different psychological characteristics suggested as the origin of crime.

A wide variety of learning disabilities were suggested as the sources of crime. As discussed in an earlier chapter, Hirschi himself largely abandoned his sociological version of control theory for the essentially psychological theory that crime could be traced to a breakdown of self-control, the one form of control that was really crucial (Gottfredson & Hirschi, 1990). Although the theory was less biologically oriented than some that were becoming popular, it did not link crime to weakness in society in the manner of strain theory, conflict theory, or even labeling theory; instead it focused on the failure of the institutions of socialization, especially child-rearing practices of the family, to inculcate the inner, self-control necessary for an individual to resist the temptations of crime.

By the late 1970s the IQ theory that had fallen into disrepute decades earlier was being reasserted (Hirschi & Hindelang, 1977). Wilson and Herrnstein (1985) suggested that low intelligence is associated with inability to reason morally, reestablishing the notion that it represented not only a cognitive but also a moral backwardness. By the late 1980s, those accepting as facts the arguable assumptions (a) that intelligence is a single, unitary faculty, (b) that IQ scores are valid measures of this capacity, and (c) that the capacity is essentially inherited rather than environmentally developed were using them to explain racial differences in crime and delinquency (Gordon, 1987). In somewhat oversimplified terms one might say that the early 1990s saw a restoration of elements of social Darwinism, with suggestions that Blacks, for example, were both cognitively and morally inferior by nature and that this inferiority explained much of the crime problem.

Permissive society and crime. In addition to rational choice approaches and those stressing possible psychological deficits, some of the more conservative theorists have linked crime to a distinctive type of social influence: the permissive culture in U.S. society (see Murray, 1984). Although minimizing the criminogenic effects of class and social inequality, they argued that family and schools were failing to discipline and punish effectively (see also Hirschi, 1983). Underlying these claims is the notion that unless humans' baser instincts are tamed they will embark on lives of crime.

Assessment. These observations on crime should not be dismissed out of hand. Some offenders do calculate crime's profitability; some think differently; and some become lawbreakers due to lax child rearing. Empirical evidence, however, is equivocal on the extent to which complex decision making by offenders can be reduced to a simple model of weighing costs and benefits; simply raising the costs of crime does not seem an effective crime control strategy (Finckenauer, 1982). Similarly, cognitive approaches to understanding offenders' thinking have merit, but simple constructs— such as a criminal mind—have not been demonstrated to exist across offenders. Yochelson and Samenow's study was limited to a highly specialized, institutionalized group of offenders, and such approaches leave unexplained the critical causal point: Where do criminal minds come from (Pfohl, 1985)? Families and schools clearly have an impact on criminal involvement (Blumstein, Cohen, Roth, & Visher, 1986), but as Elliott Currie (1985) pointed out, crime seems to be associated not with permissiveness per se but with child-rearing practices that are overly neglectful or overly harsh, failing to nurture human development.

A more general criticism, however, can be leveled at these types of conservative theorizing: "They treat larger social arrangements and forces as inconsequential" (Currie, 1985). Even if offenders make decisions on costs and benefits, we are told little of why society is structured in such a way as to make joining a gang "pay" for some youths and going to college pay for other youths. The existence of criminal minds, as noted, is taken for granted, with little thought given to the social circumstances that may have shaped this unhealthy development. Parents and teachers are warned that tough discipline is a panacea for misbehavior, but we learn little of how poverty, loss of manufacturing jobs in cities, and neighborhood disintegration strain families and schools and thereby reduce their ability to furnish youth with a nurturant environment (see also W. J. Wilson, 1987). In short, by seeing crime as simply a matter of bad choices, bad personalities, or the failure to tame bad impulses, attention is deflected away from defects in the social structure that form the wider context of crime causation.

Consequences of Conservative Theory:
Policy Implications

Before proceeding further, we need to make an important qualification: Not all individualistic theories are inherently conservative nor would many of the authors of these theories necessarily consider themselves on the political right. For example, some psychological theories—particularly those stressing social learning—differ only in emphasis from sociological perspectives such as differential association theory (Sutherland & Cressey, 1970; see also Akers, 1994). Further, more than a few authors of individualistic theories would favor using information on differences between criminals and noncriminals to create more effective rehabilitation programs for offenders entrenched in crime and to assist families at risk for producing troubled youths (see Andrews & Bonta, 1994).

Despite these caveats, we identify the revitalization of individualistic theory as conservative for two main reasons. First, as noted above, by looking inside people for the sources of crime, individualistic theories do not consider what is going on outside people. There is a tendency to take the existing society as a given and to see crime as the inability of deficient individuals to adjust to that society. There is no consideration of how long-standing patterns of inequality in power and in living conditions are implicated in these criminogenic "deficiencies." Crime as a social problem is thus transformed into a problem of individual pathology; society is taken as good, offenders as bad. In this approach, criminology forfeits its "critical" potential: It risks masking, if not excusing, the inequities rooted in the social order.

Second, at least in the United States, the revitalization of individualistic theories has not resulted in an era of progressive practices in criminal justice. Although individualistic theories may not be (at least in most instances) inherently conservative, they often are used—or at times misused—to justify "get tough" policies. The events of recent years are instructive.

The revitalized conservative theories of the 1980s and early 1990s involve two policy agendas—incapacitation and deterrence. Although incapacitation has made a comeback in forms such as the castration of sex offenders and the deterrence theme has manifested itself in a variety of approaches to crime prevention such as drug use prevention campaigns with tactics such as mandatory urine testing, the major policy agenda of the new conservative theorizing centers around incarceration of larger numbers for longer periods, at least until methods of behavioral prediction and effective intervention techniques can be developed. Over the past two decades, the U.S. prison population has more than doubled, escalating to unprecedented numbers and giving the United States the highest rate of incarceration in the world (Irwin & Austin, 1994).

Two aspects of conservative theorizing make incarceration seem a prudent practice. First, in revitalizing classical theory, conservatives emphasize the need to ensure that crime does not pay and see lengthy prison terms as an effective means of increasing the cost of offending. Rational choice theory suggests that some will pursue crime as long as the benefits outweigh the costs. Although one could interpret this to imply that everyone who has "nothing to lose" will turn to crime and that policies should be developed to ensure that citizens have enough of a "stake in conformity" that they are afraid to risk it by criminal activity, the logic is now taken to mean that lawbreakers will be deterred best from further offenses by long incarceration experiences and that those contemplating crime will be deterred from acting on their criminalistic impulses by examples of stricter incarceration of offenders. Second, in revitalizing positivist theory, conservatives are expressing their belief that a proportion of offenders— whether due to a criminal mind or to a criminal nature—are beyond reform and must be incapacitated behind thick walls and sturdy bars.

"Wicked people exist," observed James Q. Wilson (1975). "Nothing avails except to set them apart from innocent people" (p. 235).

There can be little doubt that such thinking has justified, if not actively encouraged, the ready use of prisons as a solution to crime. If conservatives gain comfort from rising inmate populations, they have far less reason to be sanguine about the effects of this policy. Research on the deterrent effects of imprisonment is equivocal at best; getting tough does not seem to scare past or future offenders straight (Currie, 1985; Finckenauer, 1982; but see Wright, 1994). Similarly, although locking up offenders in large numbers reduces crime, its overall effect is modest. A doubling of the prison population, for example, has achieved only a small decrease (less than 10%) in crime rates (Visher, 1987). More disturbing, with construction costs of $30,000 to $80,000 a cell and the yearly cost for housing an inmate in excess of $10,000, this modest reduction in crime was achieved only at substantial drain on state treasuries nationwide (Camp & Camp, 1987).

The financial burdens of prison in fiscally tight times have provided ample motivation to search for alternative methods of social control. Still, in turning to community corrections, conservatives have brought a distinctive look. These conservative times have resulted in a redefinition of the meaning and importance of community, public, and privacy. Just a few short years ago it would have been highly offensive to the American public to turn a home into a prison, a bedroom into a cell. But by the mid-1980s, several states followed the lead of Florida and Kentucky in passing laws permitting house arrest and electronic monitoring (see Ball & Lilly, 1985; Ball, Huff, & Lilly, 1988; Lilly & Ball, 1993). An idea rejected in the United States in the 19th century reappeared in the 1980s: charging offenders a daily fee for their supervision and keep. Although it has several drawbacks, by the late 1980s communities in California, Ohio, Michigan, and Maryland were charging inmates between $20 and $85 per day (*USA Today*, 1987, p. 8A).

These high economic costs of incarceration and the search for reasonable alternatives, however, were viewed by some observers as part of a larger trend. Early in the 1990s it was reported that corrections in the United States and other parts of the world were part of a "corrections-commercial complex," not unlike the military industrial complex President Eisenhower warned about in 1961. The central point of this argument is that the costs of corrections cannot be explained by high crime and incarcerate rates alone, because corporations providing goods and services to corrections, as well as corrections officials and political interests, profit economically from "get tough" policies, including President Clinton's "three strikes and you're out" proposal for life sentences for repeat offenders. Observers of this development also contend that it is not only a U.S. phenomenon but one that is transnational and which at times influences justice policies for profit in foreign countries (see Lilly, 1992; Lilly & Deflem, 1993; Lilly & Knepper, 1992, 1993).

The biological approach has had one of its most dramatic policy applications in the pharmacologic treatment of sex offenders. Although discussion of actual physical castration of sex offenders has resurfaced, the major biologically oriented technique has become a form of chemical castration through antiandrogen agents such as Depo-Provera administered to reduce the sex drive. The problem here lies in the fact that sex offenders seem to be responding to complex interacting factors so that a simple technique such as antiandrogen therapy may not have the expected effects (Demsky, 1984).

Interestingly enough, few of the conservative theorists have focused much attention on the potential impact of improved prenatal care as proposed by some researchers (Moffitt, Mednick, & Gabrielli, 1989). Minor physical anomalies (MPAs) that result from problems in fetal development, for example, are considered by some to be indicators of deeper anomalies such as impairment of the central nervous system, and a relatively high incidence of MPAs has been detected among hyperactive and criminally violent populations. Because MPAs are believed to result from fetal traumas provoked by such problems as poor diet, stress, and drug use on the part of the mother, significant improvements in prenatal care could be expected to have a major impact here.

At the same time, public humiliation or public punishment reappeared. In Portland, Oregon, for instance, a sex molester not only received the usual sentence of no alcohol, no drugs, counseling, orders to stay away from parks and school yards, plus a jail sentence, but also on release from jail was required to put a sign on his front door that read "Dangerous Sex Offender, No Children Allowed" (New York Times, 1987j, p. 10). A similar form of public humiliation was used in one Oklahoma city in which convicted drunk drivers were required to put bumper stickers on their cars that read "I am a convicted DWI, driving while intoxicated, DUI, driving under the influence. Report any erratic driving to the Midwest City Police" (ABC News Nightline, 1986).

Even when offenders remain in the community, then, the more conservative policy approach of the 1980s and 1990s tends to pay less attention to the societal roots of crime than was the case in the 1960s and early 1970s. Operating on the assumption that social circumstances are either unimportant or unfixable, these policies tend to restrict their attention to finding inexpensive ways to incapacitate offenders (e.g., chemical castration or house arrest), deter crime by increasing its psychological costs (e.g., public humiliation), or inculcate more acceptable values through advocacy of certain forms of traditional family values or use of such programs as DARE, a drug abuse prevention program that consists of using police officers to go into schools for antidrug discussions.

Conclusion

The 1980s saw a return to ways of thinking about crime that although packaged in different language, revitalized the old idea that the sources of lawlessness reside in individuals, not within the social fabric. The rekindling of this type of theorizing, we believe, was no coincidence. Like other theories before it, conservative theory drew its power and popularity from the prevailing social context. And as we have seen, conservative thinking has had its day in influencing the direction of criminal justice policy. Locking people up in unprecedented numbers only makes sense if one believes prisons reduce lawlessness by deterring the calculating and by incapacitating the wicked.

Unfortunately, there is little evidence that incarceration deters and a great deal of evidence that it exacerbates the problem. Furthermore, it is extremely expensive, draining funds from hard-pressed taxpayers and limiting funds that could be spent in areas such as education and health care. It is somewhat paradoxical that these theories that purport to be the epitome of rationalism tend to produce policy consequences of such dubious rationality.

As biological research progresses, it may be that the recent resurgence of biological or biosocial theories will find greater empirical support. To date, the evidence is not very striking, although the potential dangers of the "medicalization of deviance" (Conrad & Schneider, 1993) give cause for concern. The psychological theories that trace crime to pathological mental states have achieved major media coverage, such as in the case of serial killers, but social policy hardly can be based on extreme cases. Policies developed on the basis of the various theories tracing crime to failures of the institutions of socialization may offer more hope, although strain theorists and conflict theorists alike would criticize them as too narrow to get at the root of the problem.

As we move closer to the 21st century, it remains to be seen whether individualistic theories of crime will continue to enjoy favor. Although these theories have considerable public appeal—if for no other reason than their simplicity—research has yet to demonstrate that such explanations have greater practical value in reducing crime than focusing attention and resources on the social environment. As noted, the failure of America's crime rate to fall despite enormous increases in the prison population over the past two decades is an embarrassing empirical reality for conservative theories that logically predict the power of punishment to reduce criminality. Further, as one Harvard neurobiologist warned, "I would say, don't hold your breath if you think looking for genes is going to help you understand violence. I would put my money on clever environmental manipulation, because in the end you're going to go there anyway" (Balaban, 1994, sec. 4, p. 3). But neither is it clear that the near future will see any major shift away from these theories, the conservative explanations of crime, and the get tough policies of the past two decades.

The confusion about which direction criminological theorizing and policy development will take in the near future stems in part from the fact that the political context of the United States is in a state of flux. The 1992 election of President Clinton, along with some of his subsequent policy positions, illustrates this point. During his presidential campaign and first year in office Clinton often espoused traditionally liberal policies on such issues as gays in the military, civil rights, gun control, and help for women who are the victims of violence. At the same time, however, many of his popular crime-fighting policies were much more akin to what had been supported by his more conservative Republican predecessors than what some expected from a Yale and Oxford University-educated liberal Democrat whom some saw as a Vietnam draft dodger. This new political mix seems to reflect a reshuffling of traditional patterns of social thought in the minds of many Americans.

All this was well illustrated by President Clinton's second State of the Union message in early 1994. In this speech he called for 100,000 more police on the streets, mandatory life sentences for three-time convicted violent offenders ("three strikes and you're out"), a dramatic increase in the number of federal death sentences, and $3 billion in matching funds for regional prisons (*New York Times*, 1994c). At the same time, he advocated traditionally liberal policies for education, training, and health care.

This led one observer to remark that on the national debt Clinton was Perotist, on crime a conservative Republican, and on family and traditional values a cross between Dan Quayle and a Baptist preacher (Fineman, 1994). Although the political ideology advocated here is unclear in traditional terms, there is no doubt that the public now places crime at the top of its list of major concerns. This alone may be enough to maintain conservative approaches to crime well into the future.

In short, our discussion of conservative theory reflects the central point of this book: Ideas about crime—or what we call theories—are a product of society that develop in a particular context and then have their consequences for social policy. We hope that this theme has served as a useful framework for understanding criminological theory's stages of development and its impact on the criminal justice system. We hope also, however, that our observations on the intimate link among context, theory, and policy will have a personal relevance to readers. A look to the past illuminates the risk of taking for granted one's existing social reality. Whether criminologists or simply interested citizens, we are immersed in a social context that shapes our beliefs about crime and its control. We cannot fully escape this context, but as reflexive creatures we can explore our biases, think more clearly about crime, and embrace policies less contaminated by our prejudices.

Note

1. Quotes in this chapter from the *New York Times* are copyright © 1987/88/94 by The New York Times Company. Reprinted by permission.

REFERENCES

ABC News Nightline. (1986, May 20). Public humiliation [television news story].

Adler, F. (1975). *Sisters in crime: The rise of the new female criminal.* New York: McGraw-Hill.

Agnew, R. (1985). A revised strain theory of delinquency. *Social Forces, 64,* 151-167.

Agnew, R. (1989). A longitudinal test of the revised strained theory. *Journal of Quantitative Criminology, 5,* 373-387.

Agnew, R. (1992). Foundation for a general strain theory of crime and delinquency. *Criminology, 30,* 47-87.

Agnew, R., & White, H. R. (1992). An empirical test of general strain theory. *Criminology, 30,* 475-499.

Aichorn, A. (1936). *Wayward youth.* New York: Viking.

Akers, R. L. (1977). *Deviant behavior: A social learning approach* (2nd ed.). Belmont, CA: Wadsworth.

Akers, R. L. (1994). *Criminological theories: Introduction and evaluation.* Los Angeles: Roxbury.

Akers, R. L., Krohn, M. D., Lanza-Kaduce, L., & Radosevich, M. (1979). Social learning and deviant behavior: A specific test of general theory. *American Sociological Review, 44,* 636-655.

Alexander, F., & Healy, W. (1935). *Roots of crime.* New York: Knopf.

Allen, F. A. (1973). Raffaele Garofalo. In H. Mannheim (Ed.), *Pioneers in criminology* (2nd ed., pp. 318-340). Montclair, NJ: Patterson Smith.

Allen, M. (1977). James E. Carter and the trilateral commission: A southern strategy. *Black Scholar, 8,* 27.

Andrews, D. A., & Bonta, J. (1994). *The psychology of criminal conduct.* Cincinnati: Anderson.

Arneklev, B. J., Grasmick, H. G., Tittle, C. R., & Bursick, R. J., Jr. (1993). Low self-control and imprudent behavior. *Journal of Quantitative Criminology, 9,* 225-247.

Aronowitz, S. (1973). *False promises: The shaping of American working class consciousness.* New York: McGraw-Hill.

Balaban, E. S. (1994, January 23). Quoted in Elementary, Dr. Watson: The neurotransmitters did it. *New York Times*, Sec. 4, pp. 1, 3.

Ball, R. A. (1966). An empirical exploration of the neutralization hypothesis. *Criminologica, 4*, 22-32.

Ball, R. A. (1978). The dialectical method: Its application to social theory. *Social Forces, 57*, 785-798.

Ball, R. A. (1979). Toward a dialectical criminology. In M. D. Krohn & R. L. Akers (Eds.), *Crime, law, and sanctions* (pp. 11-26). Beverly Hills, CA: Sage.

Ball, R. A., Huff, R. C., & Lilly, J. R. (1988). *House arrest and correctional policy: Doing time at home.* Newbury Park, CA: Sage.

Ball, R. A., & Lilly, J. R. (1982). The menace of margarine: The rise and fall of a social problem. *Social Problems, 29*, 488-498.

Ball, R. A., & Lilly, J. R. (1985). Home incarceration: An international alternative to institutional incarceration. *International Journal of Comparative and Applied Criminal Justice, 9*, 85-97.

Baran, P. A., & Sweezy, P. M. (1966). *Monopoly capitalism: An essay on the American economic and social order.* New York: Monthly Review Press.

Barnes, H. E. (1930). Criminology. In *Encyclopedia of the social sciences* (E.R.A. Seligmann, Ed., Vol. 4). New York: Macmillan.

Bartollas, C. (1985). *Juvenile delinquency.* New York: John Wiley.

Bayer, R. (1981). Crime, punishment, and the decline of liberal optimism. *Crime and Delinquency, 27*, 169-190.

Bazemore, G. (1985). Delinquency reform and the labeling perspective. *Criminal Justice and Behavior, 12*, 131-169.

Beccaria, C. (1963). *On crimes and punishments* (H. Paolucci, Trans.). Indianapolis: Bobbs-Merrill. (Original work published 1764)

Becker, H. S. (1963). *Outsiders: Studies in the sociology of deviance.* New York: Free Press.

Beckwith, J. (1985). Social and political uses of genetics in the United States: Past and present. In F. H. Marsh & J. Katz (Eds.), *Biology, crime and ethics: A study of biological explanations for criminal behavior* (pp. 316-326). Cincinnati: Anderson.

Bellah, R. N., Madsen, R., Sullivan, W. M., Swindler, A., & Tipton, S. M. (1985). Habits of the heart: Individualism and commitment in American life. Berkeley: University of California Press.

Bellah, R. N., Madsen, R., Sullivan, W. M., Swindler, A., & Tipton, S. M. (1991). *The good society.* New York: Knopf.

Bennett, G. (1987). *Crimewarps: The future of crime in America.* New York: Anchor/Doubleday.

Benson, M. L., & Moore, E. (1992). Are white-collar offenders and common criminals the same? An empirical and theoretical critique of a recently proposed general theory of crime. *Journal of Research in Crime and Delinquency, 29*, 251-272.

Bentham, J. (1948). *An introduction to the principles of morals and legislation* (L. J. Lafleur, Ed.). New York: Hafner.

Berger, P. C., & Luckmann, T. (1966). The social construction of reality. Garden City, NY: Anchor.

Bernard, M. A. (1969). Self-image and delinquency: A contribution to the study of female criminality and women's image. *Acta Criminologica: Etudes sur la Conduiter Antisociale, 2*, 71-144.

Bernard, T. J. (1984). Control criticisms of strain theories: An assessment of theoretical and empirical adequacy. *Journal of Research in Crime and Delinquency, 21*, 353-372.

Binder, A., & Geis, G. (1984). Ad populum argumentation in criminology: Juvenile diversion as rhetoric. *Crime and Delinquency, 30*, 309-333.

Blumstein, A., Cohen, J., Roth, J. A., & Visher, C. A. (1986). *Criminal careers and "career criminals"* (Vol. 1). Washington, DC: National Academy Press.

Bohm, R. M. (1982). Radical criminology: An explication. *Criminology, 19,* 565-589.

Bonger, W. (1969). *Criminality and economic conditions.* Bloomington: Indiana University Press. (Original work published 1916)

Boulding, E. (1992). *The underside of history: A view of women through time* (Vol. 1). Newbury Park, CA: Sage.

Bowers v. Hardwick, 478 U.S. 186 (1986).

Braithwaite, J. (1989). *Crime, shame and reintegration.* Cambridge, UK: Cambridge University Press.

Brownfield, D., & Sorenson, A. M. (1993). Self-control and juvenile delinquency: Theoretical issues and an empirical assessment of selected elements of a general theory of crime. *Deviant Behavior, 14,* 243-264

Brownmiller, S. (1975). *Against our will: Men, women, and rape.* New York: Simon & Schuster.

Bureau of Justice Statistics. (1994). *Criminal victimization in the United States, 1992.* Washington, DC: U.S. Department of Justice.

Burgess, E. W. (1967). The growth of the city: An introduction to a research project. In R. E. Park, E. W. Burgess, & R. D. McKenzie (Eds.), *The city* (pp. 47-62). Chicago: University of Chicago Press. (Original work published 1925)

Burgess, R. L., & Akers, R. L. (1966). A differential association-reinforcement theory of criminal behavior. *Social Problems, 14,* 128-146.

Burton, V. S., Jr., & Cullen, F. T. (1992). The empirical status of strain theory. *Journal of Crime and Justice, 15*(2), 1-30.

Burton, V. S., Jr., Cullen, F. T., Evans, D. T., & Dunaway, R. G. (in press). Reconsidering strain theory: Operationalization, rival theories, and adult criminality. *Journal of Quantitative Criminology.*

Camp, G. M., & Camp, C. G. (1987). *The corrections yearbook.* South Salem, NY: Criminal Justice Institute.

Campbell, A. (1981). *Girl delinquents.* Oxford, UK: Basil Blackwell.

Celis, W. (1991, January 2). Growing talk of date rape separates sex from assault. *New York Times,* p. A-1.

Chambliss, W. J. (1964). A sociological analysis of the law of vagrancy. *Social Problems, 12,* 67-77.

Chambliss, W. J. (1969). *Crime and the legal process.* New York: McGraw-Hill.

Chambliss, W. J. (1975). Toward a political economy of crime. *Theory and Society, 2,* 149-170.

Chambliss, W. J. (1984). The saints and the roughnecks. In W. J. Chambliss (Ed.), *Criminal law in action* (2nd ed., pp. 126-135). New York: John Wiley.

Chambliss, W. J. (1987). I wish I didn't know now what I didn't know then. *Criminologist, 12,* 1-9.

Chambliss, W., & Seidman, R. T. (1971). *Law, order, and power.* Reading, MA: Addison-Wesley.

Chesney-Lind, M. (1973). Judicial enforcement of the female sex roles: The family court and the female delinquent. *Issues in Criminology, 8*(2), 51-69.

Cincinnati Enquirer. (1985a, September 5). Meese: Execute teen-age killers, pp. 1, 6.

Cincinnati Enquirer. (1985b, October 6). Officials to probe brain use, p. C-12.

Cincinnati Enquirer. (1985c, October 28). [Editorial], p. C-12.

Clinard, M. (1957). *Sociology of deviant behavior* (3rd ed.). New York: Holt, Rinehart & Winston.

Cloward, R. A. (1959). Illegitimate means, anomie, and deviant behavior. *American Sociological Review, 24,* 164-176.

Cloward, R. A., & Ohlin, L. E. (1960). *Delinquency and opportunity: A theory of delinquent gangs.* New York: Free Press.

Cloward, R. A., & Piven, F. F. (1979). Hidden protest: The channeling of female innovation and resistance. *Signs, 4,* 651-669.

Cohen, A. K. (1955). *Delinquent boys: The culture of the gang.* New York: Free Press.

Cohen, A. K., & Short, J. F., Jr. (1958). Research in delinquent sub-cultures. *Journal of Social Issues, 14,* 20-37.

Cohen, L. E., & Felson, M. (1979). Social change and crime rate trends: A routine activities approach. *American Sociological Review, 44,* 588-608.

Cohen, S. (1981). Footprints in the sand. In M. Fitzgerald, G. McLenna, & K. Pease (Eds.), *Crime and society: Readings in history and theory* (pp. 220-267). London: Routledge & Kegan Paul.

Cohen, S. (1988). *Against criminology.* New Brunswick, NJ: Transaction Books.

Cole, S. (1975). The growth of scientific knowledge: Theories of deviance as a case study. In L. A. Coser (Ed.), *The idea of social structure: Papers in honor of R. K. Merton* (pp. 175-200). New York: Harcourt Brace Jovanovich.

Coles, R. (1993). *The call of service: A witness to idealism.* New York: Houghton Mifflin.

Colvin, M., & Pauly, J. (1983). A critique of criminology: Toward an integrated structural-Marxist theory of delinquency production. *American Journal of Sociology, 89,* 513-551.

Conrad, P., & Schneider, J. W. (1993). Medicine as an institution of social control: Consequences for society. In P. Conrad & J. W. Schneider (Eds.), *Deviance and medicalization: From badness to sickness* (pp. 241-260). Philadelphia: Temple University Press.

Cooley, C. H. (1902). *Human nature and social order.* New York: Scribner.

Cooley, C. H. (1909). *Social organization.* New York: Scribner.

Cooley, C. H. (1922). *Human nature and social order* (rev. ed.). New York: Scribner.

Cornish, D., & Clarke, R. V. (1986). *The reasoning criminal: Rational choice perspectives on offending.* New York: Springer.

Corrections Magazine. (1975, November-December). Deinstitutionalization: Special report.

Cullen, F. T. (1984). *Rethinking crime and deviance theory: The emergence of a structuring tradition.* Totowa, NJ: Rowman & Allanheld.

Cullen, F. T. (1988). Were Cloward and Ohlin strain theorists? Delinquency and opportunity revisited. *Journal of Research in Crime and Delinquency, 25,* 214-241.

Cullen, F. T., & Burton, V. S., Jr. (Eds.). (1994). *Contemporary criminological theory.* Aldershot, UK: Dartmouth.

Cullen, F. T., Clark, G. A., & Wozniak, J. F. (1985). Explaining the get tough movement: Can the public be blamed? *Federal Probation, 49,* 16-24.

Cullen, F. T., & Cullen, J. B. (1978). *Toward a paradigm of labeling theory.* Lincoln: University of Nebraska Press.

Cullen, F. T., & Gilbert, K. (1982). *Reaffirming rehabilitation.* Cincinnati: Anderson.

Cullen, F. T., Maakestad, W. J., & Cavender, G. (1987). *Corporate crime under attack: The Ford pinto case and beyond.* Cincinnati: Anderson.

Curran, D. J., & Renzetti, C. M. (1994). *Theories of crime.* Boston: Allyn & Bacon.

Currie, E. (1974). Book review. *Issues in Criminology, 9,* 123-142.

Currie, E. (1985). *Confronting crime: An American challenge.* New York: Pantheon.

Currie, E. (1989). Confronting crime: Looking toward the twenty-first century. *Justice Quarterly, 6,* 5-25.

Currie, E. (1993). *Reckoning: Drugs, cities, and the American future.* New York: Hill Wang.

Dahrendorf, R. (1958). *Class and class conflict in industrial society.* Palo Alto, CA: Stanford University Press.

Dahrendorf, R. (1968). Toward a theory of social conflict. *Journal of Conflict Resolution, 2,* 170-183.

Daly, K., & Chesney-Lind, M. (1988). Feminism and criminology. *Justice Quarterly, 5,* 497-535.

Darwin, C. (1871). *The descent of man.* London: John Murray.

Darwin, C. (1872). *Expressions of emotion in man and animals.* London: John Murray.

Darwin, C. (1981). *The origin of species* (rev. ed.). Danbury, CT: Grolier. (Original work published 1859)

Davis, K. (1948). *Human society.* New York: Macmillan.

Demsky, L. (1984). The use of depo-provera in the treatment of sex offenders. *Journal of Legal Medicine, 5,* 295-322.

Dinitz, S., Scarpitti, F. R., & Reckless, W. C. (1958). A self gradient among potential delinquents. *Journal of Criminal Law, Criminology and Police Science, 49,* 230-233.

Dinitz, S., Scarpitti, F. R., & Reckless, W. C. (1962). Delinquency vulnerability: A cross group and longitudinal analysis. *American Sociological Review, 27,* 515-517.

Dimtz, S., Reckless, W. C., & Kay, B. (1958). A self gradient among potential delinquents. *Journal of Criminal Law, Criminology and Police Science, 49,* 230-233.

Downes, D., & Rock, P. (1982). *Understanding deviance.* Oxford, UK: Clarendon.

Dugdale, R. L. (1877). *The Jukes.* New York: Putnam.

Durkheim, E. (1933). *The division of labor in society.* Glencoe, IL: Free Press.

Durkheim, E. (1951). *Suicide: A study in sociology* (J. A. Spaulding & G. Simpson, Trans.). New York: Free Press. (Original work published 1897)

Durkheim, E. (1964). *The elementary forms of the religious life.* Glencoe, IL: Free Press.

Edwards, R. C., Reich, M., & Weisskoph, T. E. (1972). *The capitalist system: A radical analysis of American society.* Englewood Cliffs, NJ: Prentice Hall.

Ellis, H. (1913). *The criminal* (4th ed.). New York: Scribner.

Empey, L. T. (1979). Foreword: From optimism to despair: New doctrines in juvenile justice. In C. A. Murray & L. A. Cox, Jr. (Eds.), *Beyond probation: Juvenile corrections and the chronic delinquent* (pp. 9-26). Beverly Hills, CA: Sage.

Empey, L. T. (1982). *American delinquency: Its meaning and construction* (rev. ed.). Homewood, IL: Dorsey.

Empey, L. T., & Erickson, M. L. (1972). *The Provo experiment: Evaluating community control of delinquency.* Lexington, MA: Lexington.

Empey, L. T., & Lubek, S. (1971). *The Silverlake experiment: Testing delinquency theory and community intervention.* Chicago: Aldine.

Erickson, K. T. (1966). *Wayward Puritans: A study in sociology of deviance.* New York: John Wiley.

Estrabrook, A. H. (1916). *The Jukes in 1915.* Washington, DC: Carnegie Institute.

Etzioni, A. (1993). *The spirit of community: Rights, responsibilities, and the communitarian agenda.* New York: Crown.

Eysenck, H. J. (1964). *Crime and personality.* Boston: Houghton Mifflin.

Federal Bureau of Investigation. (1993). *Uniform crime reports: Crime in the United States, 1992.* Washington, DC: Government Printing Office.

Ferri, E. (1929-1930). *Sociologia criminale* (5th ed., 2 vols.). Turino, Italy: UTET.

Finckenauer, J. O. (1982). *Scared straight! And the panacea phenomenon.* Englewood Cliffs, NJ: Prentice Hall.

Fineman, H. (1994, January 7). The four faces of Bill Clinton. *Newsweek,* pp. 16-17.

Fishbein, D. H. (1990). Biological perspectives in criminology. *Criminology, 28,* 27-72.

Flanagan, T. J. (1987). Change and influence in popular criminology: Public attributions of crime causation. *Journal of Criminal Justice, 15,* 231-243.

Frazier, C. E., & Cochran, J. K. (1986). Official intervention, diversion from the juvenile justice system, and dynamics of human services work: Effects of a reform goal based on labeling theory. *Crime and Delinquency, 32,* 157-176.

Freud, S. (1920). *A general introduction to psychoanalysis.* New York: Boni & Liveright.

Freud, S. (1927). *The ego and the id.* London: Hogarth.

Freud, S. (1930). *Civilization and its discontents.* New York: Cape & Smith.

Friedan, B. (1963). *The feminine mystique.* New York: Norton.

Friedlander, K. (1949). Latent delinquency and ego development. In K. R. Eissler (Ed.), *Searchlights on delinquency* (pp. 205-215). New York: International University Press.

Friedrichs, D. O. (1979). The law and legitimacy crisis: A critical issue for criminal justice. In R. G. Iacovetta & D. H. Chang (Eds.), *Critical issues in criminal justice* (pp. 290-311). Durham, NC: Carolina Academic Press.

Galliher, J. F., & Walker, A. (1977). The puzzle of the social origins of the Marijuana Tax Act of 1937. *Social Problems, 24,* 367-376.

Gamble, A. (1989). Privatization, Thatcherism, and the British state. *Journal of Law and Society, 16,* 1-20.

Garfinkel, H. (1956). Conditions of successful degradation ceremonies. *American Journal of Sociology, 61,* 420-424.

Garofalo, R. (1885). *Criminology.* Naples, Italy: N.p.

Geis, G., & Goff, C. (1983). Introduction. In E. H. Sutherland, *White collar crime: The uncut version* (pp. ix-xxxiii). New Haven, CT: Yale University Press.

Geis, G., & Goff, C. (1986). Edwin H. Sutherland's white-collar crime in America: An essay in historical criminology. *Criminal Justice History, 7,* 1-31.

Gelsthorpe, L. (1988). Feminism and criminology in Britain. *British Journal of Criminology, 28,* 93-110.

Gibbons, D. C. (1979). *The criminological enterprise: Theories and perspectives.* Englewood Cliffs, NJ: Prentice Hall.

Gibbons, D. C., & Garabedian, P. (1974). Conservative, liberal and radical criminology: Some trends and observations. In C. E. Reasons (Ed.), *The criminologist: Crime and the criminal* (pp. 51-65). Pacific Palisades, CA: Goodyear.

Gibbs, J. P. (1975). *Crime, punishment and deterrence.* New York: Elsevier.

Gibbs, J. P. (1985). Review essay. *Criminology, 23,* 381-388.

Giordano, P. C., Kerbel, S., & Dudley, S. (1981). The economics of female criminality: An analysis of police blotters, 1890-1975. In L. H. Bower (Ed.), *Women and crime in America* (pp. 65-82). New York: Macmillan.

Glueck, S., & Glueck, E. (1950). *Unraveling juvenile delinquency.* New York: Commonwealth Fund.

Goddard, H. H. (1912). *The Kallikak family.* New York: Macmillan.

Goddard, H. H. (1914). *Feeblemindedness: Its causes and consequences.* New York: Macmillan.

Goddard, H. H. (1921). Feeblemindedness and delinquency. *Journal of Psycho-Asthenics, 25,* 168-176.

Goddard, H. H. (1927). Who is a moron? *Scientific Monthly, 24,* 41-46.

Goodstein, L. (1992). Feminist perspectives and the criminal justice curriculum. *Journal of Criminal Justice Education, 3,* 154-181.

Gordon, D. M. (1971). Class and the economics of crime. *Review of Radical Political Economy, 3,* 51-75.

Gordon, R. A. (1987). SES versus IQ in the race-IQ delinquency model. *International Journal of Sociology and Social Policy, 7,* 29-96.

Goring, C. (1913). *The English convict: A statistical study.* London: HMSO.

Gottfredson, M. R., & Hirschi, T. (1990). *A general theory of crime.* Palo Alto, CA: Stanford University Press.

Gouldner, A. (1973). Foreword. In I. Taylor, P. Walton, & J. Young, *The new criminology* (pp. xi-xiv). New York: Torchbooks.

Gove, W. R. (Ed.). (1975). *The labeling of deviance: Evaluating a perspective.* Beverly Hills, CA: Sage.

Gove, W. R. (Ed.). (1980). *The labeling of deviance: Evaluating a perspective* (2nd ed.). Beverly Hills, CA: Sage.

Grasmick, H. G., Tittle, C. R., Bursik, R. J., Jr., & Arneklev, B. J. (1993). Testing the core empirical implications of Gottfredson and Hirschi's general theory of crime. *Journal of Research in Crime and Delinquency, 30,* 5-29.

Greenberg, D. (1977). Delinquency and the age structure of society. *Contemporary Crises, 1,* 189-233.

Greenberg, D. F. (1981). Introduction. In D. F. Greenberg (Ed.), *Crime and capitalism* (pp. 1-35). Palo Alto, CA: Mayfield.

Griffin, S. (1971, September). Rape: The all-American crime. *Ramparts.*

Habermas, J. (1970). *Knowledge and human interests.* Boston: Beacon.

Habermas, J. (1971). *Toward a rational society.* Boston: Beacon.

Hagan, J. L. (1973). Labeling and deviance: A case study in the "sociology of the interesting." *Social Problems, 20,* 447-458.

Hagan, J. (1989). *Structural criminology.* New Brunswick, NJ: Rutgers University Press.

Hagan, J., Gillis, A. R., & Simpson, J. (1990). Clarifying and extending power-control theory. *American Journal of Sociology, 95,* 1024-1037.

Hagan, J., & Kay, F. (1990). Gender and delinquency in white-collar families: A power-control perspective. *Crime and Delinquency, 36,* 391-407.

Hall, R. M., & Sandler, B. R. (1985). A chilly climate in the classroom. In A. G. Sargent (Ed.), *Beyond sex roles* (pp. 503-511). New York: West.

Hawkins, F. H. (1931). Charles Robert Darwin. In *Encyclopedia of the social sciences* (Vol. 5, pp. 4-5). New York: Macmillan.

Hawkins, G. (1976). *The prison: Policy and practice.* Chicago: University of Chicago Press.

Hawley, F. F., & Messner, S. F. (1989). The southern violence construct: A review of arguments, evidence, and normative context. *Justice Quarterly, 6,* 481-511.

Heidensohn, F. M. (1968). The deviance of women: A critique and an enquiry. *British Journal of Sociology, 19,* 160-176.

Heidensohn, F. M. (1985). *Women and crime: The life of the female offender.* New York: New York University Press.

Heusenstamm, F. K. (1975). Bumper stickers and the cops. In D. J. Steffensmeier & R. M. Terry (Eds.), *Examining deviance experimentally: Selected readings* (pp. 251-255). Port Washington, NY: Alfred.

Hill, G., & Atkinson, M. P. (1988). Gender, familial control, and delinquency. *Criminology, 26,* 127-151.

Hinkle, R. C., & Hinkle, G. J. (1954). *The development of modern sociology.* New York: Random House.

Hirschi, T. (1969). *Causes of delinquency.* Berkeley: University of California Press.

Hirschi, T. (1975). Labeling theory and juvenile delinquency: An assessment of the evidence. In W. R. Gove (Ed.), *The labeling of deviance: Evaluating a perspective* (pp. 181-201). Beverly Hills, CA: Sage.

Hirschi, T. (1983). Crime and the family. In J. Q. Wilson (Ed.), *Crime and public policy* (pp. 53-68). San Francisco: Institute for Contemporary Studies.

Hirschi, T., & Hindelang, M. J. (1977). Intelligence and delinquency: A revisionist review. *American Sociological Review, 42,* 571-586.

Hofstadter, R. (1955a). *Age of reform.* New York: Knopf.

Hofstadter, R. (1955b). *Social Darwinism in American thought.* Boston: Beacon.

Hofstadter, R. (1963). *The progressive movement: 1900 to 1915.* New York: Touchstone.

Hooton, E. A. (1939). *Crime and the man.* Cambridge, MA: Harvard University Press.

Howard, J. (1973). *The state of the prisons* (4th ed.). Montclair, NJ: Patterson Smith. (Original work published 1792)

Hughes, E. C. (1945). Dilemmas and contradictions of statuses. *American Journal of Sociology, 50,* 353-359.

Hunt, M. M. (1961, January 28). How does it come to be so? Profile of Robert K. Merton. *New Yorker,* pp. 39-64.

Inciardi, J. (1986). *The war on drugs: Heroin, cocaine, crime, and public policy.* Palo Alto, CA: Mayfield.

Inciardi, J. A. (Ed.). (1980). *Radical criminology: The coming crises.* Beverly Hills, CA: Sage.

Irwin, J., & Austin, J. (1994). *It's about time: America's imprisonment binge.* Belmont, CA: Wadsworth.

Jenkins, P. (1987). *Mrs. Thatcher's revolution: The ending of the socialist era.* London: Pan Books.

Jensen, G. F., & Thompson, K. (1990). What's class got to do with it? A further examination of power-control theory. *American Journal of Sociology, 95,* 1009-1023.

Josephson, E., & Josephson, M. (1962). *Man alone: Alienation in modern society.* New York: Dell.

Kamin, L. L. (1985, April). Is crime in the genes? The answer may depend on who chooses the evidence. *Scientific American,* pp. 22-25.

Katz, J., & Abel, C. F. (1984). The medicalization of repression: Eugenics and crime. *Contemporary Crises, 8,* 227-241.

Keane, C., Maxim, P. S., & Teevan, J. J. (1993). Drinking and driving, self-control, and gender. *Journal of Research in Crime and Delinquency, 30,* 30-46.

Kennedy, P. (1987). The (relative) decline of America. *Atlantic, 260,* 29-38.

Kitsuse, J. I. (1964). Societal reaction to deviant behavior: Problems of theory and method. In H. Becker (Ed.), *The other side* (pp. 87-102). New York: Free Press.

Klein, D. (1973). The etiology of female crime: A review of the literature. *Issues in Criminology, 8,* 3-30.

Klein, M. W. (1979). Deinstitutionalization and diversion of juvenile offenders: A litany of impediments. In N. Morris & M. Tonry (Eds.), *Crime and justice: An annual review of research* (Vol. 1, pp. 145-201). Chicago: University of Chicago Press.

Klein, M. W. (1986). Labeling theory and delinquency policy: An experimental test. *Criminal Justice and Behavior, 13,* 47-79.

Kobrin, S. (1959). The Chicago area project: A 25-year assessment. *Annals of the American Academy of Political and Social Sciences, 332,* 19-29.

Kornhauser, R. R. (1978). *Social sources of delinquency: An appraisal of analytical models.* Chicago: University of Chicago Press.

Kretschmer, E. (1925). *Physique and character* (W. J. Sprott, Trans.). New York: Harcourt Brace Jovanovich.

Krisberg, B., & Austin, J. (1978). *The children of Ishmael: Critical perspectives on juvenile justice.* Palo Alto, CA: Mayfield.

Lasch, C. (1978). *The culture of narcissism.* New York: Norton.

Latessa, E. J. (1987). The effectiveness of intensive supervision with high risk probationers. In B. R. McCarthy (Ed.), *Intermediate punishments: Intensive supervision, home confinement, and electronic surveillance* (pp. 99-112). Monsey, NY: Criminal Justice Press.

Laub, J. H. (1983). *Criminology in the making: An oral history.* Boston: Northeastern University Press.

Lederer, G. (1961). *A nation of sheep.* New York: Fawcett.

Lemert, E. M. (1951). *Social pathology.* New York: McGraw-Hill.

Lemert, E. M. (1972). *Human deviance, social problems, and social control* (2nd ed.). Englewood Cliffs, NJ: Prentice Hall.

Lilly, J. R. (1992). Selling justice: Electronic monitoring and the security industry. *Justice Quarterly, 9,* 493-504.

Lilly, J. R., & Ball, R. A. (1993). Selling justice: Will electronic monitoring last? *Northern Kentucky Law Review, 20,* 505-530.

Lilly, J. R., & Deflem, M. (1993, June). Penologie en profit. *Delinkt en Delinkent,* pp. 551-557.

Lilly, J. R., & Jeffrey, W., Jr. (1979). On the state of criminology: A review of a classic. *Crime and Delinquency, 25,* 95-103.

Lilly, J. R., & Knepper, P. (1992). An international perspective on the privatization of corrections. *The Howard Journal of Criminal Justice, 31,* 174-191.

Lilly, J. R., & Knepper, P. (1993). The corrections-commercial complex. *Crime and Delinquency, 39,* 150-166.

Link, B. G., Cullen, F. T., Frank, J., & Wozniak, J. F. (1987). The social rejection of former mental patients: Understanding why labels matter. *American Journal of Sociology, 92,* 1461-1500.

Lipset, S. M., & Schneider, W. (1983). *The confidence gap: Business, labor, and government in the public mind.* New York: Free Press.

Liska, A. E. (1981). *Perspectives on deviance.* Englewood Cliffs, NJ: Prentice Hall.

Loeber, R., & Dishion, T. (1983). Early predictors of male delinquency: A review. *Psychological Bulletin, 94,* 68-99.

Lofland, L. H. (1973). *A world of strangers: Order and action in urban public space.* New York: Basic Books.

Lombroso, C. (1876). *On criminal man* (1st ed.). Milan, Italy: Hoepli.

Lombroso, C. (1920). *The female offender.* New York: Appleton. (Original work published 1903)

Lombroso-Ferrero, G. (1972). *Criminal man according to the classification of Cesare Lombroso.* Montclair, NJ: Patterson Smith.

Madge, J. (1962). *The origins of scientific sociology.* New York: Free Press.

Mankoff, M. (1971). Societal reaction and career deviance: A critical analysis. *Sociological Quarterly, 12,* 204-218.

Marcuse, H. (1960). *Reason and revolution.* Boston: Beacon.

Marcuse, H. (1964). *One dimensional man.* Boston: Beacon.

Marcuse, H. (1972). *Counter-revolution and revolt.* Boston: Beacon.

Martindale, D. (1960). *The nature and types of sociological theory.* Cambridge, MA: Houghton Mifflin.

Marx, K., & Engels, F. (1992). *Communist manifesto.* New York: Bantam. (Original work published 1848)

Mathiesen, T. (1974). *The politics of abolition.* New York: Halstead.

Matthews, R., & Young, J. (1986). Editors' introduction. In R. Matthews & J. Young (Eds.), *Confronting crime* (p. 1). London: Sage.

Matthews, R., & Young, J. (Eds.). (1992). *Issues in realist criminology.* London: Sage.

Matza, D. (1964). *Delinquency and drift.* New York: John Wiley.

Matza, D. (1969). *Becoming deviant.* Englewood Cliffs, NJ: Prentice Hall.

McCarthy, B., & Hagan, J. (1992). Mean streets: The theoretical significance of situational delinquency among homeless youths. *American Journal of Sociology, 98,* 597-627.

McDermott, M. J. (1992). The personal is empirical: Feminism, research methods and criminal justice education. *Journal of Criminal Justice Education, 3,* 237-249.

Mead, G. H. (1934). *Mind, self, and society* (C. W. Morris, Ed.). Chicago: University of Chicago Press.

Mednick, S. A. (1977). A biological theory of the learning of law-abiding behavior. In S. A. Mednick & K. O. Christiansen (Eds.), *Biosocial bases of criminal behavior* (pp. 1-8). New York: Gardner.

Mednick, S. A., & Christiansen, K. O. (Eds.). (1977). *Biosocial bases of criminal behavior.* New York: Gardner.

Mednick, S. A., Gabrielli, W., & Hutchings, B. (1984). Genetic influences in criminal convictions: Evidence from an adoption cohort. *Science, 224,* 891-894.

Mednick, S. A., Gabrielli, W., & Hutchings, B. (1987). Genetic factors in the etiology of criminal behavior. In S. A. Mednick, T. E. Moffitt, & S. A. Stack (Eds.), *The causes of crime: New biological approaches* (pp. 74-91). New York: Cambridge University Press.

Mednick, S. A., Moffitt, T. E., & Stack, S. A. (Eds.). (1987). *The causes of crime: New biological approaches.* New York: Cambridge University Press.

Mednick, S. A., Pollack, V., Volavka, J., & Gabrielli, W. F. (1982). Biology and violence. In M. E. Wolfgang & N. A. Weiner (Eds.), *Criminal violence* (pp. 21-79). Beverly Hills, CA: Sage.

Mednick, S. A., & Shoham, G. (1979). *New paths in criminology.* Lexington, MA: Lexington.

Mednick, S. A., Volavka, J., Gabrielli, W. F., & Itil, T. M. (1981). EEG as a predictor of antisocial behavior. *Criminology, 19,* 219-229.

Merton, R. K. (1938). Social structure and anomie. *American Sociological Review, 3,* 672-682.

Merton, R. K. (1957). Priorities in scientific discovery: A chapter in the sociology of science. *American Sociological Review, 22,* 635-659.

Merton, R. K. (1959). Social conformity, deviation, and opportunity structures: A comment on the contributions of Dubin and Cloward. *American Sociological Review, 24,* 177-189.

Merton, R. K. (1964). Anomie, anomia, and social interaction: Contexts of deviant behavior. In M. B. Clinard (Ed.), *Anomie and deviant behavior* (pp. 213-242). New York: Free Press.

Merton, R. K. (1968). *Social theory and social structure.* New York: Free Press.

Merton, R. K., & Montagu, A. (1940). Crime and the anthropologist. *American Anthropologist, 42,* 384-408.

Messerschmidt, J. W. (1986). *Capitalism, patriarchy, and crime: Toward a socialist feminist criminology.* Totowa, NJ: Rowman & Littlefield.

Messner, S. F. (1988). Merton's "social structure and anomie": The road not taken. *Deviant Behavior, 9*(1), 33-53.

Messner, S. F., & Rosenfeld, R. (1994). *Crime and the American dream.* Belmont, CA: Wadsworth.

Michalowski, R. J., & Bolander, E. W. (1976). Repression and criminal justice in capitalist America. *Sociological Inquiry, 46,* 95-106.

Miles, R. (1989). *The women's history of the world.* London: Paladin.

Milibrand, R. (1969). *The state in capitalist society.* New York: Basic Books.

Miller, A. D., & Ohlin, L. E. (1985). *Delinquency and community: Creating opportunities and controls.* Beverly Hills, CA: Sage.

Miller, W. (1979). Lower class culture as a generating milieu of gang delinquency. In J. E. Jacoby (Ed.), *Classics of criminology* (pp. 155-168). Oak Park, IL: Moore.

Moffitt, T. E. (1983). The learning theory model of punishment: Implications for delinquency deterrence. *Criminal Justice and Behavior, 10,* 131-158.

Moffitt, T. E., Mednick, S. A., & Gabrielli, W. F., Jr. (1989). Predicting careers of criminal violence: Descriptive data and predispositional factors. In D. A. Brizer & M. Crowner (Eds.), *Current approaches to the prediction of violence.* Washington, DC: American Psychiatric Press.

Mohr, G. J., & Gundlach, R. H. (1929-1930). A further study of the relation between physique and performance in criminals. *Journal of Abnormal and Social Psychology, 24,* 36-50.

Monachesi, E. (1973). Cesare Beccaria. In H. Mannheim (Ed.), *Pioneers in criminology* (2nd ed., pp. 36-50). Montclair, NJ: Patterson Smith.

Morash, M. (1982). Juvenile reaction to labels: An experiment and an exploratory study. *Sociology and Social Research, 67,* 76-88.

Morris, A. (1987). *Women, crime and criminal justice.* New York: Blackwell.

Morris, N., & Hawkins, G. (1970). *The honest politician's guide to crime control.* Chicago: University of Chicago Press.

Moynihan, D. P. (1969). *Maximum feasible misunderstanding: Community action in the war on poverty.* New York: Free Press.

Murray, C. (1984). *Losing ground: American social policy, 1950-1980.* New York: Basic Books.

Nagin, D. S., & Paternoster, R. (1993). Enduring individual differences and rational choice theories of crime. *Law and Society Review, 27,* 467-496.

New York Times. (1985, September 17). Brain defects seen in those who report violent acts, pp. 17, 19.

New York Times. (1986a, August 10). Fighting narcotics is everyone's issue now, p. 25.

New York Times. (1986b, October 23). Meese says court doesn't make law.

New York Times. (1986c, June 3). A study of 15 convicted murderers shows that all had once suffered head injuries.

New York Times. (1987a, March 21). T.V. evangelist resigns, citing sexual blackmail.

New York Times. (1987b, June 15). U.S. churches gain members slowly: Rate of increase keeps pace with population growth, p. 13.

New York Times. (1987c, April 5). Lack of figures on racial strife fueling dispute, p. 13.

New York Times. (1987d, February 15). Report traces 45 cases of attacks on minorities, p. 22.

New York Times. (1987e, September 23). Reports of bias attacks on the rise in New York, p. 19.

New York Times. (1987f, January 27). Anti-Semitic acts were up 12 percent in 1987, p. 13.

New York Times. (1987g, June 19). Goetz case: Commentary on nature of urban life, p. 11.

New York Times. (1987h, January 22). Meese seen as ready to challenge rule on telling suspects of rights, p. 13.

New York Times. (1987i, February 26). Defective gene tied to form of manic depression illness, p. 1.

New York Times. (1987j, August 27). Unusual sentence stirs legal dispute, p. 10.

New York Times. (1988a, February 29). 20 years after the Kerner report: Three societies, all separate, p. 13.

New York Times. (1988b, January 28). Death row appeals assailed, p. 7.

New York Times. (1988c, March 16). The Gideon case 25 years later, p. 27.

New York Times. (1988d, February 12). Scientists urge high project to chart all human genes, pp. 1, 13.

New York Times. (1991, September 20). Many rape victims finding justice through civil courts, p. A-1

New York Times. (1994a, January 14). British scandals jeopardizing party's "back to basics" effort, p. A-3.

New York Times. (1994b, January 13). Wife tells jury of love story, then "torture," p. A-8.

New York Times. (1994c, January 27). Tough and smart on crime? p. A-14.

New York Times. (1994d, June 29). U.S. had more than 7,000 hate crimes in 1993, FBI head says, p. A-9.

Newsweek. (1986a, August 11). Trying to say no, pp. 14-19.

Newsweek. (1986b, November 3). Edwin Meese lifts his lance, p. 9.

Newsweek. (1986c, October 6). The president's angry apostle, p. 27.

Newsweek. (1986d, Summer). Sweet land of liberty [Special issue].

Newsweek. (1987a, April 6). God and money: Sex scandal, greed and lust for power split the TV preaching world, pp. 16-22.

Newsweek. (1987b, June 19). A trial that wouldn't end, pp. 20-21.

Newsweek. (1988a, February 22). Argentining of America, pp. 22-45.

Newsweek. (1988b, January 4). The eighties are over, pp. 40-44.

Nye, I. F. (1958). *Family relationships and delinquency behavior.* New York: John Wiley.

Observer. (1993, November 21). Assault on the welfare state, p. 1.

Palamara, F., Cullen, F. T., & Gersten, J. C. (1986). The effect of police and mental health intervention on juvenile deviance: Specifying contingencies in the impact of formal reaction. *Journal of Health and Social Behavior, 27,* 90-105.

Palen, J. J. (1981). *The urban world* (3rd ed.). New York: McGraw-Hill.

Panel on High-Risk Youth. (1993). *Losing generations: Adolescents in high-risk settings.* Washington, DC: National Academy Press.

Passas, N. (1990). Anomie and corporate deviance. *Contemporary Crises, 14,* 157-178.

Paternoster, R., & Iovanni, L. (1989). The labeling perspective and delinquency: An elaboration of the theory and assessment of the evidence. *Justice Quarterly, 6,* 359-394.

Pepinsky, H. (1976). *Crime and conflict: A study in law and society.* New York: Academic Press.

Persell, C. H. (1984). An interview with Robert K. Merton. *Teaching Sociology, 11,* 355-386.

Pfohl, S. J. (1977). The "discovery of child abuse." *Social Problems, 24,* 310-323.

Pfohl, S. J. (1985). *Images of deviance and social control: A sociological history.* New York: McGraw-Hill.

Piliavin, I., & Briar, S. (1964). Police encounters with juveniles. *American Journal of Sociology, 70,* 206-214.

Pivar, D. J. (1973). *Purity crusade: Sexual morality and social control, 1868-1900.* Westport, CT: Greenwood.

Platt, A. M. (1969). *The child savers: The invention of delinquency.* Chicago: University of Chicago Press.

Pollak, O. (1950). *The criminality of women.* Philadelphia: University of Pennsylvania Press.

Pound, R. (1942). *Social control through law.* New Haven, CT: Yale University Press.

Provine, W. B. (1973). Geneticists and the biology of race crossing. *Science, 182,* 790.

Quinney, R. (1969). *Crime and justice in society.* Boston: Little, Brown.

Quinney, R. (1970a). *The problem of crime.* New York: Dodd, Mead.

Quinney, R. (1970b). *The social reality of crime.* Boston: Little, Brown.

Quinney, R. (1974a). *Criminal justice in America: A critical understanding.* Boston: Little, Brown.

Quinney, R. (1974b). *Critique of the legal order: Crime control in capitalist society.* Boston: Little, Brown.

Quinney, R. (1977). *Class, state, and crime: On the theory and practice of criminal justice.* New York: McKay.

Quinney, R. (1980). *Class, state, and crime: On the theory and practice of criminal justice* (2nd ed.). New York: McKay.

Radzinowicz, L. (1966). *Ideology and crime: A study of crime in its social and historical context.* New York: Columbia University Press.

Reckless, W. C. (1943). *The etiology of criminal and delinquent behavior.* New York: Social Science Research Council.

Reckless, W. C. (1961). *The crime problem* (3rd ed.). New York: Appleton-Century-Crofts.

Reckless, W. C. (1967). *The crime problem* (4th ed.). New York: Meredith.

Reckless, W. C., & Dinitz, S. (1967). Pioneering with self-concept as a vulnerability factor in delinquency. *Journal of Criminal Law, Criminology and Police Science, 58,* 515-523.

Reckless, W. C., Dinitz, S., & Kay, B. (1957). The self component in potential delinquency and nondelinquency. *American Sociological Review, 22,* 566-570.

Reckless, W. C., Dinitz, S., & Murray, E. (1956). Self concept as insulator against delinquency. *American Sociological Review, 21,* 744-764.

Redl, F., & Wineman, D. (1951). *Children who hate.* New York: Free Press.

Reich, R. B. (Ed.). (1988). *The power of public ideas.* Cambridge, MA: Harvard University Press.

Reiman, J. (1979). *The rich get richer and the poor get prison.* New York: John Wiley.

Reiss, A. J. (1949). *The accuracy, efficiency, and validity of a prediction instrument.* Unpublished doctoral dissertation, University of Chicago, Department of Sociology.

Reiss, A. J. (1951). Delinquency as the failure of personal and social controls. *American Sociological Review, 16,* 196-207.

Rennie, Y. (1978). *The search for criminal man: A conceptual history of the dangerous offender.* Lexington, MA: Lexington.

Renzetti, C. M. (1993). On the margins of the malestream (or they *still* don't get it, do they?): Feminist analyses in criminal justice education. *Journal of Criminal Justice Education, 4,* 219-234.

Rock, P. (1977). Review symposium on women, crime and criminology. *British Journal of Criminology, 17,* 393-395.

Roe v. Wade, 410 U.S. 113 (1973).

Rosenfeld, R. (1989). Robert Merton's contribution to the sociology of deviance. *Sociological Inquiry, 59,* 453-466.

Rothman, D. J. (1971). *The discovery of the asylum: Social order and disorder in the new republic.* Boston: Little, Brown.

Rothman, D. J. (1978). The state as parent: Social policy in the progressive era. In W. Gaylin, I. Glasser, S. Marcus, & D. Rothman (Eds.), *Doing good: The limits of benevolence* (pp. 69-96). New York: Pantheon.

Rothman, D. J. (1980). *Conscience and convenience: The asylum and its alternatives in progressive America.* Boston: Little, Brown.

Rubington, E., & Weinberg, M. S. (1971). *The study of social problems.* New York: Oxford University Press.

Sampson, R. J. (1986). Effects of socioeconomic context on official reaction to juvenile delinquency. *American Sociological Review, 51,* 876-885.

Sampson, R. J., & Laub, J. H. (1993). *Crime in the making: Pathways and turning points through life.* Cambridge, MA: Harvard University Press.

Scarpitti, F. R., Murray, E., Dinitz, S., & Reckless, W. C. (1960). The good boys in a high delinquency area: Four years later. *American Sociological Review, 25,* 922-926

Scheff, T. J. (1966). *Being mentally ill.* Chicago: Aldine.

Scheingold, S. A. (1984). *The politics of law and order: Street crime and public policy.* New York: Longman.

Schlossman, S., Zellman, G., & Shavelson, R., with Sedlak, M., & Cobb, J. (1984). *Delinquency prevention in South Chicago: A fifty-year assessment of the Chicago area project.* Santa Monica, CA: RAND.

Schur, E. M. (1965). *Crimes without victims: Deviant behavior and public policy.* Englewood Cliffs, NJ: Prentice Hall.

Schur, E. M. (1973). *Radical non-intervention: Rethinking the delinquency problem.* Englewood Cliffs, NJ: Prentice Hall.

Schur, E. M., & Bedeau, H. A. (1974). *Victimless crimes: Two sides of a controversy.* Englewood Cliffs, NJ: Prentice Hall.

Schuessler, K. (Ed.). (1973). Introduction. In E. H. Sutherland, *On analyzing crime* (pp. ix-xxxvi). Chicago: University of Chicago Press.

Schutz, A. (1962). *The problem of social reality.* The Hague, The Netherlands: Martinus Nijhoff.

Sellin, T. (1938). *Culture conflict and crime.* New York: Social Science Research Council.

Sellin, T. (1973). Enrico Ferri. In H. Mannheim (Ed.), *Pioneers in criminology* (2nd ed., pp. 361-384). Montclair, NJ: Patterson Smith.

Shannon, L. W. (1982). *Assessing the relationship of adult criminal careers to juvenile careers: A summary.* Washington, DC: U.S. Department of Justice.

Shaw, C. R. (1930). *The jack-roller: A delinquent boy's own story.* Chicago: University of Chicago Press.

Shaw, C. R., & McKay, H. D. (1972). *Juvenile delinquency and urban areas.* Chicago: University of Chicago Press.

Shaw, C. R., with the assistance of McKay, H. D., & MacDonald, J. F. (1938). *Brothers in crime.* Chicago: University of Chicago Press.

Shaw, C. R., in collaboration with Moore, M. E. (1931). *The natural history of a delinquent career.* Chicago: University of Chicago Press.

Sheldon, W. H. (1949). *Varieties of delinquent youth: An introduction to constitutional psychiatry.* New York: Harper & Brothers.

Sherman, L. W., with Schmidt, J. D., & Rogan, D. P. (1992). *Policing domestic violence: Experiments and dilemmas.* New York: Free Press.

Sherman, M., & Hawkins, G. (1981). *Imprisonment in America: Choosing the future.* Chicago: University of Chicago Press.

Short, J. F., Jr., & Strodtbeck, F. L. (1965). *Group process and gang delinquency.* Chicago: University of Chicago Press.

Simon, D. R., & Eitzen, S. D. (1986). *Elite deviance* (2nd ed.). Boston: Allyn & Bacon.

Simon, R. J. (1975). *Women and crime.* Lexington, MA: Lexington.

Sinclair, U. (1905). *The jungle.* New York: Signet.

Singer, S. I., & Levine, M. (1988). Power-control theory, gender, and delinquency. *Criminology, 26,* 627-648.

Smart, C. (1976). *Women, crime and criminology: A feminist critique.* London: Routledge & Kegan Paul.

Smith, J., & Fried, W. (1974). *The uses of the American prison: Political theory and penal practice.* Lexington, MA: Lexington.

Spitzer, S. (1976). Toward a Marxian theory of deviance. *Social Problems, 22,* 638-651.

Stanko, E. A. (1992). Intimidating education: Sexual harassment in criminology. *Journal of Criminal Justice Education, 3,* 331-340.

Starr, J. M. (1985). Cultural politics in the 1960s. In J. M. Starr (Ed.), *Cultural politics: Radical movements in modern history* (pp. 235-294). New York: Praeger.

Steffensmeier, D. J. (1978). Crime and the contemporary woman: An analysis of the changing levels of female property crime, 1960-75. *Social Forces, 57,* 556-584.

Steffensmeier, D. J. (1980). Sex differences in patterns of adult crime, 1965-1978. *Social Forces, 58,* 1080-1108.

Steffensmeier, D. J. (1981). Patterns of female property crime, 1960-1978: A postscript. In L. H. Bowker (Ed.), *Women and crime in America* (pp. 59-65). New York: Macmillan.

Steffensmeier, D. J., & Cobb, M. J. (1981). Sex differences in urban arrest patterns, 1934-79. *Social Forces, 61,* 1010-1032.

Straus, M., Gelles, R. J., & Steinmetz, S. K. (1980). *Behind closed doors: Violence in the American family.* Garden City, NY: Doubleday.

Sutherland, E. H. (1937). *The professional thief: By a professional thief.* Chicago: University of Chicago Press.

Sutherland, E. H. (1939). *Principles of criminology* (3rd ed.). Philadelphia: Lippincott.

Sutherland, E. H. (1940). White-collar criminality. *American Sociological Review, 5,* 1-12.

Sutherland, E. H. (1949). *White collar crime.* New York: Holt, Rinehart & Winston.

Sutherland, E. H. (1973). *On analyzing crime* (K. Schuessler, Ed.). Chicago: University of Chicago Press. (Original work published 1942)

Sutherland, E. H. (1983). *White collar crime: The uncut version.* New Haven, CT: Yale University Press. (Original work published 1949)

Sutherland, E. H., & Cressey, D. R. (1970). *Criminology* (8th ed.). Philadelphia: Lippincott.

Sutherland, E. H., Cressey, D. R., & Luckenbill, D. F. (1992). *Principles of criminology* (11th ed.). Dix Hills, NY: General Hall.

Sykes, G. M. (1974). The rise of critical criminology. *Journal of Criminal Law and Criminology, 65,* 206-213.

Sykes, G. M. (1978). *Criminology.* New York: Harcourt Brace Jovanovich.

Sykes, G. M., & Cullen, F. T. (1992). *Criminology* (2nd ed.). New York: Harcourt Brace Jovanovich.

Sykes, G., & Matza, D. (1957). Techniques of neutralization: A theory of delinquency. *American Sociological Review, 22,* 664-673.

Symons, J. N. (1951). Discussion. *American Sociological Review, 16,* 207-208.

Szasz, T. (1987). *Insanity: The idea and its consequences.* New York: John Wiley.

Tannenbaum, F. (1938). *Crime and the community.* New York: Columbia University Press.

Taylor, I., Walton, P., & Young, J. (1973). *The new criminology: For a social theory of deviance.* London: Routledge & Kegan Paul.

Thomas, C. W., & Bishop, D. M. (1984). The effect of formal and informal sanctions on delinquency: A longitudinal comparison of labeling and deterrence theories. *Journal of Criminal Law and Criminology, 75,* 1222-1245.

Thomas, C. W., & Hepburn, J. R. (1983). *Crime, criminal law, and criminology.* Dubuque, IA: William C. Brown.

Thomas, W. I. (1907). *Sex and society.* Boston: Little, Brown.

Thomas, W. I. (1923). *The unadjusted girl.* New York: Harper & Row.

Thrasher, F. M. (1963). *The gang: A study of 1,313 gangs in Chicago.* Chicago: University of Chicago Press. (Original work published 1927)

Tierney, K. J. (1982). The battered women movement and the creation of the wife beating problem. *Social Problems, 29,* 207-220.

Time. (1984, April 9). Sex in the 80s: The revolution is over, pp. 74-78.

Time. (1986a, August 18). Crack down: Reagan declares war on drugs and proposes tests for key officials, pp. 12-13.

Time. (1986b, July 14). Hail liberty.

Tittle, C. R. (1975a). Deterrents of labeling? *Social Forces, 53,* 399-410.

Tittle, C. R. (1975b). Labeling and crime: An empirical evaluation. In W. R. Gove (Ed.), *The labeling of deviance: Evaluating a perspective* (pp. 157-179). Beverly Hills, CA: Sage.

Turk, A. T. (1969a). *Criminality and legal order.* Chicago: Rand McNally.

Turk, A. T. (1969b). Introduction. In W. Bonger, *Criminality and economic conditions* (pp. 3-20). Bloomington: Indiana University Press.

Turk, A. (1987). Turk and conflict theory: An autobiographical reflection. *Criminologist, 12,* 3-7.

Turner, J. H. (1978). *The structure of sociological theory.* Homewood, IL: Dorsey.

USA Today. (1987, November 19). More jails are charging inmates for their stay, p. 8A.

Visher, C. A. (1987). Incapacitation and crime control: Does a "lock 'em up" strategy reduce crime? *Justice Quarterly, 4,* 513-543.

Volavka, J. (1987). Electroencephalogram among criminals. In S. A. Mednick, T. A. Moffitt, & S. A. Stack (Eds.), *The causes of crime: New biological approaches* (pp. 137-145). New York: Cambridge University Press.

Vold, G. B. (1958). *Theoretical criminology.* New York: Oxford University Press.

Vold, G. B., & Bernard, T. J. (1986). *Theoretical criminology* (3rd ed.). New York: Oxford University Press.

Ward, D. A., & Tittle, C. R. (1993). Deterrence or labeling: The effects of informal sanctions. *Deviant Behavior, 14,* 43-64.

Washington Post. (1986, June 21). Drug test called costly, often useless, p. 15.

Weaver, R. M. (1948). *Ideas have consequences.* Chicago: University of Chicago Press.

Whyte, L. (1957). *The organization man.* New York: McGraw.

Williams, F. P., & McShane, M. D. (1994). *Criminological theory* (2nd. ed.). Englewood Cliffs, NJ: Prentice Hall.

Wilson, J. Q. (1975). *Thinking about crime.* New York: Vintage.

Wilson, J. Q., & Herrnstein, R. J. (1985). *Crime and human nature.* New York: Simon & Schuster.

Wilson, W. J. (1987). *The truly disadvantaged: The inner city, the underclass, and public policy.* Chicago: University of Chicago Press.

Wirth, L. (1938). Urbanism as a way of life. *American Journal of Sociology, 44,* 1-24.

Wolff, K. H. (1964). *The sociology of George Simmel.* New York: Free Press.

Wolfgang, M. E. (1973). Cesare Lombroso. In H. Mannheim (Ed.), *Pioneers in criminology* (2nd ed., pp. 232-291). Montclair, NJ: Patterson Smith.

Wolfgang, M. E., & Ferracuti, F. (1982). *The subculture of violence: Toward an integrated theory in criminology.* Beverly Hills, CA: Sage.

Wolfgang, M. E., Figlio, R. M., & Sellin, T. (1972). *Delinquency in a birth cohort.* Chicago: University of Chicago Press.

Wood, P. B., Pfefferbaum, B., & Arneklev, B. J. (1993). Risk-taking and self-control: Social psychological correlates of delinquency. *Journal of Crime and Justice, 16*(1), 111-130.

Wright, E. O. (1973). *The politics of punishment: A critical analysis of prisons in America.* New York: Harper & Row.

Wright, R. A. (1994). *In defense of prisons.* Westport, CT: Greenwood.

Wrong, D. (1961). The oversocialized conception of man in modern sociology. *American Sociological Review, 26,* 187-193.

Wuthnow, R. (1991). *Acts of compassion: Caring for others and helping ourselves.* Princeton, NJ: Princeton University Press.

Yochelson, S., & Samenow, S. (1976). *The criminal personality.* New York: Aronson.

Young, A. (1992). Book review. *Journal of Law and Society, 19,* 289-292.

Young, J. (1976). Foreword. In F. Pearce, *Crime and the powerful* (pp. 11-21). London: Pluto.

Young, J. (1986). The failure of criminology: The need for a radical realism. In J. Young & R. Matthews (Eds.), *Confronting crime* (pp. 4-30). London: Sage.

Young, J. (1988). Radical criminology in Britain. *British Journal of Criminology, 28,* 159-183.

Young, J., & Matthews, R. (1992). *Rethinking criminology: The realist debate.* London: Sage.

Zinn, H. (1964). *SNCC: The new abolitionists.* Boston: Beacon.

Zuckerman, M. (1983). A biological model of sensation seeking. In M. Zuckerman (Ed.), *Biological basis of sensation seeking, impulsivity, and anxiety* (pp. 37-76). Hillsdale, NJ: Lawrence Erlbaum.

NAME INDEX

SUBJECT INDEX

ABOUT THE AUTHORS

J. Robert Lilly is Professor of Criminology and Adjunct Professor of Law at Northern Kentucky University. His research interests include the "commercial-corrections complex," juvenile delinquency, house arrest and electronic monitoring, criminal justice in the People's Republic of China, the sociology of law, and criminological theory. He has published in *Criminology, Crime & Delinquency, Social Problems, Legal Studies Forum, Northern Kentucky Law Review, Journal of Drug Issues, The New Scholar, Adolescence, Qualitative Sociology, Federal Probation, International Journal of Comparative and Applied Criminal Justice, Justice Quarterly,* and *The Howard Journal.* He has coauthored several articles and book chapters with Richard A. Ball, and he is coauthor of *House Arrest and Correctional Policy: Doing Time at Home* (Sage, 1988). He is the past treasurer of the American Society of Criminology. In 1988 Professor Lilly was Visiting Professor in the School of Law, Leicester Polytechnic, and Visiting Scholar at All Soul's College, Oxford. Beginning in 1992, he become Visiting Professor at the University of Durham, England.

Francis T. Cullen is Professor in the Department of Criminal Justice at the University of Cincinnati, where he also holds a joint appointment in sociology. After receiving his doctorate in 1979 from Columbia University, he was on the faculty of Western Illinois University. He is author of *Rethinking Crime and Deviance Theory: The Emergence of a Structuring Tradition*, coauthor of *Reaffirming Rehabilitation, Corporate Crime Under Attack: The Ford Pinto Case and Beyond*, and *Criminology* (2nd ed.), and coeditor of *Contemporary Criminological Theory*. He has published more than 80 articles and book chapters, including contributions to the *American Sociological Review, American Journal of Sociology, Criminology, Justice Quarterly, Crime and Delinquency, Journal of Research in Crime and Delinquency*, and *Journal of Health and Social Behavior*. He has served as editor of *Justice Quarterly* and of the *Journal of Crime and Justice* and is a past president of the Academy of Criminal Justice Sciences.

Richard A. Ball is Professor of Sociology at West Virginia University. He received his bachelor's and master's degrees from West Virginia University and his doctorate from Ohio State University in 1965. He has authored several monographs and approximately 100 articles and book chapters, including articles in the *American Journal of Corrections, American Sociological Review, The American Sociologist, British Journal of Social Psychiatry, Crime and Delinquency, Criminology, Federal Probation, International Journal of Comparative and Applied Criminal Justice, International Social Science Review, Journal of Communication, Journal of Small Business Management, Journal of Psychohistory, Justice Quarterly, Northern Kentucky Law Review, Qualitative Sociology, Rural Sociology, Social Forces, Social Problems, Sociological Focus, Sociological Symposium, Sociology and Social Welfare, Sociology of Work and Occupations, Urban Life, Victimology*, and *World Futures*. His research and interests include home incarceration, criminological theory, social problems theory, sociology of law, and women inmates. He is coauthor of *House Arrest and Correctional Policy: Doing Time at Home* (Sage, 1988).